PRAISE FOR
Good Morning

"Often I will feel lost for direction, not knowing how to focus my thoughts or intentions. I have found the 'Good Mornings' will often help guide me to have a more positive, introspective, or inspirational outlook... and the practical actions for the day can shift my focus and allow me to be more aware. The messages have helped me to not be so hard on myself, assisted me through the knowledge that ruts will happen, and encouraged me to dream beyond beliefs that limit me."

—*Liz W., New Mexico*

"Each morning the first thing I read is my 'Good Morning' quote. Each message allows me to look at my life and consider ways to improve it or a new vantage point from which to view it. How did I make it through my days with a smile before my 'Good Morning'!?!"

—*Tammy P., Texas*

"Each 'Good Morning' to me is a mini course, a direction, a new way of thinking and a new beginning."

—*Bonnie M., Pennsylvania*

"I am not the most positive person in the world. But with the help of your wisdom, I'm changing into a more optimistic and hopeful individual. The 'Good Morning' messages are priceless and get my day started on the right foot, even if I got up on the wrong side of the bed."

—*Maureen, New Jersey*

"Wow! In today's hurry-up society, it is such a blessing to be able to relax for a few minutes and enjoy a daily inspirational and encouraging message that we all can relate to at one time or another in our busy lives. Thank you for providing this organized, enlightening, and powerful website for all readers, young and old (and everyone of us in between!)."

—*Patricia M., Pennsylvania*

"I remember your first good morning...it seems so long ago. Do you remember? I emailed you and said, "Hey, I need more of that." And you did it. You started sending them out within the week or two and haven't stopped in all these years. So, I'm proud to be your first good morning fan. They keep me on track and give me a daily reminder of what's important and why I'm doing what I am doing...which can get foggy in the middle of a woman's hectic life."

—Paige K., Virginia

"Reading the 'Good Morning' inspiration each day is like taking a spiritual vitamin that keeps me focused and encouraged!"

—Mary S., New York

"If more people would wake up and read Brook Noel's 'Good Morning' messages... the world would be a happier place. I look forward to them each morning and they always help me start my day off on a positive note."

—Amy C., Michigan

"I have found many of the 'Good Morning' quotes to be the impetus for self-examination and for making changes that I might not have ordinarily noticed. Sometimes I get in such a rut that these inspirations help me explore what's really going on in my life—and what priorities I let rule my life—so that I can put things back into balance."

—Christine P., Indiana

"In a world that greets us each day with soul-jangling headlines, receiving my 'Good Morning' words of inspiration is like a breath of fresh air!"

—Donna H., California

"Absolutely the best motivation to get my day moving in the right direction. The affirmation at the end of each 'Good Morning' is invaluable to refer to over and over. I have index cards all over my house with Brook's affirmations. It's amazing how well the 'Good Mornings' just flow into the stage of life I'm at each day."

—Debra P., Ohio

"I love the 'Good Mornings.' There are some days when I feel a little low but when I open your email, I can refocus my day. Some resonate and touch me as though you were actually reading my mind and know that I needed just that thought at that moment. Others make me think, long after I have read them. Thank you for all you do to enhance our lives and to help us learn to know ourselves better."

—*Maggie D., Virginia*

"I look forward to my 'Good Morning' because I can count on that to remind me what is really important in life. No matter what kind of day you are having, reading the 'Good Morning' positions you to accept whatever comes your way with a positive attitude! No matter what the message is, you can always relate it to something in your own life. These messages are powerful."

—*Michelle M., North Carolina*

"I look forward to Brook's 'Good Mornings' to start each day on an uplifting note. The quotes are always relevant to making wise life choices and guiding changes that will surely bring positive outcomes. They have been a tool in my journey of self-examination and improvement. Thanks, Brook!"

—*Felicia D., Maryland*

"I treasure the 'Good Morning' messages I receive each day. They are a wonderful, positive way to start each and every day."

—*Lori L., Florida*

"'Good Mornings' are just a little bit of wisdom, making it easy to use, so that you may redirect your thoughts for the day. I have used the thought-provoking quotes to change my thinking and help me to feel uplifted on many occasions. My favorite is so simple but says so much: 'I can dance with life.' How perfect for this time in my life! I now dance through life instead of sitting by and watching everyone else."

—*Kathy P., Texas*

good morning

365 Positive Ways to Start Your Day

BROOK NOEL

SOURCEBOOKS, INC.®
NAPERVILLE, ILLINOIS

Published by Sourcebooks, Inc.
P.O. Box 4410, Naperville, Illinois 60567–4410
(630) 961–3900
Fax: (630) 961–2168
www.sourcebooks.com

Library of Congress Cataloging-in-Publication Data

Noel, Brook.
Good morning : 365 positive ways to start your day / Brook Noel.
p. cm.
1. Women—Conduct of life—Miscellanea. 2. Affirmations. I. Title.
BJ1610.N644 2008
646.7082—dc22

                    2008020582

        Printed and bound in the United States of America.
                CHG 10 9 8 7 6 5 4 3

For my big brother Caleb,
who taught me the art of the
"Good Morning"

Nothing is worth more than this day.

—Goethe

Introduction

In 1998 I started a simple routine, unaware of the profound impact it would have on me in the years to follow. This simple routine has since been adopted by over ninety thousand women.

Each morning I wake and stumble toward the kitchen for a glass of water and a mug of morning java. Coffee in hand, I walk outside or to a large window. I soak in all I can see and then say a silent "thank you" for the day ahead and my opportunity to be a part of it. I stand in this silent thanks for a couple of minutes and then say, with heartfelt conviction: *Something great is going to happen today... I can't wait to see what it is!*

Something great happens each and every day. And because I am aware, I never miss it. Sometimes it is major—for example, a new business deal or an unexpected opportunity. Sometimes the gift is less obvious—a beautiful bird landing at my feeder, an email from a friend, the smile of a child, the pleasure from a great idea, or the joy that comes from complimenting someone. But sure enough, life brings a gift to my doorstep each and every day.

The gifts, of course, have always been there, but I was not an active recipient or participant until my wake-up call in 1997. In the fall of that year my older brother died suddenly at the age of twenty-seven. As I wandered through the maze of grief, I looked for a way to honor Caleb. I had noticed that each morning when he awoke he would walk to the front porch and look out over the lake for about two minutes before starting his day. I don't know what he was looking at—or looking for—but I hope he has found it. I wanted Caleb to live on within me and I added his morning reflection to the start of my days.

Prior to this routine, I spent many years looking for a key to fill a void deep within me. I could feel this void, yet I could not explain or define it. I knew not where it came from, or how to satiate it. I looked in all directions, searching and scouring for the answer. But the answer remained elusive and my search turned to frustration.

When I began this morning routine, I stopped looking for something outside of myself and affirmed that my key was already right where I was. I simply needed to receive it. Instead of looking around, I began looking within. Instead of waking in a haze and propelling through a daily fog, I began waking to greet the world with positive intention, anticipation, and expectation.

How to Get the Most Out of Each Good Morning

Timing

Read the Good Morning message as early as possible. Consider keeping the book near your bed or breakfast table as a reminder of this important emotional breakfast. Visit www. brooknoel.com to download free printable Good Morning reminder cards for your bathroom mirror, car, or wallet.

Your Turn

Each daily inspiration includes a call to action to apply the Good Morning theme to your life. When you finish reading the morning entry, choose a way to apply the "Your Turn" and write it in your calendar or a journal

Record Your Journey

Using a blank calendar, journal, or notebook to record your reflections and affirmations will enrich your journey.

Today's Affirmation

Affirmative statements (or affirmations) are positively phrased sentences in the present tense. We strip out the "I should, I will, I'm going to..." and replace them with empowering words like "I am." Positive affirmations, especially when written, dramatically improve our lives.

Studies have shown that those who use written affirmations are 86 percent more likely to accomplish what they have written than those who do not use written affirmative statements. Reflect on each day's affirmation and then write it down on an index card, in a journal, or on a daily calendar or planner.

Join in the Discussion

I began writing Good Morning messages and broadcasting these inspirations by email in 2003. Readers often share favorite quotes, feedback, and stories, which I incorporate into future messages. (You will see the names of readers throughout the book.) Consider sending a favorite quote or joining in the discussion at my Good Morning blog, www.brooknoelstudio. com/goodmorning.

Each day, join the tens of thousands of women who write or speak aloud the original affirmation of "Something great is going to happen today—I can't wait to see what it is!" This simple affirmation has turned skeptics into faithful Good Morning followers.

Highlights

Scattered throughout this book you will also find the following boxes:

- Inspirations
- Going Further
- Reflection Questions

Inspirations include online resources to inspire or expound on the daily theme.

Going Further boxes offer ways you can explore beyond the "My Turn" if the topic is especially relevant to your life

Reflection Questions are journaling prompts for further reflection and exploration of the daily topic. If you join with a group of women practicing the Good Morning, these reflection questions can be used as topic starters for group discussion.

But I hate mornings!

I used to have a membership to the I-hate-mornings-club, but I relinquished it. It really didn't help me. I am far from a morning person, which is all the more reason to create a Good Morning routine. Even if you say the words skeptically, you are still creating awareness, and you will be amazed at the good things that begin coming your way. Don't take my word for it. Try it for thirty days and see for yourself.

But what if my life is an utter disaster and it isn't good?

Then say it twice! There is no better way to maintain a disastrous life than by continuing to do what you are doing or focusing on how disastrous your life is. Like attracts like.

Getting Started...

Stand up. Go to the nearest window or step outside. Say a silent thank you or shout it at the top of your lungs. Stand in your thanks for a couple of minutes. If you are reading this and thinking, *What a lovely idea,* but have no plans of standing, please put the book down. It takes only minutes. It will transform your life. Then begin using this book tomorrow by opening to the current date.

January 1

> *"And what are you prepared to do?"*
> —*Sean Connery,* **The Untouchables**

Good morning! Here it is in all its glory... a New Year: 365 new days and over 8,700 hours waiting for your exploration. There is no denying the world changes dramatically over twelve months (often, it changes dramatically overnight!). When you stand in this space a year from now, what will you be saying as you reflect back on the days that are now yet to come?

As we begin a new year, take a moment to answer this great movie quote, "And what are you prepared to do?" Hone in on one area above all others. Commit and schedule ten minutes each day to create a future you will proudly reflect on. Then, let the action begin! A new year is here: let there be no delays, no excuses, and no fear—pursue the life you have imagined with abandon.

Your Turn:

Spend some quiet moments today reflecting on where you will be one year from now. Find a blank notebook to act as your companion throughout the year to come. Journal the actions you are committed to and willing to take in order to step forward. Then take a first step. Do not hesitate. Run toward your dreams... they are waiting.

Today's Affirmation:

I am ready, prepared, and committed to small daily action. I greet this New Year with enthusiastic expectation.

Going Further: A Step a Day

Visit www.brooknoelstudio.com/goodmorning/ at the start of each month to print a special Step a Day Calendar. Aim to fill each box on the monthly calendar with a step toward your goal.

January 2

"And now let us welcome the New Year
Full of things that have never been."
—*Rainer Marie Rilke*

Good morning! As the holiday festivities come to an end and we begin taking down trees, packing decorations, and returning to our daily lives, pack carefully. While wrapping glass ornaments and memories of another year now past, hold onto the wonder of the holiday season and the gift of opportunity a New Year brings.

The New Year has always been one of my favorite holidays. Something about a fresh palette of days fills me with a childlike joy usually reserved for young children on gift-filled celebrations.

I have learned that even in the darkest times, life is always magical. Although my years, like yours, are a compilation of the good, the not-so-good, the magical, and the dark, I know each day holds gifts and opportunities. The New Year reminds me that each day can be a new beginning, each hour a fresh start.

Time does not stand in our way—we do. For ages we did not have clocks or calendars directing our actions. Today we find people hunt for time, need more of it, or excuse their inactions because of it. Yet humans created time. In 700 BC, the Romans introduced the first calendar. The calendar was not intended to trap and constrain, but to act as a tool for guiding our days. If humans created time, then humans can also manage it.

We can set a new resolution every midnight: We can decide to greet each day with hope and opportunity. Nothing stops us from experiencing childlike wonder every day except our own perceptions. We can change our perceptions and change our lives.

Your Turn:

Spend a moment or two reflecting on these two questions: What could you possibly lose by treating each day as a gift with childlike wonder? What might you gain?

Today's Affirmation:

This year I will not stand in my way. Today and every day I take control and realize true joy in my life.

Reflection Questions

When in your life have you prevented progress by waiting for a better day or better time to move ahead?

How might this year be different if you accepted that each day *is* the better day and the perfect time for change?

January 3

"Getting organized is one of the top five New Year's resolutions people make."

—*Standolyn Robertson, president of the National Association of Professional Organizers (NAPO)*

Good morning! This quote makes a lot of sense to me, because the New Year is a time of "fresh starts." Our external environment is often a reflection of our internal thoughts, and a cluttered home reflects a cluttered mind.

Here are some tips to tackle clutter and get organized during January (which just happens to be National Get-Organized Month).

Light Up Your Life: Feng shui experts have found that well-lit areas tend to have less clutter. Look around your home and see if this is true for you. If you find that it is, consider adding brighter lamps to light up darker, more cluttered areas.

A Home for Loose Items: As you work through your rooms, watch out for items that tend to be spread throughout the house or throughout a room. Two good examples are remote controls and magazines, which often stray from their "homes." Find a basket for each type of loose item so that it has a place to live (besides on top of the table or surface you are trying to keep clear!).

Store Items Close to Where They Are Most Often Used: Are your items located conveniently to where they are used? For example, if you frequently play games in the living room, are the games stored in a nearby closet, making them easy to retrieve and put away? Try to keep often-used items near the area where they are most often used—that makes cleanup more likely.

Avoid Mail-Paper Piles: Try the following for a quick way to manage your incoming mail and bills. Purchase three magnetic envelope-size holders. Place these on the side of your refrigerator. Use the top one for bills you need to pay with your first paycheck each month. Use the second for bills you will pay with your second monthly paycheck. Use the last to house any other mail.

Your Turn:

Make a list of five cluttered areas in your home you would like to regain control of this January. To help you make this wish a reality, paste this list in your planner or post it on your refrigerator. For maximum efficiency, enlist the help of family members to help you get more done.

Today's Affirmation:

I keep my life and my home in order.

Going Further

During National Get-Organized Month, NAPO's dozens of chapters and thousands of members hold public events throughout the country to help you get started. You can learn about these events online at www.napo.net. You can also join me online the last Saturday of every January for a motivational cleaning marathon in which we tackle our homes in thirty-minute intervals. To learn more, visit www.brooknoel.com.

January 4

> *"Try not. Do, or do not. There is no 'try'."*
> —*Yoda*

Good morning! Every year I host an online "goal" class, devoting six weeks to creating a solid goal foundation for the year ahead. In one of the goal groups, I have noticed how ingrained the concept of "trying" has become. People (especially women) confidently affirm, "I will try." But when it comes to affirming action with the words "I will do," the words come much slower, if at all.

Most of us are great at setting goals; in fact, we are goal-setting experts. We have set goals a thousand times or more. What we are not so great at is reaching them. In order to help ourselves reach our goals, we have to follow Yoda's wisdom. We need to replace "try" with "do." Write your goal down in one sentence and be sure to make it S.M.A.R.T.

The S.M.A.R.T. acronym stands for:

SPECIFIC: Make sure your goal specifically states what you desire to accomplish. "Become healthier," is not a specific goal. "Improve my health by adding one new healthy habit each week for fifty-two weeks," is a specific goal.

MEASURABLE: Make sure your goal can be measured, so that you will know if you have achieved your objective. The above example is measurable, because you can clearly measure whether or not you reach the goal.

ATTAINABLE: Do a soul-search to determine if you have the resources (and energy/attitude) needed to reach this goal during the time line you set for its completion. If you do not have the resources, make sure to include the process of attaining them within your goal plan.

REALISTIC: Many people take an all-or-nothing approach to goals. A great example is a woman who wants to pursue healthy-lifestyle changes. She sets a goal on January 1: She is going to join a health club, exercise every day, change all her eating habits and give up sweets—STARTING the next day! We have to remember that part of any goal is forming new habits, which often means replacing and reprogramming old habits. This doesn't happen overnight. While we might be able to adhere to a schedule like this for a short time, it will be hard to sustain long-term. If you have set up a goal like this, now is the perfect time to revisit it and make a realistic plan.

TIMELY: Make sure to have an end date for your goal. This is what transforms a wish into a goal. Wishes don't have deadlines—goals do! In addition to an end date, identify key milestones at the 25 percent, 50 percent and 75 percent mark to track your progress.

Your Turn:

Start the year with a S.M.A.R.T. goal. Summarize it in one or two clear sentences. Then, decide what practical steps you can take this week to move toward this goal. Journal your answers, making each step specific, measurable, attainable, realistic, and timely. Then, throughout the week (and all your weeks ahead), do not go out and try—go out and "do."

Today's Affirmation:

I set smart goals and take action.

January 5

"One must always maintain one's connection to the past and yet ceaselessly pull away from it."
—Gaston Bachelard

Good morning! In order to find true contentment and lasting joy, we have to live in the present. If we become overly reflective of the past or overly concerned about the future, we begin living in our minds instead of in the physical world surrounding us. We must be present to what is actually happening *this minute* and our role in the here and now. Thoughts of yesterday or tomorrow pull us away from creating today.

This quote inspires my realization of a healthy connection to both past and future. However, beyond making this connection, we must pull away from letting either past or future control our daily lives. We can learn from the past, but let's not dwell in it. Let's not focus on the past and give it energy to repeat itself in our present. Instead, let's learn its lessons and apply them today. We can be "researchers" in our own lives, noting what has influenced us, made us happy, and what we regret, and apply this research to maximize the good in today.

Of course, this is easier said than done. The human mind is very good at worrying and anticipating obstacles. But, time spent worrying is wasted time we will never recover. Statistically, 99 percent of what we worry about never happens. Likewise, we are overcritical of our past mistakes. Often, looking back on events in the past, we are quick to find something we should, could, or would have done differently. But we cannot go back. We cannot do anything for yesterday's mistakes, errors in judgment, hurts, or injustices. So why do we hold onto this pain? What will it give us? If the food in our refrigerator was rotten, would we keep it as a reminder to not be wasteful in the future? What good do either of these practices do besides sap our energy from living "in the now?"

When we are attentive to today, we can work to apply new knowledge and have fewer regrets to reflect upon when we move forward. When we are attentive to today, we create our future.

Let us look forward to the future with passion, excitement, and expectation, knowing that by living "in the now" we can create the tomorrow we desire.

Your Turn:

Notice today how many times you spend living in the past or worrying about the future. Consciously draw your attention back to "now"; the only place where we can create true change.

Today's Affirmation:

I keep a healthy relationship with the past and a hopeful heart for the future.

 January 6

"Rethink your approach…"
—*The theme for a series of Neutrogena print ads*

Good morning! During interviews, I am often asked how I have achieved certain accomplishments. In the past, answering this question was always challenging. I found it difficult to articulate a "core" of achievements until stumbling on this Neutrogena advertisement. "Rethink your approach" summarizes a vital and crucial component between achieving and abandoning a goal.

Imagine you are driving to a very important, long-planned, family get-together. While driving, you encounter a closed road. What do you do? Do you rethink your approach? My guess is that you would retrieve your map or just wing it by taking an alternate route; perhaps you might call someone at the gathering and ask what route he used to maneuver around the roadblock.

When faced with blocks on the road of dreams, too often people do not reach for a map or try an alternate route. Instead they idle, or they park, or sometimes simply wait for "something" to happen. When it comes to personal problems, rarely do we demonstrate the same alternative thinking we use to solve more practical problems like a roadblock.

If I were to park, idle, or wait, I would likely starve or freeze while sitting in my car and waiting for the roadblock to clear (I live in Wisconsin and road-construction projects seem to average three years). Similarly, many people starve their dreams or freeze on the path to achievement, versus rethinking their approach and moving ahead.

I have always loved solving puzzles—word searches, crosswords, logic problems, or the latest craze: Sudoku. Even more than puzzles, I love solving daily life challenges. *"What if I tried this?" "What if I looked at it from this angle?" "What if I..."* I incessantly evaluate, ask questions, and rethink my approach again and again until I maneuver past the block.

Your Turn:

Think of a challenge you currently face. Incorporate the process of rethinking your approach by completing the following sentence at least ten different ways: "What if I..." If you have a hard time getting started, brainstorm with a friend. Come up with outlandish solutions—anything to get the creativity going. Let the list sit for a day. Then, highlight one approach and try it. Instead of idling when challenge comes, choose to view it as a puzzle to be solved.

Today's Affirmation:

When faced with a challenge, I rethink my approach. I ask questions and implement answers.

 January 7

> *"Have the gumption to try something new, and the grit to see it through."*
> —*Karen Fonstad*

Good morning! Lately, I have been talking with a lot of people about energy—more specifically, lack of energy. Each January, fatigue seems to challenge many of us. Perhaps it is the cold, or the shorter days, or maybe we are all just a little worn out after the busy holiday season.

Recently I read that "boredom breeds fatigue." When we live on autopilot, the cousin of boredom, we do not create new energy and zest in our lives. How can we change this? One quick cure is reinvigorating ourselves through a passionate interest. What do you really enjoy doing? What would you really like to try in your life? Is there a hobby that you have been neglecting, or one you have always wanted to pursue?

Your Turn:

Make a list in your journal of ten activities or interests that stir your passions. Schedule ten to twenty minutes a couple of times per week to pursue an activity from this list. The energy and excitement you gain from this will radiate in every area of your life.

Today's Affirmation:

I create a space for my passions in my daily life.

Inspirations

Choose one of the ten activities on your list and take action. Fuel your ambition at www.gutenberg.org: a free online library with thousands of books covering a huge variety of topics.

January 8

"Vision without action is a daydream.
Action without vision is a nightmare."
—Japanese Proverb

Good morning! I chuckled at the truth hidden within this quote. How often have you had a clear vision, but lacked action? Conversely, how often have you launched into action without a clear vision?

All effective change needs both components: action and vision. Working toward change without both of them, is like trying to make macaroni and cheese with just macaroni or just cheese.

Your Turn:

Creating a personal vision statement is a good January exercise to help us hone in on personal goals. Create a simple statement of purpose. Each day, take one action to help you live your vision.

Today's Affirmation:

I have a clearly defined path for my life.

Going Further

Today is National Clean Off Your Desk Day. Use this day to clean off your desk, replacing clutter with clear space for action. Once your desk is clean, go ahead and write your vision statement!

January 9

"We spend January 1 walking through our lives, room by room, drawing up a list of work to be done, cracks to be patched. Maybe this year, to balance the list, we ought to walk through the rooms of our lives... not looking for flaws, but for potential."
—Ellen Goodman

Good morning! What a wise woman Ellen is. This is the perfect time of year to map out the "rooms" of your life, just as an architect would draw a floor plan. Generate your "room" list by writing down the responsibilities you have in life: for example, volunteer, wife, mother, daughter, artist, author, and church member. In each "room," record the potential that exists for growth. This activity and reflection will inspire more greatness than an external to-do list.

Your Turn:

As the architect of your life, think about the life you want to build. Sketch out the rooms of your life and write down how you might grow, change, or remodel them in the year ahead.

Today's Affirmation:

I am the architect of my reality. I design a rich and fulfilling daily experience.

Going Further

One of the exercises in my online goal class is to create a goal poster. One technique we cover is the "room method," inspired by class participant Rhonda Miga. Rhonda drew a house on a large piece of poster board and then labeled the "rooms" she uncovered. In each room, she wrote a sentence reflecting her goal for the year ahead. She added visual images she cut out from magazines to enhance the poster and then displayed it where she will see it regularly.

January 10

"It is not enough to take steps which may someday lead to a goal; each step must be itself a goal and a step likewise."
—Goethe

Good morning! Today's quote provides insight for pursuing the lives we desire and for helping us to realize our resolutions.

Most changes or goals require a lengthy investment in both dedication and time. To last for the long run, each step forward must be a goal in and of itself. Each step is an accomplishment, deserving the same celebration as a reached goal.

With each step we gain self-respect, determination, and confidence. We are now ten days into the New Year. What steps have you taken so far? Instead of looking at the steps yet to be taken, celebrate your accomplishments to date. If you have yet to take a step forward, then take a step today—and then celebrate this step! Change begins whenever you choose to let it do so.

Your Turn:

If you have made progress in your goals, take time today to celebrate and recognize your accomplishment, or to journal about your progress. Reward yourself with a new book, long bath, new CD, or enjoyable coffee at a local café. If you have yet to take a step, why not take one today? Then, reward yourself for beginning the journey.

Today's Affirmation:

Every positive step I take feeds my confidence and determination. My motto: I can and I do.

 *January 11*

> *"The greatest wealth is health."*
> *—Virgil*

Good morning! Two of the most common resolutions made every year are to be fit and/or lose weight, and to spend more time with family. In an effort to keep both resolutions, try turning your family time into health and fitness time. Former U.S. Surgeon General and founder of Shape Up America!, Dr. C. Everett Koop stated in the introduction to *99 Tips for Family Fitness Fun*, "... I encourage you to choose activities you can do together and support and reward each other's efforts to be more active at home, at school, at work, and in your communities... The pleasure of your company is the best reward your child can receive and the best gift you can give."

January is Family Fit Lifestyle Month, and it is a month brimming with resources to help you meet your fitness goals. Here are a couple of ideas to get you started:

Family Fitness Kit: Secrets to making you and your family healthier, starting today, without fancy gadgets or exercise equipment. Visit http://www.healthymainepartnerships.org/tips.aspx to download the PDF and browse other family-friendly health resources.

Visit Shape Up America to learn about the 10,000 Step Program, and download a PDF guidebook for getting started (http://www.shapeup.org/shape/10000steps_2006fs.pdf). While you're there, check out the online cyber-kitchen to help choose a calorie goal, select menus and build a healthy shopping list with recipes (http://www.shapeup.org/atmstd/kitchen/page0.php).

Your Turn:

Take a small step today to begin a walk toward improved health. Schedule two nights a week to focus on fitness, either with friends or as a family.

Today's Affirmation:

Today is the best day to take steps toward a healthier lifestyle.

January 12

"One day Alice came to a fork in the road and saw a Cheshire cat in a tree. 'Which road do I take?' she asked. 'Where do you want to go?' was his response. 'I don't know,' Alice answered. 'Then,' said the cat, 'it doesn't matter."
—Alice in Wonderland

Good morning! The tales of Lewis Carroll have always intrigued me, because many universal truths lie within their pages. Many of us are like Alice in *Alice in Wonderland:* We struggle with which path to take instead of struggling with the more important question: Where is it we want to go? As the Cheshire cat says, if we have no specific destination, then any road will get us there.

Many of us have difficulty articulating our "wants." We might be used to expressing our needs, but we do not give much thought to what we truly want from life. We think about getting from this day to the next, or about improving our immediate future, but we lose sight of a bigger vision that rejuvenates and inspires us. Let's do something fun to break out of this mold—let's make a crazy list.

I stumbled onto the idea of a crazy list early last year. I had just finished telling someone why I couldn't do something. I can't remember the exact thing to which I was referring but the sentence was, "I don't have enough time to _____" (and frankly, it was a lousy excuse—it even sounded lousy when I was saying it). However, since many of us are so talented at making excuses, it can be easy for us to actually begin to believe them.

Later that night, something within me stirred and said, "Wait a second… why can't you do that?" Whenever I find myself engaging in a negative pattern, I challenge it as quickly as I can. In this case, within minutes I was creating a crazy list of all the things I would like to do before I die. The list contained many things—get my pilot's license, climb Mount Hood, go on a safari, paint a series, run a marathon, ski in Colorado, skydive, learn calligraphy, spend New Year's Eve in Times Square, start a self-esteem group for girls, on and on and on the list went—some of the list items more challenging than others. As I created this list, I found it easier to begin articulating the "wants" of my life.

These lists had no limitations. Money was not an object. Time was not an object. Location was not an object. These were indeed Crazy Lists.

I didn't stop and ask, "Is this realistic?" because something had started to occur to me during this process: I think many things become unrealistic simply because we deem them to be unrealistic. For example, I might say, "I don't have an hour a day to devote to that…. It is unrealistic." The truth is, I actually could find an hour, and I just choose not to find it. I *choose* to make it unrealistic.

Our minds have great power. We must be careful with what we deem to be realistic versus unrealistic.

Your Turn:

Start a Crazy List for the year. Spend at least ten minutes this week brainstorming ideas for the year. Tuck this list inside your daily calendar.

Today's Affirmation:

I make time to reach my goals—even the crazy ones.

 # January 13

> *"Before I built a wall I'd ask to know what*
> *I was walling in or walling out."*
> —*Robert Frost*

Good morning! Frost's quote reminds us that whenever we build a wall, we not only keep something in, but we also keep something out. Have you ever built a wall in your life? Perhaps an emotional wall to avoid hurt in some area, or a wall around your confidence because you are scared to fail? Perhaps you've built a wall to keep away a certain type of person?

Building a wall is not easy—bricks and time are required. Removing a wall is also difficult. We would be smart to follow Frost's advice and, before building any more walls in our emotional or physical lives, make sure the wall serves a purpose we are willing to live with.

Your Turn:

Are there any walls you need to tear down this year to create room for personal growth?

Today's Affirmation:

I release destructive patterns and put positive action in their place.

Reflection Questions

What physical and emotional walls have you created in your life?

Which of these walls helped you? Which hurt you?

January 14

> *"Expect nothing; live frugally on surprise."*
> —*Alice Walker*

Good morning! When a friend of mine was going through some challenging times, I asked her what solutions she could brainstorm to help her get through her difficulties. Each of her solutions relied on someone else.

"If only she could..."

"If they would just..."

"He should have..."

Sometimes the expectations we have of others can interfere with our ability to live a rich and rewarding life. When expectations prevent our taking action and responsibility, we limit personal power and build a roadblock on the path to happiness.

We cannot control other people, regardless of how well we know them or how close we are. Anytime we do control another, we are engaging in unhealthy patterns and manipulation. We are not qualified to control other people; we have a hard enough time controlling our own thoughts and actions. The journey of life calls on us to learn to control our own thoughts and actions.

To "expect nothing," as Alice encourages, is not about giving up hope, but about releasing expectations. Instead of placing our needs in the hands of others, we place them where they belong—in our own hands and in our own faith.

When we put our needs in our own hands, then the positive actions of others become blessings versus expectations. We don't feel "let down" if something doesn't happen, but rather inspired when something does.

Your Turn:

What needs have you given to others to fulfill for you? What have the results been? Who are you waiting on in order to move forward? Do you blame anyone for holding you back in any area? What step can you take today to recall your needs and place them in the only place they can be fulfilled—your own hands?

Today's Affirmation:

The only expectation I hold is to personally commit daily to living my best life.

January 15

*"My formula for living is quite simple. I get up
in the morning and I go to bed at night.
In between, I occupy myself as best I can."*
—Cary Grant

Good morning! Grant's quote makes the formula for a happy life seem so simple, doesn't it? Confucius said, "Life is simple, it is we who insist on making it complicated." Each day, why not try the simple advice in this quote: Occupy yourself in the best way you can. For, at the end of any day, if we have done our best in all the things we have touched, we can ask for nothing more.

Your Turn:

As you go throughout your day today, keep it simple. Occupy yourself in the best way that you can.

Today's Affirmation:

I remember to "keep it simple."

Going Further:

Tonight, relax and reflect on how you can keep life simple. Since January is National Hot Tea Month, consider mixing up a healthy homemade tea to enjoy during your reflection.

2 cups brewed tea

1/8 cup honey

2 cinnamon sticks

2 cloves

Combine all ingredients in a saucepan. Bring to a simmer over medium heat and continue heating, without boiling, for five minutes. Strain into mugs and enjoy. Makes 2 servings.

January 16

> *"When we can't access our inner resources, we come to the flawed conclusion that happiness and fulfillment come only from external events."*
> —*Sarah Ban Breathnach,*
> *Simple Abundance*

Good morning! I don't know about you, but I have made this mistake before. I have spent time continually looking for happiness in external events. The problem with that search is that our happiness becomes codependent. Instead of having a well to draw on from within, we require external events to "lift us up." Not only is that unfair to the events or people we are relying upon, it is unfair to ourselves, because the happiness we create is conditional.

We all deserve unconditional joy and happiness within our own hearts. We deserve to have a sense of internal peace, regardless of what is happening around us. The intensity of that happiness might fluctuate with what our external world offers, but it is there nonetheless.

Sarah is very accurate in her assessment. When we can't (or choose not to) access our inner resources, is when we look to the external to "fill us up." Because we can't figure out how to create the reality we need, we turn to others and ask or expect them to do it for us.

To break out of that mold, we have to access our inner resources. We have to learn the skills to turn our questions inward instead of outward. We have to accept responsibility that happiness begins right where we are, not somewhere outside ourselves.

How do we do this? There are many things in life we can't or don't control, but we do control our attitude and our perceptions. Once we accept this fact, we create a space in our life to access those inner resources. We create quiet time, reflection time. We engage in activities that promote self-awareness, self-discovery, and self-reflection. We feed our souls with positive affirmations and positive people. We turn away and don't accept the negative into our thoughts and perceptions. We embrace that which nurtures us, and we reject the rest.

Your Turn:

Get out your calendar and schedule in a space for self-reflection and self-discovery. Choose to look inward instead of outward in order to begin discovering lasting joy in your daily life.

Today's Affirmation:

Within me is everything I need to experience lasting joy.

January 17

> *"We control what we look at. Start looking at what you can control."*
> —*Brook Noel*

Good morning! Often, we desire change in our lives during those times when we feel completely *overwhelmed*! Because we feel weighed down by life, we desire change. It is a catch-22: The change we desire is hard to reach *because* we feel so overwhelmed. Welcome to the number-one reason that people start to change, and also the number-one reason most people fall off the wagon.

To honor the self we begin each day with a simple good morning. We begin by learning to complete steps that build us up instead of tear us down.

There is a great story in *Level Six Performance* by Stephen Long, about how a hammer isn't actually a tool until someone picks it up. Until that point it is just a funny-looking shape; it may as well be an art object. The hammer doesn't derive purpose as a tool until someone uses it. I have heard a similar analogy with the postage stamp. Until you put it on something, it is just a little square piece of sticky paper. We can buy all the tools in the world, look at them, and study them, but they don't actually become tools until we start *using* them.

Imagine that you had never properly used a hammer before, so you sign up for a building class. Oddly, the first assignment the instructor gives is to build a house. How do you think you would do? I don't think it would work real well. Why? Well, not only do you not have any practice with the hammer, but a house would also require many other tools that you likely don't have experience with. How would you master the hammer and all the other tools? I don't know about you, but I think I would drop out of that class.

While the hammer and house story may sound silly, many of us are trying to build something even bigger—our lives—without first mastering the simplest tools.

On any given day, if any of us were to look at the whole picture of life, surely it would be overwhelming. So, why look at it? It only paralyzes us and stops us from making any progress in the place where we can be effective—today—right now! You don't need to build your entire life right now: just build today. Make today matter.

Your Turn:

Instead of looking at the whole picture, focus in on a single area. Ask: *What can I do right now that makes a difference?* And then take that little step, and another little step, and another little step. There will always be things that aren't done— but today we both have twenty-four hours (less sleep time) to do what matters. Let's get it done.

Today's Affirmation:

I focus my attention and energies on making today matter.

January 18

> *"I will never take a step backward. Sideways, diagonally, up, down, but never back."*
>
> —A Toyota insert in the June 2005 issue of O, **The Oprah Magazine**

Good morning! I was flipping through old magazines while looking for some positive sayings for a goal poster. I came across an insert in the June 2005 issue of *O* that I wanted to share with you. The campaign was done by Toyota under the slogan "Moving forward." In it were three small cards detailing ideas for moving forward; on the back was space for writing down how you would move forward yourself. One of the cards included the quote above. The other two are: "I will contemplate my own limitations and then exceed them," and "I will become my own role model." How empowering each of these statements can be if we don't just read them, but instead truly live them.

Your Turn:

Choose one of these quotes as a theme for "moving forward" this month and write it down in your calendar. Create an action list of how you will live the quote in your life.

Today's Affirmation:

I move forward in life. I am unstoppable.

January 19

*"And the day came when the risk to remain
tight in the bud was more painful than the
risk it took to blossom."*
—Anaïs Nin

Good morning! As we challenge our way through the first month of the year, have you been feeling restless? Have you found yourself thinking, "I know I can do better?" Have you been unsettled about the life you are living? If so, consider that your time to blossom has come.

Don't be scared of unsettling feelings or relentless self-questioning. Realize that these are seeds of change. It is through these feelings and questions that we reach the place where we are ready to change—for good.

Your Turn:

Read today's quote several times and consider how it might apply to your life.

Today's Affirmation:

I blossom into the beautiful world I deserve.

Going Further

Make this your year to Make Today Matter. Join me online for a step-by-step exploration of life, purpose, balance, and contentment. Visit www.brooknoelstudio.com to learn more, or sign up for my free Make Today Matter newsletter.

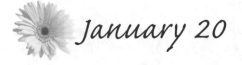 *January 20*

> *"Pay attention to what's good about your life.*
> *Rather than worrying about what you don't have,*
> *seek to make the best of all the good things you do*
> *have. There are a lot of things right with your life.*
> *Give your attention to them and they will grow."*
> *—Ralph S. Marston Jr.*

Good morning! Michelle sent in this quote, along with the following note:

I have this quote up on the wall where my whole family and myself can see it as we pass by... it helps us to remember that we have so many blessings and things right with our lives... and focusing on those things, paying attention to them, helps keep our few minor and some huge disappointments or struggles in proper proportion.

I followed Michelle's lead and posted this quote where my family would see it often. It does just as Michelle says: It helps us keep perspective. When we focus on the good, when we greet the day with expectation, when we write down what we are thankful for, we attract and nourish the good in our lives. Likewise, when we focus on the bad, when we maintain lists filled with stressors and greet each day with trepidation, we nourish the negative in our lives. You are the gardener of your life. What crop will you grow?

Your Turn:

Print a copy of this quote and post it where your family will see it often. Create a Family Thankfulness Journal, encouraging each family member to list a few things they are grateful for each evening. Let guests share.

Today's Affirmation:

I nourish the positive in my life, with both thought and action.

January 21

> *"Without goals, and plans to reach them, you are like a ship that has set sail with no destination."*
> —*Fitzhugh Dodson*

Good morning! For many people, the magic of the New Year is replaced by the stressors of daily life, and goals are put on the shelf or delayed, somewhere near the end of January. If you have found yourself tempted to shelve your goals (or already have) I would encourage you to reconsider your actions, with these tips.

Aim for improvement, not perfection: Many people make rigid goals—that is, exercise EVERY day for twenty minutes. Or drink sixty ounces of water EVERY day. Every day is a lot of days! When setting a goal, it is important to optimize your opportunities for success and also to create the opportunities to EXCEED your goal. If you set a goal for seven days per week, it is impossible to exceed the goal unless you have a magic machine that creates an eighth day (if so, please send it my way!). Instead, be realistic, and set a goal for five days or less per week.

Take control of your time: Schedule the time you will need to complete your goal on your planner. Obviously, this goal is important to you or you wouldn't have set it. Respect this "goal time" as you would any other appointment.

Be accountable: Whether it is an online group, a friend, coach, doctor, spouse, or child—share your goal plan with someone who will hold you accountable.

Inventory your obstacles: There is a quote that states if we wait for the right time, it never comes. The truth is that we are unlikely to hit a long space of time where we can focus on our goals without obstacles and interruptions. Instead of using interruptions and obstacles as excuses to "back off" a goal, create a notebook for listing obstacles and interruptions. Brainstorm solutions and options for as many of these as you can. As you hit more obstacles (which is part of any process) add them to the list. Brainstorm solutions with others if needed.

Revise... don't abandon: If you hit a roadblock and go off track in your goal, don't abandon your goal and wait for "another time." Instead, sit down and revise your plan, using the knowledge you have gained to create a more concrete plan for the next time around. What separates those who achieve their goals from those who don't is simply perseverance. I have created more than two dozen goal plans to reach a single goal—each one carried me a bit further than the last. When we persevere, we will get there.

Your Turn:
Today, recommit to your goal. If you have veered off track, revise versus abandoning your goals.

Today's Affirmation:
I pursue my goals with drive, dedication, and determination.

Going Further

Need inspiration and accountability? As you read about earlier, each year I host an online goal class, devoting six weeks to creating a solid goal foundation for the year ahead. To learn more, visit www.brooknoel.com.

January 22

> *"Three Rules of Work: (1) Out of clutter, find simplicity.*
> *(2) From discord, find harmony.*
> *(3) In the middle of difficulty lies opportunity."*
> —*Albert Einstein*

Good morning! Einstein's clear approach to work offers a basic strategy we can apply to life as well.

Out of clutter, find simplicity. We all know that it is easier to operate well and be effective when we are in peaceful, instead of chaotic, surroundings. Our surroundings influence our thought patterns, attitudes, and general energy levels. A desk full of piles of work induces stress and saps energy, whereas a clean, organized work area allows us to focus on the task at hand. Likewise, if our homes are messy or disorganized, much of our energy is spent worrying about organizing, or searching for some missing object. When our surroundings are peaceful, we are able to spend our energy focusing on family.

From discord, find harmony. It can be more difficult to uncover the practical application of this second rule, but after thinking about it at length I discovered what it means to me. "Discord" is usually found in our relationships with other people. There is a clash, conflict, or general tension. When we can identify a relationship in which we are experiencing discord, we can also identify the opposite of that relationship. We can ask ourselves, "What would harmony look like?" And further, "What steps do I need to take to work toward harmony?" We can also experience discord in our mind and our general daily activities in the form of stress, irritability, or frustration. More often than not, negative emotions are created when we veer from our core values. We find harmony by living in tune with our core values and passions.

In the middle of difficulty lies opportunity. Often, when faced with difficulty, either we become overwhelmed or we let the difficulty influence our overall outlook. We can reframe how we look at difficulty. Each time we face a challenge, instead of becoming bogged down in negativity we can ask, "What can I learn here that will improve me as a person? What skill can I develop? What new experiences await me if I learn how to proactively deal with this difficulty?" Looking at the problem never gets us closer to the solution—looking at the opportunity does.

Your Turn:

These three "rules of work" could well be the rules of contentment, happiness, and a rich life. They are three easy-to-remember practices that we can engage in regularly if we keep them present in our mind. Copy down these rules and post them where you will see them often. Ask yourself, "What do each of these rules mean to me?" Choose one rule to work with first and take a step toward implementing it in your life today.

Today's Affirmation:

I create simplicity, harmony, and opportunity.

January 23

"Life's ups and downs provide windows of opportunity to determine… [your] values and goals… Think of using all obstacles as stepping stones to build the life you want."
—*Marsha Sinetar*

Good morning! What one person perceives as a challenge or "down" might be perceived as an opportunity, or "up" by another person. That doesn't make one person right or the other person wrong, but it does demonstrate that we are all unique individuals with unique values and goals. What makes me happy may be quite different from what makes you happy. Each up and down provides us "the window to determine our values and goals" and to discover what we desire in our life.

One approach I have found very helpful in building the ideal life (and in my own self-discovery in general) is the process of elimination. It isn't always easy to uncover what would make us happy. We might think we know what it would be, but often we get to that place and discover that what we thought we needed isn't really the "key" to our happiness. Sometimes it is easier to observe what doesn't make us happy. By keeping a list of what doesn't work, we become like an inventor: Each combination that doesn't work leads us closer to finding the combination that will.

Your Turn:

Instead of allowing your moods and energy to flow with "ups and downs," take a step back and observe each up and down as an opportunity to learn more about inventing the life you desire.

Today's Affirmation:

Each day is filled with opportunities to expand, refine, and improve my life direction.

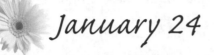 *January 24*

> *"We could learn a lot from crayons: some are sharp, some are pretty and some are dull. Some have weird names, and all are different colors, but they all have to live in the same box."*
> —*Robert Fulghum*

Good morning! What a wonderful quote to celebrate our diversity and uniqueness! If you stick with the crayon analogy, there will always be crayons you "favor" over others (I'm a periwinkle fan myself), but each crayon has its purpose and its time to shine—and each crayon adds color to the world in its own unique way.

We are the same—we each have our purpose, our time, and our ability to add color to the world. While it is important to discover our own uniqueness and what we can offer to the world, it is equally important to respect those we meet and celebrate what they bring to this world.

We live in a society that can be quick to label and judge. Labeling and judging ourselves or others quickly destroys possibility. If we replaced labeling with compliments and judging with support, what a wonderful world this would be.

Your Turn:

While we can't change the way everyone else thinks, we *can* change our own thinking. Strive to replace labeling with compliments, and judging with support, as you go about your days.

Today's Affirmation:

I release labeling and judging... and use compliments and encouragement instead.

Inspirations

Caring through Compliments: Celebrated every January 24, Compliment Day was created in 1998 by Kathy Chamberlin and Debby Hoffman. Join in the celebration by trying to give at least five compliments to five different people.

Try these ideas to incorporate compliments: Consider creating a compliment journal. Throughout the year record all the compliments you receive. Reflect on these pages when you need a quick pick-me-up. Create a family compliment board: Use a bulletin board with index cards to post a weekly compliment to each family member.

For ideas on how to give compliments and what to say, visit www.complimentday.com and http://www.write-express.com/compli08.html.

January 25

> *"When your life flashes before your eyes, make*
> *sure that you've got plenty to watch."*
> —*Author unknown*

Good morning! Today's quote offers the important reminder that we need to live life to its fullest—not just when it is convenient for us, but every day. It can be tempting to let our dreams, goals, and relationships pile up on our to-do list while we tend to the daily logistics of living, but we must remember that our dreams, goals, and relationships are what build a life. We never know what tomorrow brings, which makes it all the more important to make today count.

Your Turn:

What dreams, ambitions, or relationships have you put "on hold" while tending to the day-to-day logistics of living? How can you incorporate these important areas at the center of your day-to-day life?

Today's Affirmation:

I live each day to the fullest.

January 26

> *"You are only given a little spark of madness.*
> *You mustn't lose it."*
> —*Robin Williams*

Good morning! Robin Williams's humor and wisdom also extends to his quotes. He is right, we are each given a "little spark of madness": that little part of the soul that isn't scared to dream or fly or laugh or trust or dance or sing.

Unfortunately, we live in a world that is often eager to extinguish the spark. I was talking to my best friend the other day and she was pointing out how many "don't" messages we receive in our lifetimes. She recounted how as children we are told: Don't run. Don't touch. Don't talk back. Then we get older and hear: Don't park here. Don't speed. Don't cross. Don't drink coffee (or do, then don't, depending on the latest study). Don't eat processed foods. Don't be late. Don't walk.

In the wake of all of life's "don't messages," we must be sure to feed that little spark of madness that still wants to "do, do, do."

Your Turn:

When was the last time you "let go" and had fun for the sake of having fun? When was the last time you let that little spark of madness burn brightly?

Today's Affirmation:

I let the spark of my soul shine.

Going Further

Light the spark: Choose one action to do today with
the simple goal of having fun.

January 27

*"We choose, and in doing so, we design our lives.
Learn to master the moment of decision and
you will live a life uncommon."*

**—from The Rhythm of Life: Living Every Day
with Passion & Purpose,
by Matthew Kelly**

Good morning! The Nike slogan: "Just Do It" is pretty catchy,
isn't it? I wonder how successful it would have been if Nike
would have used, "Just think about it," or "Just wallow in indecision." It doesn't have a real ring to it, does it? But that is
what many of us do. Instead of "deciding," we "debate." Instead of moving forward, we tread water. Instead of making "it
happen," we weigh what might happen. In these moments of
indecision, life continues on without us.

This quote by Matthew Kelly really brings us back to that fundamental point: "Learn to master the moment of decision and
you will live a life uncommon." Uncommon, because so few
people actually decide anything. Instead, we dabble and debate and discuss. What progress have you made in your goals
so far this year? Are you dabbling and debating? Or did you
make a decision and move forward? If you have, you have seen
change. If you haven't, you're likely looking at the same old

scenery. But each day brings many decisions, and each decision you make creates power and momentum.

As a business owner, I make many decisions, both large and small, each day. They aren't always right, but I would rather make a wrong decision than no decision at all. Instead of wallowing in indecision, I would rather gain information and learn what *doesn't* work so I can pursue what *does* work. Each time we make a decision, even if it is the wrong one, we get closer to making the right decision.

Your Turn:

Today, don't put any decisions on the back burner or in the "debate and dabble" column. Trust yourself and make a decision while the situation is in front of you. Feel the action and empowerment that comes with decision making.

Today's Affirmation:

I make decisions with confidence and optimism.

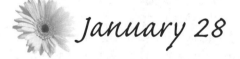 *January 28*

> *"It's not that I'm so smart, it's just that*
> *I stay with problems longer."*
> —*Albert Einstein*

Good morning! I love the fact that Einstein, one of the greatest minds ever, offered this wisdom-filled quote. When I first read it, I immediately wondered if perhaps the definition of "smart" is: *staying with a problem until the answer is found.* Maybe many people who "look smart" don't necessarily grasp things more quickly, but instead have persistence and perseverance.

Although I am far from being an Einstein myself, I can relate to this quote. Many people have asked how I have overcome certain obstacles or created certain processes. It certainly wasn't a stroke of genius, brilliance, or a lightbulb flash above my head. I simply stayed with the problem longer. I believe every problem must have a solution. A personal commitment to discovering the solution is what makes the difference.

As we learn to problem solve, our problem-solving skills develop and become stronger. The only thought pattern required to implement positive problem-solving skills in your own life is a curious mind and the belief that each problem must have a solution.

Your Turn:

Work on increasing your problem-solving skills. Instead of shrinking away from a challenge or problem, realize that each challenge or problem does have a solution—become a detective with the aim of uncovering it. Some solutions can be discovered in a day, some may take months—but the solutions are there. Try writing down a problem you are facing. Then ask yourself questions to begin exploring solutions. Some questions you might try include: How did this problem come into being? Who do I know that might be able to give me ideas or strategies for solving this problem? What would the answer/solution look like? What steps are needed to get that answer or solution? What role did I play in the creation of this problem and, if I reversed my actions/thought patterns, would that impact a solution? What are five crazy solutions I can dream up to help solve this problem? (Brainstorming quick lists—no matter how outrageous—helps us become creative in our approach and solution-focused.)

Today's Affirmation:

For every challenge or problem, I know there is a solution. I also know that I can find it.

 *January 29*

> *"Life is short. Stay awake for it!"*
> —*Caribou Coffee slogan*

Good morning! What a cute and valid quote to remind us of the importance of being present in the moment. During our waking hours it is important to be "awake and present" to embrace all that life offers. Every moment has something to offer, but if we are preoccupied, distracted, or thinking of something else, we might miss what it is. In order to find the magic in a moment, we have to stay in the moment.

Lose yourself in the moment at hand instead of contemplating the moment to come. When you play a game with a child, don't think about what you need to do after the game. Instead, jump into the game, absorb it, laugh, be. When having a conversation with someone, listen with your heart and mind instead of thinking about what is around the corner, or what you will say next. Becoming more attentive, moment to moment, is one of the quickest ways to a more joyful heart and rich life.

Your Turn:

Create a visual reminder to pull you back to the present. I wear a bracelet that says "Make Today Matter" and I use it as a visual prompt to engage in the moment at hand.

Today's Affirmation:

Every day, I practice being present.

Inspirations

You can find Make Today Matter bracelets, journals, magnets, mirrors, and reminder cards at www.brooknoelstudio.com.

January 30

> *"Slow down, you move too fast, you gotta make the good times last."*
>
> *—from "The 59th Street Bridge Song (Feeling Groovy)," by Simon & Garfunkel*

Good morning! I remember a Wisconsin winter where we had a really "wet snow." My daughter wanted to go out to eat as we had planned the night before. The little Mexican restaurant we often frequent is about fifteen minutes away on a non-snowy day. Given the number of accidents I had seen earlier on the freeway, I didn't think it was a good idea to go out in these conditions.

"But we have four-wheel drive, Mama," she pleaded, puffing out her lip in a pout that must have taken years of perfecting in front of a mirror.

"It will take us almost an hour to get there," I tried to reason—but I ended up succumbing to her pouty lip. I told her I would only drive on the back roads. I am a great snow-driver, but I don't necessarily trust everyone else on the road, so I decided there wouldn't be much traffic on the back roads.

We bundled up and set out on our journey. The back roads hadn't been plowed yet, so we sang "Dashing Through the Snow," as we made our way to the restaurant in a little less than my predicted hour.

After an enjoyable dinner, we made the return trek home. By then, the snow had really begun to accumulate. As I turned onto the road that leads to our home, I was taken aback by the beauty of the snow resting on the trees. It was one of those "blanket snows" that made everything look like it was outlined in lace. I pointed it out to Sammy and we drove the rest of the way even slower to enjoy the beauty to be found in each snow-covered form of nature.

Interestingly, I always find myself in a cheerful mood when the Wisconsin snow falls. Many people aren't fond of the snow, and hate driving in the "white stuff." During the wet snow, it occurred to me why I like the snow. In my daily hustle and bustle, it is easy to miss the beauty of the trees and nature that surrounds me. The snow forces me to slow down. As soon as I slow down, I can see all the beauty that surrounds me more clearly.

Your Turn:

Slow down today. Notice how slowing down helps you see more beauty in life. Do as the "Feeling Groovy" song lyrics suggest and "make the good times last."

Today's Affirmation:

I absorb and appreciate all the beauty around me.

Inspirations

Listen in... Never heard the song? Listen free online at www.rhapsody.com. Just type in "Feeling Groovy" into the search box.

January 31

> *"Don't worry about the world coming to an end today. It's already tomorrow in Australia."*
> —*Charles M. Schulz*

Good morning! This quote by *Peanuts* creator Charles M. Schulz brings home two important points: (1) How quickly a day goes by, and (2) How unhelpful it is to spend time worrying.

Worrying doesn't feel good; it makes people anxious and stress-filled. So why do people worry? Worrying, like many negative emotions, is a defense mechanism. We worry to protect ourselves from "what might happen." We worry in order to avoid taking "the next step." However, like many other defense mechanisms, "worry" doesn't protect us. Instead, it creates a wall that blocks off possibility. Worry invites us to be immobile, to stay still, and to wait "for a better time."

Respected biblical scholar Thomas S. Kepler wrote about a woman who realized her fears were ruining her life. She began to track her worries and discovered:

40 percent of the things she worried about were about things that would never happen.

30 percent of the things she worried about were about things that had already happened, and were now water under the bridge.

12 percent of the things she worried about were about others' opinions. When she thought about *that*, she realized that criticisms are often made by those that are jealous or insecure, and that therefore unjust criticism is a disguised compliment.

10 percent of the things she worried about were needless health worries, which only made her health worse as she worried.

8 percent of the things she worried about were "legitimate," since life has some real problems to meet.

These statistics have been adapted by many psychologists and professionals as a fairly accurate analysis of worry breakdown.

Life isn't lived behind a wall. Life is lived out in the wide-open when we take chances and chase down dreams. When we use worry as a wall in our world, we not only block out our fear of "what might happen," but we also block out possibility. If we spend our time worrying, we lose valuable time that could be spent on what we do want to happen in our lives.

Your Turn:

Where have you been using worry to hide from life? Take a step toward knocking down the wall of worry by choosing one area not to worry about at all. Direct your thoughts toward possibilities instead of limits. Break down the wall that worry builds to see how wonderful opportunity is on the other side.

Today's Affirmation:

I climb over worry and into joy.

February 1

> *"You've got to get up every morning with a smile on your face, And show the world all the love in your heart."*
> —*Carole King*

Good morning! Smiling may not come as easily during the long winter days as it does other times of year, but Carole is right: When we wake up, determined to show the world the love in our heart, we feel better.

Reflect on how you began the last few mornings. Are you beginning the day with a smile for yourself? What about for other family members and colleagues? Are you greeting those you care about with a smile?

Your Turn:

On the top of your to-do list for today, make a small heart. Whenever you see this heart, let it remind you to do as Carole suggests and "show the world all the love in your heart."

Today's Affirmation:

Today, I will show the world all the love in my heart.

Going Further

Spread the love... Stop by www.brooknoel.com and view the printable resources there to download a February calendar with a heart for each day of the month. Print a copy for each family member and work to express love to others in one small way each day. Record the ways you do this in the heart calendar and share over a family dinner at the end of the month.

February 2

> *"BE HERE NOW."*
> *—Ram Dass*

Good morning! Welcome to the second month of the year. On this second day of February, I want to encourage you to look at the past month. Don't let this year be one of those years that "drifts by" and is gone before you know it. The year is young: Let's embrace it and transform it into something wonderful!

What goals did you set as the New Year greeted us a short thirty-two days ago? What steps have you taken toward them? If you had to grade yourself on your progress, what would your progress report reveal? Are you pleased with the answer? If not, then embrace today's quote—BE HERE NOW—and take a step today to make next month's progress report one that you can be proud of.

Your Turn:

Take a moment to reflect on your progress report for the year. Then, jot down five action steps you can take over February to "make the grade" toward your goals.

Today's Affirmation:

I am present in every moment, consciously creating the life I desire and deserve.

February 3

> *"You cannot control what happens to you, but you can control your attitude toward what happens to you, and in that, you will be mastering change rather than allowing it to master you."*
> —*Brian Tracy*

Good morning! Mastering the art of change is essential to life happiness. Most of life's pains come from trying to "hold on" or "freeze" some specific moment in time. I have seen many women attempt to re-create moments that have passed.

"If I could just get back to 130 pounds."

"I know it would be better if we could find the spark we had at the beginning of our relationship."

"I was happier when I used to_____ (fill in the blank). If I could just do that again..."

We must remember that life is fluid. Thus, a component to our happiness is learning how to be fluid with life. Within our attitude, within our own mind, and within our own heart, we hold the key to living a full life. It is not what we have, how much we accomplish, or any other measurable component. The key to living a full life is dependent on how we view the world; this choice of view lies solely within each of us. Are you using a rearview mirror to look at your life?

Your Turn:

How have you been looking at the world? Given that it only takes a moment to decide to look at the world differently, could you benefit from any viewpoint adjustments?

Today's Affirmation:

I accept change. I dance with life.

February 4

> *"No one would have crossed the ocean if he could have gotten off the ship in the middle of a storm."*
> —*Charles F. Kettering*

Good morning! Okay, maybe someone would have still crossed the ocean, but Kettering's point is very valid. Most people would have bailed when that storm became tremulous if there were any safe way to shore. Imagine being one of the first to cross the ocean—think of all the fear involved as you sailed through wild storms to an uncertain destination. I am sure these mariners and passengers were filled with fear and regret, and greatly questioned their choice and endeavor.

Now imagine the first sight of land after crossing that ocean and the beauty of the first sunrise or sunset in that undiscovered territory. How do you think that must have felt? I would think relief, gratefulness, accomplishment, and bliss would be among a long list of emotions.

Your Turn:

Picture your life as an ocean. Are you in the calm or are you in the storm? What does "land" look like for you? Remember that any journey worth taking will have both stormy and calm times—beauty is found by those who keep going.

Today's Affirmation:

I enjoy the journey.

 # *February 5*

> *"What you leave behind is not what is engraved in stone monuments, but what is woven into the lives of others."*
> *—Pericles*

Good morning! Today and every day gives us opportunities to "weave" our own positives into the lives of others. Each day, as we go about our business, we interact with those both in and outside of our family. Each time we do, we leave a history. The type of history we leave is completely within our control.

Your Turn:

Today, I challenge you to evaluate the history you are weaving into the lives of others. What gifts are you giving from the heart? Are you making each day and interaction count? If not, try doing so for the rest of this week and notice how wonderful you feel.

Today's Affirmation:

Every day I share and weave positive energy into the lives of others.

 February 6

> *"Try making two small changes every day. Take a different street, try a new restaurant, change your toothpaste, smile at someone you don't know, eat dessert first. There's a lot of landscape to explore off the beaten path."*
> —*Joan Borysenko, PhD*

Good morning! If we do not nurture curiosity, we can quickly become enmeshed in habits and overlook all the opportunity and newness within our reach. Today, try to have the curiosity of a child as you go about your daily routine.

Your Turn:

Today and for at least one week, try making two small changes every day, as Joan suggests. Enjoy the sense of discovery!

Today's Affirmation:

Every day I make a joyous new discovery about myself and my world.

Going Further

What are five new things you can try in February? How about a new recipe, new restaurant, new route to work, new book, new morning or evening routine, new exercise, or new prayer?

February 7

> *"Shrink your worry list. Examine areas in your life where anxiety rules. Does your worrying really make a positive difference in those situations? If not, dump the worry."*
> —*from* **Checklists for Life**

Good morning! Worry has many similar characteristics to guilt, and it hurts us much more than it helps. While a little worry or a little guilt keeps our consciences clean and our focus clear, incessant worry and guilt are destructive.

How do you know if these worry/guilt emotions are constructive or destructive in your own life? Ask yourself this simple question: Did my (worry/guilt/insert any emotion) make a positive difference in the situation?

If your answer is "no," then you are needlessly bringing yourself down, and you are likely bringing down the people around you.

Your Turn:

As you encounter guilt, worries, and other emotions today, ask yourself: "Is this making a positive difference in this situation?" If the answer is no, say a positive affirmation to dilute the negative emotion.

Today's Affirmation:

I release negative emotions from my life and replace them with positive and constructive thoughts.

Going Further

Visit the Newsletters & Free Stuff link at www.maketoday matter.net to find articles that will help you make the most of each day.

February 8

> *"Motivation is what gets you started. Habit is what keeps you going."*
> —**Jim Rohn**

Good morning! The combination of motivation and habit are key ingredients in the recipe for a successful life. Motivation is the spark that often gets us moving. But within that initial motivation, we must work hard to develop positive and effective habits to keep us moving. Success is made from both motivation and habits, not one or the other.

Staying positive and solution-oriented will help to sustain a high level of motivation while we create new habits. Connecting with others who are also making positive life changes also fosters motivation.

Your Turn:

Does your plan for change contain equal parts motivation and excitement? If not, brainstorm ways to create more of whichever quality is needed.

Today's Affirmation:

I seek out the positive in people and in life's situations.

Going Further

Who can you turn to for support when your motivation runs low? Create a Master Motivation List in the front of your address book and write down the contact information of at least three people who inspire you.

February 9

> *"If you have built castles in the air, your work need not be lost; that is where they should be. Now put foundations under them."*
> —*Henry David Thoreau*

Good morning! What are your goals and wildest dreams? Have you built castles in the air? If your answer is yes, good for you! That's where dreams must begin.

Although I have never built a castle, I would guess it is a time-intensive project. After building our dreams, we must put the foundation beneath them.

Your Turn:

How is your foundation coming along? Are you taking practical, daily steps forward (no matter how small)? We can't get to our goal when we are not moving. Are you moving toward success? If not, what little step can you take today to recommit and get yourself back on track?

Today's Affirmation:

Each day I take a step toward success. I know there is no such thing as a "small step." Every step is important.

Inspirations

Recognize the progress you make as you move toward your goals with this free, easy-to-use goal tracker: www.joesgoals.com/.

February 10

> *"Life's challenges are not supposed to paralyze you, they're supposed to help you discover who you are."*
> —*Bernice Johnson Reagon*

Good morning! Have you ever had a day or a week or a month in which you feel you are walking around under one of those black rain clouds and the rain is only falling on you? That each step forward you take is counteracted by two steps back?

The more we attempt to move forward and the more we aspire to accomplish, the more rain clouds we will run into. Why? Because change and challenge require that we push beyond our boundaries and step outside of our comfort zone. What feels like a rain cloud is often just water fertilizing the soil for a fresh dream or direction.

Your Turn:

The next time you feel like a rain cloud is following you, look up and thank it for being present. Realize this is the fertilizing of fresh ground for a new dream and aspiration. Keep on challenging life—that is how we discover who we are.

Today's Affirmation:

I grow in positive ways from each challenge I face in life.

 February 11

> *"I've learned that people will forget what you said, people will forget what you did, but people will never forget how you made them feel."*
> —*Maya Angelou*

Good morning! This quote is a wonderful self-check on what we say versus what we do. It is often easy to make promises, but do our actions support them? While we talk about being respectful, caring, optimistic people, do we then treat those around us with respect and caring?

Maya has it right. Long after we interact with someone, they may not remember our words, but they will never forget how we made them feel. Are you leaving good memories?

Your Turn:

As you go about your day, ask yourself if you are leaving positive memories. Are you proud of the way those you interact with will remember you? If not, take an instant step to change the memory you are creating for them.

Today's Affirmation:

I live with love and caring and leave loving and caring memories.

Going Further

What outstanding promises do you have in your life? Take a moment to think them through and write down your answers. Connect with these people. Give them an update. If circumstances have changed, tell them so. For the promises yet to be completed, assign one or two to the month of February. On your calendar, write out the steps you will take and when.

February 12

"Life is great, if you're tough enough to live it."
—Aunt Connie Gill

Good morning! Perhaps this quote exemplifies what some of us are missing—a "toughness" that enriches our lives. I created the Make Today Matter program and authored *The Change Your Life Challenge* as a means to help myself and other women "toughen up" and challenge ourselves to rise above challenges and live our best lives. To me, "becoming tough" is parallel to becoming "personally accountable." We become tough when we quit diffusing blows to outward circumstances and events, and, instead, work to improve ourselves.

Maybe the word is not tough, but *brave.* To stand up for ourselves and what we believe in and what we deserve requires courage and bravery. It is much easier to walk away from a dream than it is to pursue it. Pursuing a dream involves falling down, bruises, tears, and getting back up one hundred times plus. I've walked both paths—chasing a dream and abandoning one—and the scenery is vastly different. I would take the scenery of a dream, complete with its bumps and bruises, over the "easy" path any day.

Your Turn:

What do you love enough to be brave and courageous for? What do you believe in so strongly, you are willing to risk a bump and a bruise and become "tougher" so that you may diligently pursue the dream?

Today's Affirmation:

I am brave and courageous in the pursuit of my dreams.

Going Further

If you are ready to take another step of courage toward living the life you desire, visit www.brooknoel.com to learn more about the Make Today Matter Life System and *The Change Your Life Challenge* book.

February 13

"Love is… being patient, even when you're tired—especially when you're tired."
—Danae Jacobsen, age sixteen

Good morning! How smart this sixteen-year-old is! This comes from a piece of writing she did, titled "Things I've Learned Lately." She adds many wonderful phrases to this list, including trusting in someone when you're scared, writing a note of encouragement, caring—even when it's hard and you don't feel like it.

Your Turn:

What does "love" mean to you in your everyday life? How can you show and share this emotion? Which of Danae's ideas and tips could you try today?

Today's Affirmation:

I freely show and share my love for others.

Going Further

Ten Simple Ways to Show You Care:

See how many of the items below you can check off today and tomorrow.

❏ Give or get a hug

❏ Show respect and kindness

❏ Play a game

❏ Spend one-on-one time with someone and give them your undivided attention

❏ Prepare or share a meal together

❏ Share dreams and goals

❏ Give compliments

❏ Make a sacrifice

❏ Reach out and call someone you need to connect with

❏ Send a note saying you care

February 14

*"Love does not consist of gazing at each other,
but in looking outward together in
the same direction."*
—Antoine de Saint-Exupery

Good morning! I was working on finding a quote for this morning and I have to tell you it was really a toss-up between this one and "I married the first man I ever kissed. When I tell this to my children, they just about throw up," said by former First Lady Barbara Bush. (Thought you might like the chuckle this morning.)

Actually, I was quite blessed when I was working on my Good Mornings for February, as a note came in just as I began to contemplate Valentine's Day. It was a note from Good Morning reader Beverly, and she wrote:

I often tell the significant others in my life—family and friends, that I love them more today than yesterday and less than I shall tomorrow. I do not remember where I found that quote, but for me it is an affirmation that my love will continue to grow, develop and expand each day.

I thought that was so beautifully articulated. And what is Valentine's Day? It is a time when we articulate our feelings toward our loved ones. Often it is done through browsing for the perfect card, but why not take a moment today and write a special handwritten note? Then take it a step further and make an effort to verbally express and affirm your love as Beverly does.

My daughter and I have a fun routine that started when she was around four years old. Somehow in one of our phone calls (I was traveling) we ended up (in our ever-competitive way) bantering back and forth with "I love you" statements. I had said I love you, she had responded with the same, and I had said "I love you, plus one." This has led to many variations over the years: "I love you more than mountains are high;" "I love you more than every number plus itself squared." My daughter finally took the cake with, "I love you more than more." Ever since we have bantered and shared our affection through creative "I love you" statements, and I anticipate many more wonderful years (in between her not talking to me in her teen phase) of "I love you" statements.

Your Turn:

How often do you say "I love you," to those you love? Do the words roll off your tongue in routine, or are they said with heartfelt meaning? Think of ways you can articulate and share your feelings for those you love. Take a moment today to write a handwritten note and express your love to someone.

Today's Affirmation:

I express my love for others easily and often.

 ## *February 15*

> *"A vision without a task is but a dream, a task without vision is drudgery, a vision with a task is the hope of the world."*
> *—On the cornerstone of a church in England, dated 1730. Author unknown*

Good morning! I felt so blessed to stumble across this quote that has existed in stone for centuries and has now traveled across oceans to be shared with us. If you take the time to read it, and really think it through, there is so much truth to the simple words. Often, we have great visions—but we do not break down the tasks in order to complete them. Other times, we have tasks, but we don't have a vision or purpose to make them fulfilling. Combine a vision with proper tasks, and we become engines and vehicles of change.

Your Turn:

What is your vision? Don't let it be just a dream. Take a few moments today to consider your action steps. Take the next step.

Today's Affirmation:

I change the world through my vision and my action steps.

 *February 16*

Good morning! One of my readers shared this anonymous poem. I thought it was worth a read and contemplation.

I am your constant companion.
I am your greatest helper or your heaviest burden.
I will push you onward or drag you down to failure.
I am completely at your command.

Half the things you do, you might as well turn over to me,
And I will be able to do them quickly and correctly.
I am easily managed; you must merely be firm with me.
Show me exactly how you want something done,
And after a few lessons I will do it automatically.

I am the servant of all great individuals
And, alas, of all failures as well.
Those who are great I have made great.
Those who are failures I have made failures.

I am not a machine,
Though I work with all the precision of a machine
Plus the intelligence of a human being.
You may run me for profit, or run me for ruin;
It makes no difference to me.

Take me, train me, be firm with me,
And I will put the world at your feet.
Be easy with me, and I will destroy you.
Who am I? I am habit!

Your Turn:

After discovering that the subject of this poem is "habit," read it a second time. Which habits do you have that are building you up? Which habits are holding you back? What are some observations you can make about habits in your own life?

Today's Affirmation:

I control my habits. My habits are healthy.

Inspirations

February is National Heart Month, a month devoted to raising women's awareness about how to improve heart health and reduce the number-one killer of women: cardio-vascular disease. The WISEWOMAN program offers down-loadable cookbooks, planning tools, and assessments to improve heart health. Learn more at http://www.cdc.gov/wisewoman/resources.htm.

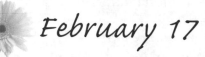

February 17

*"To think too long about doing a thing of
ten becomes its undoing."*
—Eva Young

Good morning! When was the last time you felt truly over-whelmed? Maybe it was last week, or last month, or maybe it is right now, this very minute. Have your "to-dos" piled up so high that they are robbing the joy from your days and taking the skip from your step?

When we are overwhelmed, we can often trace the feeling to one of four sources:

1. When we fail to allow enough time for the unexpected, tasks pile up and all of a sudden we find ourselves anxious or struggling to stay above water.

2. There is some specific "to do" that you just don't like do-ing. That single to-do is ignored more than any others, until it gets to a point of crisis, and must be dealt with.

3. The project seems insurmountable—since we don't know where to start, we just don't start.

4. Like today's quote, we confuse planning with doing, and spend too long in the planning phase and not enough time in the action phase.

Regardless of the source of your overwhelmed feelings, the quickest way to release them is through action. Spending even five concentrated minutes on a task helps us to feel we have control over the "to-do" versus it controlling us.

Your Turn:

Make a list of the things that are overwhelming to you right now. Choose one to work with this week. Each day, set your timer for at least five minutes and take focused action. Notice how the action begins to make the anxious and overwhelmed feelings dissolve.

Today's Affirmation:

I do not succumb to feelings of being overwhelmed. Instead, I am inspired to take action.

Going Further

Choose one area of your life where you need to stop planning and start acting. Visit www.online-stopwatch.com and set the stopwatch for five or ten minutes. Then stop thinking and take action.

February 18

> *"When you make a mistake, don't look back at it long. Take the reason of the thing into your mind and then look forward. Mistakes are lessons of wisdom. The past cannot be changed. The future is yet in your power."*
> —*Hugh White*

Good morning! When I was about sixteen, I had one of those lightbulb moments. As a teen, I battled obsessive compulsive disorder (and still do today), but at that point I had not yet been diagnosed and my thoughts and emotions were all over the board. I often felt discouraged, would beat myself up, or feel guilty—many times for things that were completely outside of my control.

I also lived in a very small town, about three hundred residents in all. There was a local café where many people would cluster and discuss the town gossip. I was amazed at how much of this gossip focused on the negative and on the past. As I listened, I realized that in my mind, I was doing much the same thing. I was rehashing the past, feeling guilt for it, and losing the present moment as I battled something from yesterday.

The lightbulb moment came when I asked myself, "How would my life change if I spent nine-tenths of that time focusing on changing the *present* instead of rehashing the past?" Not only did I ask the question, I began living the answer. My life changed in phenomenal ways. By living in the moment, yet learning from the past, the concept of regret became a rare one for me, because I was making today count.

At sixteen, I didn't realize that moment would become the first building block for living a content and complete life. I didn't know that would be the building block for the *Change Your Life Challenge* program that has helped over ten thousand women find the same contentment in all areas of their lives.

Your Turn:

What if you devoted nine-tenths of the time you now spend thinking about the past to changing the present? I know you would realize wonderful things. Try it for thirty days. This simple concept can revolutionize your life.

Today's Affirmation:

I learn from the past, but I don't sit in detention… instead I move forward and maximize the moment.

February 19

> *"Your life is what you make it."*
> —*Nana Messler*

Good morning! I had an interesting conversation with a girlfriend the other day. She was telling me about this woman who "has it all." My friend perceives this woman as having the perfect and caring husband; beautiful, talented, and respectful children; a well-kept and beautiful home; and the woman herself is beautiful with a great attitude. The description concluded with an exclamation like: "I just hate her!" (said tongue-in-cheek).

I started laughing. She asked me what was so funny. I posed this question: "If this woman had an awful husband, ugly children, a shack, and a bad attitude—would that make YOUR life better?"

She asked me what that had to do with anything. I proceeded to ask her why she was spending so much time analyzing this woman's life. What possible purpose did it serve? She explained that if this woman could "have it all" then certainly she could as well. "But what if this woman *didn't* have it all?" I pressed on. "Would that mean you couldn't have it all?"

Whether this woman owned a llama farm, was an attorney, First Lady, or the first female president of the United States has no bearing on my friend's life. Each moment she spent looking at this woman and comparing their lives was taking her focus off where it needed to be—*her own life*. Whatever this woman's life looks like is completely irrelevant to all of us. It doesn't change our own life one iota. The only thing that can change our lives is *us*. As Nana's quote states, "Your life is what you make it"—not what others make it.

Your Turn:

We rarely compare ourselves to those who have less than we do to increase our self-esteem, but women often compare themselves to those who have more, and so undermine their own esteem. Today, embrace the concept of looking at your own life, instead of the lives of others. Don't be distracted with the destructive thinking found in comparing yourself to another person—remember, you can never truly walk in his or her shoes.

Today's Affirmation:

Today, I only compare myself to the "me" I was yesterday.

Reflection Questions

Who do you compare yourself to?

How do these comparisons hinder or help you?

How would it feel to let go of measuring your life against the lives of others?

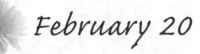 ## *February 20*

> *"Why not go out on a limb?*
> *That's where all the fruit is!"*
> *—Will Rogers*

Good morning! Take a moment to think about the times in your life when you felt the most esteemed, proud, excited, and fulfilled. What happened to create those feelings? Were you going through your day on autopilot and just doing the same-old, same-old? Or was something different?

I am going to take a wild guess that something was different. I am going to guess that when you felt that way, it was because you had reached further, discovered something new, challenged yourself, or taken a chance. And you surprised yourself by learning that chance, change, and challenge can be good things. Feelings of esteem, pride, excitement, and fulfillment are derived from an "I CAN" attitude. An "I CAN" attitude leads to an "I DO" world.

Your Turn:

Today's quote reminds us that to reach life's fruit, we have to go out on a limb and get it. We can sit and wait for it to come to us, but it could be a very long wait and there is no guarantee that we would ever get "fed." What area of your life is calling for you to meet it halfway? What are you going to do about it?

Today's Affirmation:

I embrace chance, change, and challenge.

Reflection Questions

Over the past year, where have you been "waiting" instead of "reaching"?

When have you felt the most esteemed and proud of yourself?

Which of the areas on your list are you ready to reach for to renew these fulfilled feelings?

February 21

> *"If God sends us stony paths, He will*
> *provide us with strong shoes."*
> *—Alexander Maclaren*

Good morning! I don't know about you, but I have certainly had my share of days when I felt tested to the max. Sometimes it can be hard to keep a chin up when so many things are weighing us down.

I have found that on those tough and stressful days, I am continually taught the art of letting go and the art of faith. We can't control everything—and when we try to do so, life gets heavy quickly. This simple quote is one of my favorite reminders. We are equipped to handle what life sends our way—we simply must learn from the lessons than can teach us, and remember to use the tools that are given to us.

Your Turn:

Take a moment to reflect on trying times in your past and how you have pulled through. Make a list and pat yourself on the back for what you have overcome. Use this to inspire you when life gets tough. If you are in a tough situation today, remember to let go.

Today's Affirmation:

Let go and let God.

Inspirations

Consider adding a morning devotion to your Good Morning routine. There are many great online resources for free email devotionals. Check out:

proverbs31devotions.blogspot.com/

www.maxlucado.com/

www.rbc.org/odb/odb.shtml

www.crosswalk.com/devotionals/

www.beliefnet.com/

www.upperroom.org/Devotional/

www.backtothebible.org/devotions.html

February 22

"Facts do not cease to exist just
because they are ignored."
—Aldous Huxley

Good morning! When Donna submitted this quote, I knew it would have to be the subject of one of our Good Mornings. I think this quote speaks to one of the core issues many self-improvement programs miss. We can't "ignore the facts" as we strive to create a better life. While positive thinking is a great tool, if we ignore the facts, we set ourselves up for disappointment.

To change our lives for the better, we must methodically work through our "life clutter" while maintaining a positive attitude, realizing that we are taking control of our futures. A positive attitude shouldn't be something we brainwash ourselves to have. A truly positive attitude is born when we take action, take responsibility, and start regaining control of the many areas of our lives.

We can learn a lot by looking at the flipside of this. If our attitudes aren't positive, then we can assume that we are either:

1. Trying to brainwash ourselves without dealing with core issues

2. Not taking action

3. Not regaining control

4. Ignoring the facts

5. Not taking responsibility.

Those five ingredients are the mixture required for a lasting, positive outlook.

Some might argue that our outlook relies on external events. In cases of tragedy, this is often true. But in our day-to-day stresses and anxieties, I would disagree. One of my favorite quotes has always been, "Two men look out the same prison bars, one sees mud, the other sees stars." In this example, the external is the same—but the focus of the two men is different. We control our outlook.

Your Turn:

Where in your life have you been pushing to have a good attitude without taking into account "the facts?" Which of these five areas could you improve on today?

1. Not brainwashing yourself into a positive attitude by ignoring core issues

2. Taking action

3. Regaining control

4. Facing the facts or

5. Taking responsibility.

What is a step you can take in the next hour in one of those areas?

Today's Affirmation:

I am actively regaining control of every area of my life.

February 23

> *"We are never given a dream without the power to make it come true."*
> —*Richard Bach*

Good morning! When my husband is traveling, my daughter and I often take turns suggesting a "table topic" at dinner. One evening, my daughter posed this topic: What Makes a Champion? I had just finished reading *Level Six Performance* by Dr. Steve Long, which profiles the stories of seventeen Olympians and explores their secrets of success. While all the athletes used various techniques, skills, and training methods, one thing remained constant—the dedication to the dream.

Most great accomplishments aren't found at the end of smooth pathways. They are found by climbing mountains, going through dark valleys, and treading through murky water. When we start ONLY looking at the mountain, or a dark valley, or murky water, it is easy to lose sight of the dream. But Richard Bach reminds us that, "We are never given a dream without the power to make it come true." While we will get sidetracked and look other directions at times, we have to remember to hold the vision of our dream like we would a precious jewel.

Think of all the people who have had great visions and dreams: Martin Luther King, the Wright brothers, Alexander Graham Bell, Walt Disney... the long and varied list is endless. Had one of these individuals chosen not to cherish their dream and nurture it, our world would be vastly different.

Your Turn:

What is your precious jewel of a dream? It can be simple or complex, but whatever it is, do not lose sight of it. The realization of a dream will have a profound influence on your home, your community, the country, or the world.

Today's Affirmation:
I am living my dream.

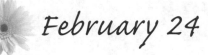

February 24

> *"I'm getting better every day in every way."*
> —*Joel Osteen*

Good morning! I have heard variations of this quote in different affirmation workbooks, and it truly is a powerful one to recite regularly.

Often, we tend to want to do so much, in so little time, we push and push and push and then get frustrated with what we perceive to be shortcomings or imperfections. These imperfections can quickly consume our focus if we let them. Of course, when we focus on our imperfections, we magnify them and give them more power than they need to have.

None of us will ever be "perfect." But we can actively be "living the challenge" through daily improvement. Some days those improvements may be large, and sometimes they may be as simple as sharing an extra smile or word of encouragement with someone.

Your Turn:
Remember that when we give up on judging ourselves, we have more to give to others. When we focus on our imperfections, we sap our own energy and have less to give to ourselves and

to those whom we care for. Today, when you find yourself pushing yourself backward instead of forward, recite the quote, "I am getting better every day in every way."

Today's Affirmation:
I am getting better every day in every way.

Reflection Questions
Where do you have a tendency to be overly critical of your efforts?

How much emotional energy could you reclaim by releasing self-judgment?

February 25

> *"Fill each day with purpose—not problems."*
> *—Shared by Good Morning reader, Cathy Rudder*

Good morning! Today's quote accompanied an email from Cathy Rudder of Dallas, Texas. She wrote:

I coined this phrase when I first started selling real estate, and my income was 100 percent commission. I used this motto to overcome my fears. These words were inspired by a quote from Ben Sweetland, referring to how trapeze acrobats keep their "act together" and make the triples happen—all in sync. His quote was, "Put your heart over the bar and the rest will follow."

That was twenty-five years ago. For the past ten years, I've owned my own firm.

This quote is truly an inspiring vision for greeting each day. When we "get out of our own way," and focus on our purpose, our problems are easier to conquer. But many of us take an opposite approach to our days: We focus on the problems at hand and believe we will "get to our purpose," once the problems are solved. We don't realize that we have it all backward. We must focus on the purpose at hand, for our purpose is always bigger than our problems.

Your Turn:

When we stay centered on our purpose and our vision, problems shrink instead of grow. When we put our problems before our vision, they become roadblocks. How have you been living your days? Is your primary focus problems or purpose? Try filling your day with purpose, and watch the dramatic shift it will create in your life.

Today's Affirmation:

I fill my days with purpose—not problems.

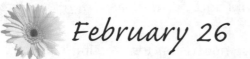

February 26

> *"Life is a competition, not with others, but with ourselves. We should seek each day to live stronger, better, truer lives; each day to master some weakness of yesterday; each day to repair a mistake; each day to surpass ourselves."*
> —David B. Haight

Good morning! When I read this quote, I felt it truly embraced what it means to be a Champion in life. If each of us were to embrace this quote, how could we not feel good come nightfall?

Each day, we compete in the arena of life and self-improvement. If we embrace the teachings of today's quote, a personal gold medal is within the reach of each of us.

Your Turn:

Today, do at least one of the following:

- live a stronger, better, truer life
- master some weakness of yesterday
- repair a mistake
- surpass yesterday

Today's Affirmation:

I become stronger every day.

Reflection Questions

In what ways could you live a stronger, better, truer life?

What weaknesses of the past are you ready to master in the present?

What mistakes will you repair in the months ahead?

February 27

> *"Insanity: doing the same thing over and over again and expecting different results."*
> —*Albert Einstein*

Good morning! I have found that most women greet positive change with open arms when given the proper tools. Yet there are some people who just can't commit to a new approach. They waiver in their efforts and eventually go back to old, destructive patterns, and become frustrated when they don't realize the changes they desire in their lives.

Einstein is right—doing the same thing over and over and expecting the result to be different is insanity. Imagine typing two-plus-two into your calculator over and over and over and over again. Do you think it would magically equal six at some point? Of course not: That would be insane! But that is what many of us do in our lives. We want a different result—but we don't modify our actions or our attitude. We might want a more fulfilling relationship, but we don't change how we communicate. We might want a more rewarding career, but we don't change our efforts. We might want to be healthier, but we don't change our unhealthy routines. To think we will reach our desired outcome without doing some work and changing our approach is insanity.

We have to learn to think of change and personal evolvement as fun! It is a chance to think outside the box, try new things, live a richer life, ask good questions, and discover new truths.

Your Turn:

Where in your life have you been desiring change without modifying your action or attitude? Pick one area and make a behavior modification that you can stick with.

Today's Affirmation:

Change is the chance to challenge and improve my life.

 February 28

> *"A man can do only what he can do. But if he does that each day he can sleep at night and do it again the next day."*
> —*Albert Schweitzer*

Good morning! I believe: "Just because our lives are complicated, doesn't mean our systems have to be"—and today's quote helps me to realize that our lives don't need to be complicated either. Schweitzer has articulately stated what it means to have a "fulfilling day," regardless of what happens between sunrise and sundown.

Somewhere along the way, we have learned to make our days more complicated than they need to be by focusing on things that are not within our control. Or, we spend a large part of our day getting sidetracked by the past or preoccupied with the future. If we keep our hearts and minds focused on the day at hand and "give it all we've got," then we can rest soundly at night.

Your Turn:

Today, push back thoughts of yesterday and worries about tomorrow. Stay focused on the day and moments at hand. Give it all you've got—then sleep soundly tonight.

Today's Affirmation:

I give each day my all.

Going Further

Try creating a "mission statement" for the day by writing a single, clear sentence about your goals and intentions for the twenty-four hours ahead. For example, "Today I will complete the edits on this book." Keep your mission statement close at hand to help focus throughout the day.

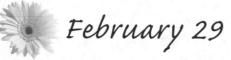 *February 29*

*"To be successful you must accept all challenges
that come your way. You can't just accept
the ones you like."*
—*Mike Gafka*

Good morning! The first time I read this quote, I smiled knowingly. When I started my first business, at age twenty-two, I still believed in a very black-and-white concept of fairness. I believed that if I worked hard enough, good results would come my way in work endeavors. I believed that if I lived in a loving, caring, and compassionate way, my personal life would be full of loving, caring, and compassion.

I am now in my mid-thirties and realize that life is fair in the long-term, even though it rarely seems fair in the short-term. Often what *we* think is fair, is actually one-sided, and we can't see fairness until we have grown, stretched, and visited other perspectives and places.

I do know that the quickest way to make life unfair and stay "stuck" is to not accept everything life brings. When we become picky or choosy about what we accept—trying to extract the good and leave the bad—we shut down to the balance and fairness of life. Often "the bad" comes for a reason. It comes to make us grow; it comes to make us see something new; it comes to challenge our spirit and build our soul. When we refuse to welcome this "bad," we refuse to welcome that growth.

Some of my most tragic and difficult life experiences were actually my best teachers. They carried me to places I never could have reached without them. Had I not gathered the courage to accept these challenges, I wouldn't be authoring this book or the many other books that have helped over 100,000 people.

Your Turn:

Where in your life have you been trying to just "take the good and leave the bad?" What challenge does life have for you, that you have been avoiding because it doesn't seem "fair?" As February comes to a close, I challenge you to accept all that life offers—the good and the bad. During the month of March, I encourage you to meet a challenge eye to eye, welcome it, and see where it might carry you.

Today's Affirmation:

I understand that each of life's challenges is vital to reaching my full potential. I embrace and welcome these challenges with open arms.

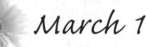 *March 1*

> *"We increase whatever we praise."*
> —*Charles Fillmore*

Good morning! One of the methods most often used in couple's therapy is praising the good we see in our spouses. Our tendency can be to dwell on the negative, or to "nag" about what we do not like. We can fall into the same patterns with friends, children, and colleagues. However, this negativity will only strengthen the very actions or behaviors we feel negative about.

The best strategy (and a much more pleasant way to live) is to seek out the positive (even when it is hard to see!) and praise it up and down. Think of it this way—whatever we give attention to will grow. If we give attention to bothersome behaviors/

actions through negativity or nagging, they will grow. If we give attention to the positive, it will grow.

Your Turn:

Today, squelch the negative and feed the positive. Look for something to praise in each person you have contact with. Watch how your attitude and day becomes brighter as well!

Today's Affirmation:

I praise the positive.

Inspirations

March 1 marks Be Positive Day. Visit www.bepositiveday. com to view the Be Positive Day Handbook. The handbook is a developing resource guide full of ideas as to things that can be done to make our world a more positive place.

March 2

> *No matter how long the winter,*
> *spring is sure to follow.*
> *—Proverb*

Good morning! As we emerge from winter's darkness and the sun begins peeking through our windows this spring, it can feel magical and warming. Yet, it can also magically help us catch sight of all the dust that piles up on short winter days.

During an interview on the "Ask Heloise" show, Amy (her daughter who now hosts the show) and I were discussing my approach to priority planning and choosing things to do each day that matter. Heloise had a similar approach, which was specific to cleaning. She advised her daughter to choose three things in the home and maintain those things vigorously. They could be clean windows, a desire for fresh flowers, clean appliances, or the like.

Take Heloise's advice and focus your efforts. Choose three priorities for your home and then maintain them rigorously.

Your Turn:

Choose your three-item priority household list. Just as a painter signs his work, consider this your "signature" in your household.

Today's Affirmation:

I prioritize and focus on efforts I take pride in.

Reflection Question

Could any other areas of your life use a "signature"? Consider developing a three-priority list for a relationship, work, hobby, fitness, family time, or any other area.

March 3

"Be GOOD and do GOOD"
—*Nikki Turner*

Good morning! Nikki sent in today's quote with the following message:

I lost my hearing in 1996 and in 2000 was implanted with a cochlear implant and met my now-fiancé through a mutual friend. On his first email to me, he had this quote in the signature. When I get down, I always remind myself to BE GOOD and DO GOOD. I feel like I am living in a more open and accepting way since starting this, because I keep this in my mind throughout the day—even when life throws me a curve ball. It works.

The concept of this quote is to be good to yourself and avoid destructive habits or negative thoughts. By being good to one's self, you are open to doing good for others, too. This brings harmony to daily life and we are better able to accept life's challenges since we are in the "zone." My fiancé and I always say this to each other when saying good-bye for the day.... Be Good and Do Good.

Your Turn:

I encourage you, as I have, to gather courage from Nikki's sharing. As you go about your day today, keep this quote in your mind, "Be good and do good."

Today's Affirmation:

I am good to myself and others. I do good for myself and others.

March 4

"Expect trouble as an inevitable part of life,
and when it comes, hold your head high.
Look it squarely in the eye, and say, 'I will be
bigger than you. You cannot defeat me.'"
—*Ann Landers*

Good morning! When Ann Landers was asked to give advice about successful living, she shared the above quote, which I hadn't heard until recently, when I read it in a book I received for Christmas.

When I read Ann's words, I was filled with a feeling of: *Yes!! That is what it takes to live our best life. We don't shy from trouble, we stare it down.*

As a business owner and an entrepreneur, I have lived this quote over and over again. There is nothing more rewarding than the day you realize that you have everything you need within yourself and are perfectly capable of overcoming what-ever life throws your way. When we get to the place where we can welcome all of life—the good, the bad, and the ugly—with confidence, we know a peace beyond measure.

Your Turn:

Realize that we cannot run from trouble; it is an inevitable part of life. However, we can learn to rise above it. Welcome all of life's experiences—the good, the bad, and the ugly. Challenge yourself to look these experiences in the eye and use them as catalysts to become the very best you can be.

Today's Affirmation:

I am bigger than any troubles.

March 5

"Humility does not mean you think less of yourself.
It means you think of yourself less"
—Ken Blanchard

Good morning! Have you ever noticed the natural human tendency to put ourselves in the "middle" of everything, either as its source or its cause? For example, when someone doesn't return a phone call, our thoughts often turn to, "Did I upset her?" or "Maybe she doesn't want to talk to me." If a coworker seems to be having an off-day we may wonder, "Did I contribute to this situation?"

When we make the focus about "us," we can't focus on other people in a healthy way. In these situations, it is best to turn from our own egos, and instead look at the situation or the person involved directly. Perhaps a call wasn't returned because a child became sick, or the person went into a ditch in a snowstorm, or fell asleep while watching TV. Perhaps a coworker learned of an ill relative, or had a fight with a spouse. Perhaps it has nothing to do with us.

Your Turn:

As you go throughout your day, watch for the tendency to put yourself as a "cause" or "reason" for someone else's unhappiness. When you find yourself doing so, remove the focus from yourself and, instead, ask thoughtful and inquisitive questions about the situation you are concerned about. Remember that when we make the focus about "us" we can't focus on another person in a healthy way.

Today's Affirmation:

I remain focused on the entire situation instead of staying focused on myself.

 *March 6*

*"Don't compromise yourself;
you're all that you've got."*
—Janis Joplin

Good morning! One day a few years ago I was exhausted and decided to take a quick nap. My daughter Sammy, who was ten at the time, asked if she could come upstairs and read while I napped. Unable to fall asleep right away, I began doing a Sudoku puzzle while she read. (I had been working through the "Fiendish level" in a book a girlfriend gave me at Christmas.) Ten or fifteen minutes later, Sammy asked how I was doing on my fiendish puzzle. "I don't know, kiddo," I replied. "This is a tough one, I may not be able to solve it."

Sammy replied with, "Who are you and what have you done with my mother! The Mom *I* know can solve any Sudoku puzzle—even the fiendish." I smiled to myself and solved the puzzle in the next ten minutes.

Your Turn:

Sammy reminded me of how important the "little things" we say to ourselves are. She also reiterated the power of the mind. It will accomplish what we believe it can accomplish. I think this lesson goes nicely with today's quote. "Don't compromise yourself; you're all that you've got." Big doubts, fears, and insecurities are born from smaller ones. Today, be cognizant of the messages you send yourself. Replace: "I cannot," with "I can."

Today's Affirmation:

Each day my self-belief grows.

March 7

> *"Our workday lives are filled with opportunities*
> *to bless others. The power of a single glance*
> *or an encouraging smile must never*
> *be underestimated."*
> —*G. Richard Rieger*

Good morning! As we move through another week, let's remember the power of a glance and an encouraging smile. At a recent work meeting, our team was reviewing how 90 percent of communication is nonverbal.

What are you "saying" when you aren't "speaking?" Pay careful attention, as you might be surprised! When you aren't acting with positive intention, you leave room for negative interpretation.

Your Turn:

Pay attention to your nonverbal communication today. Work to increase your positive intentions to others through a smile or encouraging word. A simple thank-you can warm the heart.

Today's Affirmation:

I express my appreciation to those around me.

Going Further

This week heed Rieger's words and pay attention to the many opportunities to bless others. Add an index card to your daily planner and fill it with blessings you give to those around you.

March 8

"Don't say you don't have enough time. You have exactly the same number of hours per day that were given to Helen Keller, Pasteur, Michelangelo, Mother Teresa, Leonardo da Vinci, Thomas Jefferson, and Albert Einstein."
—*H. Jackson Brown Jr.*

Good morning! I have a confession. I have used the excuse, "I just don't have enough time" in my life. I even said it last week when I was discussing why I was not pursuing my martial-arts training. When I saw this quote I thought—whoa... reality check! When I say I "don't have enough time," it is really a cop-out for not knowing where to begin or not being passionate enough about the task at hand.

Excluding serious or terminal health ailments, one thing is constant—we all have the same amount of time per day. We can choose to make the day matter, or we can choose to let the day go by—its potential unrealized.

This quote helped me to realize that I don't have a lack of time. I have the same amount of time as some of the world's geniuses. It is a matter of learning to work with the clock, instead of against it, that matters the most.

Your Turn:

How often have you used the excuse "I don't have enough time" in the past thirty days? How does today's quote make you feel?

Today's Affirmation:

I create the time to do what matters.

Going Further

If procrastination is holding you back visit www.brooknoel. com to learn more about my program: Overcoming Procrastination.

March 9

> *"Always do right. This will gratify some people, and astonish the rest."*
> —*Mark Twain*

Good morning! When my daughter was in the difficult middle school years featured in movies like *Mean Girls* she lashed out at a bully who had been picking on her. When I asked her why, she explained she was following the golden rule "treating others like they were treating her." I explained that although that is how much of society lives, she had the golden rule backward. I explained that she was half-right. If the bully was practicing the golden rule, then she wouldn't pick on Sammy in the first place—but just because the bully picked on her, that didn't make it right to lash back.

Then I uttered all those wise statements that we get to say as moms like, "If a friend told you to jump off a bridge, would you?" and, "Two wrongs don't make a right." My daughter, being the inquisitive child she is, wanted to know how far the bridge was from the water (in case it would be fun, like a diving board). She also wanted to know if two wrongs don't equal a right, what they do equal, because in algebra two negatives make a positive.

I felt myself quickly losing ground in the conversation. I switched paths completely. I asked Sammy, "Do you want to be like this other girl? Is she a mentor?" My daughter rolled her eyes, appalled at the thought. I explained that one of the basic success principles is to identify what qualities you desire, find someone who has them, and emulate them. I didn't have to go any further—she understood the outcome of emulating the actions of this girl. Yet she still seemed troubled. "But that isn't fair. Why do I have to lead by example if other girls aren't?"

I asked Sammy to imagine a world where we all treated each other like other people treated us, instead of treating others how we want to be treated. We quickly saw a war-filled world, with harsh words and hurt feelings. "Someone has to find a better way," I told her. She seemed ready to end the conversation, although I could see her mind was spinning.

The next day she came home from school and told me she and another girl had encouraged the start of an anti-bully group in their school. The group has been ongoing for three years and has dramatically reduced the bullying challenges of the school.

When today's quote came across my screen, I wished I would have had it handy during my conversation with my daughter. Always do right. This will gratify some people, and astonish the rest. Often times we "do right" not by following the rules, but by forging new paths where they are desperately needed. We "do right" because we gratify and astonish others—and ourselves. A life filled with gratitude and astonishment is a much better life than one where we point fingers and live a backward golden rule.

Your Turn:

How do you live the golden rule in your own life? Do you take the higher road and "do right" even when it is the most challenging choice?

Today's Affirmation:

Every day, I make the right choices at every juncture.

 *March 10*

"We are all of us stars, and we deserve to twinkle"
—**Marilyn Monroe**

Good morning! I received today's quote from Timia, who had included this message in her email:

I also see the "star" in my kids every day—their curiosity, their enthusiasm, their (sometimes wacky!) creativity, their innocence, their love—I could go on—and I need to remember to recognize that twinkle in myself, too. It is easy to feel overwhelmed and fed-up sometimes, and you wonder some days why you bother... it's important to be in touch with what makes you "twinkle," whatever that may be!

This quote really resonated with me this morning, as my house is strangely quiet (or as quiet as a house can be with three dogs). Later this afternoon I will be on my way to Memphis and Oxford, Mississippi, for several days of appearances. Yesterday, my best friend and I drove my daughter to her grandmother, who will care for her while I am gone. Driving took most of the day, and when I arrived home I did a bit of writing, boxed up some donations for St. Vincent's, and was ready for bed.

My quiet house this morning reinforced the importance of Marilyn's quote and Timia's interpretation. Often, we get so swept up in the needs of others, our day-to-day activities, our house management... it can be challenging to create our *own* time to nourish the soul and nourish that "twinkle" within. During our child-rearing years, it is rare to have the "empty house" that challenges us to fill it with our spirit, dreams, and positive attitude. When we forget to nourish ourselves, we feel lonely when we are alone. When we create the time to nourish ourselves throughout life's journey, our peacefulness and contentment remain a constant—whether alone or within a crowd.

Your Turn:

Today, reflect on how much time you have spent nourishing yourself in the past thirty days, completely separate from other friends or family members. Today, find at least thirty minutes to nourish your own "twinkle."

Today's Affirmation:

I care for myself and for others.

Inspirations

Take some time to nourish yourself with a homemade self-care spa recipe. For 250 recipes, visit http://www.scribd.com/doc/1774/250-Bath-Body-Recipes or http://living.health.com/2008/02/28/at-home-spa-recipes

March 11

"Each day comes bearing a gift. Untie the ribbon."
—Ann Ruth Schabader

Good morning! I had seen a variation of this once before ("life is a gift, untie the ribbon") so I was pleased when a reader sent in this original quote and its source.

I think it is a beautiful reminder of how lucky we all are to be here, regardless of our circumstances or current challenges. Sometimes obstacles can seem so large or insurmountable that we forget we are still the recipients of the greatest gift— life. When faced with the seemingly insurmountable, we often forget to untie the ribbon of this gift.

Your Turn:

No matter where you are in your life, or what challenges you face short- or long-term, take a moment to be thankful for the gift of life. Then, go untie a ribbon today.

Today's Affirmation:

Life is a gift and I untie the ribbon.

Inspirations

Visit the resources at www.brooknoel.com to download printable bookmarks with Ann's wonderful quote.

 # March 12

> *"I need to stop trying to become perfect*
> *and just try to become better."*
> —*Sasha Cohen, U.S. figure skater*

Good morning! Sasha states one of those universal truths that we would all be wise to adapt. When I was teaching my Goal Class this year, I was amazed at how many people set their daily goals like this:

- Drink eight glasses of water, seven days a week
- Work out seven days a week

These goal setters were chasing perfection. But perfection doesn't exist in reality. When we strive for perfection over improvement, we end up frustrated, and often abandon our goals altogether. Why? Because they aren't attainable.

Why don't more people go stand on a ledge and jump off to see if they can fly? Because they know they can't—it's not possible. Perfection is equally impossible and insane. Chasing perfection is one of the shortest paths to living on a treadmill of incompleteness.

Your Turn:

Where in your life have you been chasing perfection instead of improvement? Take the weight off your shoulders and cast perfection aside. Instead, challenge yourself to daily improvement.

Today's Affirmation:

Each day I am getting better and better.

 # March 13

> *"Open your eyes, look within, are you satisfied*
> *with the life you're living?"*
> —*Bob Marley*

Good morning! During our days we can become so occupied with our lists, tasks, and stressors that we forget to look at the "bigger picture." Are the things we are doing taking us in the direction we want and need to go?

Take a glance at your list of tasks to complete for today. Then, bring to mind your three priorities at this stage of your life. If you don't have them written down already, go ahead and do so. Now, carefully consider each item on your to-do list. How many of them align with the priorities of your life? It is true that if you check off those to-do items, you are moving forward, but are you moving forward in a direction that is fulfilling?

Your Turn:

After identifying your priorities and checking your to-do list, what did you find? If you found that very few of your to-do items aligned with your priorities, find thirty minutes of reflection time this weekend to create a more balanced plan. Try to do at least one thing per day that coincides with your top priorities.

Today's Affirmation:

Each day, I do what matters.

March 14

> *"Daily Decisions Decide Destiny."*
> *—Kelli Sibbitt*

Good morning! Four simple words sum up an important reminder to keep with us throughout the day. Often, it seems the "big decisions" require our heart and mind and soul. But life is made up mostly from the little decisions, and these many little decisions become "our life."

Your Turn:

As you move throughout your day, realize that each decision (whether large or small) is a brick in the foundation of your destiny. Give each decision the attention of your heart and soul, remembering that there is no such thing as a "little decision."

Today's Affirmation:

I make thoughtful decisions each day.

Going Further

Indecision can be a stopping point to happiness, success, and satisfaction. If you find yourself stuck in indecision, visit www.mindtools.com to create ideas and worksheets to help you place options in perspective and begin to move forward. One of my favorites is the Six Hats exercise: http://www.mindtools.com/pages/article/new-TED_07.htm.

March 15

"Do what you can, with what you have, where you are."
—*Theodore Roosevelt*

Good morning! Have you ever heard someone say, "I'll do that once I ___ (fill in the blank) ____"? Have you ever said that yourself? This quote reminds us of the fundamental truth—in order to get anywhere different, we must begin by doing what we can, with what we have, where we are.

We can see this principle in action through a very simple example. If we want to take a trip to Orlando, a plane isn't likely to magically appear, nor will hotel reservations. First we have to do what we can, where we are. We have to research the trip, book the tickets, and pack the suitcases. By completing action after action, we then get to the wonderful trip.

Sometimes it can be hard to be as practical with our dreams and emotions and goals. They aren't as visually concrete to us as planning a vacation and taking the steps needed to get there.

Your Turn:

What goal or vision have you been thinking about instead of moving toward? What can you do, with what you have, where you are, to take a step forward today?

Today's Affirmation:

I do the best that I can, with what I have, right here, and right now.

March 16

"There are three types of people in this world: those who make things happen, those who watch things happen and those who wonder what happened. We all have a choice. You can decide which type of person you want to be. I have always chosen to be in the first group."
—*Mary Kay Ash*

Good morning! I have always loved the wisdom of entrepreneur and visionary Mary Kay Ash. Today I thought I would give you a little quiz in conjunction with her quote. Mary Kay lists three types of people.

• Those who make things happen

• Those who watch things happen

• Those who wonder what happened

Which of these three groups do you think is the happiest? Which do you think is the most unhappy, often feeling they are one of life's "victims?" Which group do you think goes through life without experiencing much joy or sadness?

Now, try this one. Which of these groups do you think is the most successful? Which do you think is most resentful? Which do you think never realizes their potential because they never explore it?

While I am sure you guessed right, here are the answers:

• Those who make things happen—happiest and most successful

• Those who watch things happen—most unhappy and resentful

• Those who wonder what happened—don't experience much joy or sadness or realize potential

Those who watch things happen or wonder what happened haven't taken the wheel to steer their life. Instead, their days are left to be blown around by external winds.

Those in group one, like Mary Kay Ash, are subject to the same external winds, but they make things happen in spite of them. Those in group one have a vision bigger than any obstacle, and that vision will always get them through the storm.

Your Turn:

Which group do you fall into? Think about your last month and what category the majority of your actions (or nonactions) fell into. If you aren't in group A, why not join? Great things are happening there!

Today's Affirmation:

I make things happen.

March 17

> *"... Be not afraid of greatness: some are born great,*
> *some achieve greatness, and some have*
> *greatness thrust upon them."*
> —**William Shakespeare**

Good morning! Our greatness can be expressed in many ways. It can be in the way we cook... be it a casserole or an extravagant dinner, a hamburger or a steak, an artful salad, or a lowly potato patty, banana boats, or just a plate of fresh fruit. Good food, lovingly prepared and artfully presented, is never anything but great! Our greatness might be in the ability to comfort a crying child, help someone overcome a fear, or take a great stride toward self-change. Sometimes we think of greatness as "what is happening around us," without realizing all the greatness for which we are responsible.

Your Turn:

As you move throughout your day today, be conscious of the fact that you have the ability to turn the "good" to "great." Take a moment to reflect on five great things you did in the last week as well. When we take the time to praise ourselves for what we do well, we will naturally do more of it.

Today's Affirmation:

I care enough to transform the good into the great.

Reflection Questions

Many of us are gifted when it comes to listing our faults and shortcomings. Practice listing your positive qualities. Today, make a list of at least twenty-five talents or characteristics that mark your greatness.

 *March 18*

"Spring is nature's way of saying 'Let's party!'"
—*Robin Williams*

Good morning! With the first official day of spring just around the corner it's the perfect time to clear our clutter. Clutter not only fills physical space in our homes but also occupies emotional energy. Here are five tips to spring into action:

1. Break your home into stations: Walk through your home and break its areas down into manageable chunks. Cleaning a kitchen might be composed of the following "stations:" emptying the pantry, cleaning appliances, emptying/sorting cabinets and drawers, cleaning surfaces. Each station should be small enough that you aren't overwhelmed before you start! Record all your stations in a notebook.

2. Choose your time line: Sit down with a calendar and choose a goal date for completing your cleaning. Assign your stations dates in order to meet your goal. Consider enlisting the help of a friend or family member to help make the work go faster.

3. Get busy: If you have a hard time getting started, use a timer and spend thirty minutes in one station of the home. You'll be relieved to hear the beep, and amazed at what you can tackle in thirty minutes.

4. Don't overorganize: Be careful not to implement a system that is too complicated to maintain. When we go to an organizing store, we can fall prey to all the wonderful-looking tools and contraptions for sale. Often, these just become a different way to store clutter.

Find a way to enjoy your cleaning time: Often, cleaning can become drudgery. Consider listening to books-on-tape or learning a new language while you clean. Doing something for yourself and learning something new can make time fly and actually make you look forward to cleaning.

For more tips on organizing or dealing with clutter, visit www. changeyourlifechallenge.com.

Your Turn:

Choose at least one tip from today's list to implement this week and get ready for spring!

Today's Affirmation:

My home is a way to express my care of family.

Going Further

Need some housekeeping inspiration? Visit www.brook-noel.com to learn about the annual Spring Cleaning challenge I host each year.

March 19

> *"Dream as if you'll live forever.*
> *Live as if you'll die today."*
> —*James Dean*

Good morning! I believe that living in the moment and maximizing each moment is the key to knowing true joy. When I first started "living in the moment," I grappled with the concept. How do I live in the moment while also keeping the long-term in mind? I wish I would have had this quote during that time, as it expresses the key to rich-living beautifully.

Even though we live in the moment, we still dream big. We look forward to the future with anticipation and expectation, but we don't "live in tomorrow." Instead, we put forward our best effort each and every day, living as though it were our last. We can only find happiness in the moment. We can't find tomorrow's happiness today. And we can't find happiness when we are waiting "for something else." To know true joy, we must embrace and recognize the joy of everything that is right here, right now.

Your Turn:

Don't search for tomorrow's happiness today. Instead, recognize and enjoy all the richness of this very moment.

Today's Affirmation:

I find joy in the moment.

Reflection Questions

In what ways have you been living "in tomorrow" instead of today?

What have you been waiting on for happiness?

How could letting go of expectations for tomorrow bring more joy today?

March 20

"I can start my day over anytime I choose."
—**Brook Noel**

Good morning! Recently, my mother and I were chatting, and she reminded me of something I had done as a little girl. Every once in a while, she would see me stop for a moment and close my eyes as if intently concentrating on something. One day, when I was doing this after lunch, she asked me what I was doing. I informed her that, "My day isn't going that good, so I am starting it over." I don't know where I learned the skill, but it has served me well.

In 2005, I was interviewed by a Penn State researcher studying the minds of media entrepreneurs. Toward the end of the interview, she asked me, "What keeps you going during the bad days?" I didn't pause for a second before responding, "I don't have bad days." While there are moments during the day that can be challenging or troubling, very rarely do I let that moment seep into the attitude of the entire day. If my morning is challenging, then, come lunchtime, I take a moment to clear my mind and "restart my day"—anticipating nothing but the best for the afternoon. Surely, there is joy to be found each and every day. If we let a challenging circumstance set the stage for the entire day, we miss the joys and opportunities of the day at hand.

Your Turn:

When you face a challenging day this week, try "restarting your day."

Today's Affirmation:

Each day brings joy, fulfillment, and love.

March 21

> *"The best time to plant a tree was twenty years ago.*
> *The second-best time is today."*
> —*Chinese Proverb*

Good morning! Rhonda Miga sent in this quote, along with the following note that is perfect for celebrating the onset of spring!

I think this applies to all of us. There are many things that we wanted to do twenty years (or ten or even five) ago but we never got around to it. I think this proverb is great because it is saying "so what, do it today!" You can't go back and change what you did not do, but there is nothing stopping us from doing it today.

I recently went back to school and made a comment to my mother-in-law: "maybe I will finish this by the time I am fifty." She said, "You are going to be fifty anyway, right? So why not be fifty and have a new degree?"

It may have been better to get this degree years ago, but now is the second-best time.

These are wonderful words of wisdom. This quote also reminds me that we need not live with regret. What we didn't do yesterday (or decades ago) can still be started today. Why live in the past, when we have the power to create our future?

Your Turn:

What has been left undone in your life that you could begin today? Take past regret and transform it into an action plan for your future.

Today's Affirmation:

Today is the perfect time for change.

Inspirations

Make a change in the world today by planting a tree in celebration or honor of someone or something. Visit the Arbor Day Foundation at www.nationaltreetrust.org/ join/tictim/ to learn more.

March 22

> *"You get the best out of others when you give the best of yourself."*
> *—Author unknown*

Good morning! What a simple and true wisdom today's quote holds. Often when we get frustrated with someone in our life, whether it is a colleague, a friend, or a family member, we begin focusing on "what's wrong," or use it as an excuse not to go the extra mile.

However, like attracts like, and when we behave like this we then attract "halfhearted efforts" from those around us. The cycle then continues until we find ourselves with a weight on our shoulders and a heaviness in our hearts.

When we give the best of ourselves, regardless of anyone's behavior, we enjoy a richer life. Likewise, we set an example for our children, friends, and all we come into contact with. We encourage others to be at their best. When we live by the creed of always doing and giving our best, we know a personal peace that can't be found through any quick-fix method. We know a personal peace that is lasting.

Your Turn:

Take a moment today to release any negativity you have been holding toward another person. Take the energy you have been focusing on their behavior, and redirect it to focus on doing and giving your best.

Today's Affirmation:

I focus all of my energies on what is productive, helpful, and makes a difference.

 *March 23*

> *"Generally, by the time you are real, most of your hair has been loved off, and your eyes drop out and you get loose in the joints and very shabby. But these things don't matter at all. Because once you are real you can't be ugly, except to people who don't understand."*
> —*Margery Williams Bianco,*
> **The Velveteen Rabbit**

Good morning! When I opened my morning email and found this quote, I felt like I was being transported back in time. I read *The Velveteen Rabbit* as a little girl (the Easter bunny left it in my basket) and I loved the passage quoted above.

Donna also shared that a close friend cross-stitched this quote for her during a rough time. She wrote:

Each morning I wake up, read it and remember that no matter what I start to "think" I may be... I am real because I am loved. I think this is one of the most beautiful and ageless tales ever written. I am blessed to have the family and friends I do. Every wrinkle for laughing and smiling and crying makes us beautiful and real because we are loved.

When we talk about self-discovery and personal peace, we are looking for that "real place." We long to be centered and have a centered (and sane!) anchor within. We long to make decisions from a peaceful and rational place, instead of as a reaction to external pressure. But we don't get to that place overnight. Like today's quote shares—it takes a long time, but it is worth it. All the little things cease to matter once we are "real."

Your Turn:

Take a moment today to center yourself and be still. Take ten deep breaths, counting to five as you inhale, and then again to five as you exhale. Remember that everything you face in life is bringing you nearer to that "real" place. Trust life.

Today's Affirmation:

I trust life.

Inspirations

If you haven't yet read *The Velveteen Rabbit*, consider picking up a copy from the children's section of your favorite bookstore, or read it online at http://www.gutenberg.org/etext/11757.

March 24

*"Angels have the ability to fly because they
take themselves lightly."*
—*Author unknown*

Good morning! As we move through our days, we are often consumed by some issue or crisis and it becomes a weight on our shoulders. What might be a "little thing" becomes a "big thing" because we make it so. Our ability to let go is weak, while our ability to blame ourselves (or someone else) is strong.

A couple of years ago, I was going through a difficult situation with some very negative people. I couldn't understand why they were doing some of the things they were doing. I found myself "wound tight" about their behavior and analyzing it with others in search of an explanation. I quickly realized that discussing or analyzing their behavior was a drain on my energy and the person I was talking with. The situation was beyond our control, and instead of "letting go" we were "holding on" by feeding it with our time and energy.

Shortly after that, I realized I had two choices: (1) Continue discussing it with others, draining my energy (and theirs!) and losing ground in moving forward with what matters; or (2) Make a conscious decision to "let go" and focus on something positive where I could make a difference.

I chose to let go. It wasn't easy. Sometimes I found my mind drifting back to the negative situation, or staying awake at night worrying about it. Continually, over and over, I had to remind myself—"LET GO!" The more I reminded myself to let go, the more able I was to do so. I found that the more I let go of the negative, the more space I created for living the positive.

Your Turn:

As you go throughout your day, treat your energy and thoughts like gold. Before you invest time and energy into a situation, ask yourself, "Does this truly matter?" If the answer is no, make the conscious choice to "let go" and focus on something positive in its place.

Today's Affirmation:

I turn away from the negative and put positive in its place.

 ## March 25

> *"Smile today… one smile can make miles and miles of smiles."*
> —*Lisa's Mother*

Good morning! Last night I received a wonderful email that is perfect to share with you as we start the day.

Lisa wrote, *I was just sending an email out to some friends and remembered something my mom has said to me since I was really young and thought I would share it with you. "Smile today... one smile can make miles and miles of smiles."*

I remember thinking about this when I was about six or seven, and I actually tried it. When you smile at a person, they almost always smile back. Even if you smile at them in passing, their smile usually lasts long enough to catch at least one other person's attention, and so the cycle begins again. I remember thinking that it was quite a powerful, yet simple thing, but it could bring so much happiness into our world.

My little ones are in bed now, but I think I just might try to teach them that tomorrow. I bet my mom will be proud to know that I did listen and even learned from what she taught. I think that I will also let her know what I remembered—I bet I make her smile too!

Thank you for sending this, Lisa. You are right—so simple, yet so profound. If each of us embraced this concept, undoubtedly we could make the world a much happier place.

Your Turn:

Embrace Lisa's mom's wisdom today and start a chain of smiles. As you do, think of other readers of this book who are doing the same. With combined efforts we can make March 25th (or any day!) one of the most smile-filled days around.

Today's Affirmation:

Each day I remember to start a chain of smiles.

 ## *March 26*

> *"It is always too early to quit."*
> —*Norman Vincent Peale*

Good morning! Last week my mother and I were discussing how, when people find strength in unknown reserves—and keep pushing forward despite the odds—they realize success. Almost every great success story has a "dark bottom," where hoping seemed difficult—if not crazy! Yet, it is in those times that we learn our true strength and develop the skill set and attitude that brings long-term success.

When I was a little girl, I used to purchase inspirational quotes on bookmarks, wallet cards, etc. They were inexpensive and always made me smile. I have one thick gold card that features a poem titled "Don't Quit." The card is about twenty-five years old now, but the message is timeless. I wanted to share it with you this morning.

Don't Quit

When things go wrong as they sometimes will.

When the road you're trudging seems all up hill.

When funds are low and the debts are high.

And you want to smile, but you have to sigh.

When care is pressing you down a bit.

Rest, if you must, but don't you quit.

Life is queer with its twists and turns.

As every one of us sometimes learns.

And many a failure turns about,

When he might have won had he stuck it out:

Don't give up though the pace seems slow -

You may succeed with another blow.

Success is failure turned inside out -

The silver tint of the clouds of doubt

And you never can tell how close you are.

It may be near when it seems so far:

So stick to the fight when you're hardest hit—

It's when things seem worst that you must not quit.

—Author unknown

I have kept this card in my wallet for most of my life and turned to it when I was "hardest hit," to remind myself that it is okay to rest, but not to quit. I am so glad that I never gave up on my dreams, or I wouldn't have the privilege of sharing with all of you today.

Your Turn:

Print out today's poem and keep it handy for times when you need a reminder to "stick to the fight when you're hardest hit."

Today's Affirmation:

When things go wrong as they sometimes will, and the road ahead seems all uphill—I may rest, but I'll never quit.

 March 27

"If you build it, they will come."
—Field of Dreams

Good morning! April submitted this fun story the other day and I wanted to share it with you. April wrote:

With our oldest daughter living in the basement until she marries (in one year!!!) we had to come up with a system for her mail. I had my husband hang the cork/white board near the basement door with 2 wall pockets underneath it. One is for my daughter's mail, the other is for markers, push pins, etc., supplies for the board. I hadn't planned on using it until I was ready to "start" my system. The family just took over—the first message was from my husband!! The kids are already using it, too—as a family message center. It made me think of that quote. We just hung it up—and they used it! Thank you.

Well the good news, April, is that you are using it the right way! What I like even better about April's story is how her family "embraced" the change. Often, we think that something we try that is "new" won't be well received, and we don't give our family the benefit of the doubt. Let's be open to the possibility that those around us may be ready for positive changes, too!

Your Turn:

Never assume that you know how someone will respond to a new routine or technique. Give everyone the chance to formulate their own response. You may be pleasantly surprised!

Today's Affirmation:

I enable positive change for those around me.

Reflection Question

Where in your life have you predicted how someone will respond and not given the person a chance to speak for him or herself?

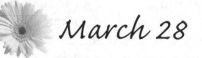

March 28

"Ring the bells that still can ring, Forget your perfect
offering. There is a crack in everything.
That's how the light shines in."
—Leonard Cohen

Good morning! I don't know about you, but I found this quote to be a wonderful relief. We all know perfection isn't possible, but still many of us chase it anyway. This quote encourages us to stop that chase. As Donna shared in an email to me:

This is one of my very favorite quotes, because it reminds me not only that imperfection is inevitable, but also a blessing, because "that's how the light shines in."

My mother is an artist. I have learned many lessons from her over the course of my life. One lesson in particular came to mind when I read this quote. When I was first learning to draw and paint as a young girl, I kept focusing on the "subject" and would quickly get frustrated when my drawing of a deer looked more like an upside-down pickup truck. My mother encouraged me to stop looking at the "object" and start looking at the "space around it." She explained that the physical object was only a small portion of the drawing—the space around the object is what actually defined the lines of the object itself. It was through that lesson I began learning to look at the "whole picture"—not just at what was obvious.

When we strive for perfection, we are just looking at "the obvious." We quickly discount all the benefits that come from the "whole picture"—from the learning curve, from the mistakes, from the space for imperfection. It is the "whole picture" that creates a rich life. It is the "whole picture" that contains the cracks that let the learning and living shine in.

Your Turn:

Today, look past the "obvious" to the "whole picture" of each situation you are in.

Today's Affirmation:

I look past the obvious and take in the "whole picture."

 *March 29*

> *"Go confidently in the directions of your dreams;*
> *live the life you've imagined. As you simplify your*
> *life, the laws of the universe will be simpler."*
> —*Henry David Thoreau*

Good morning! With spring officially here, I have been de-cluttering and simplifying. I have finally *had it* with clutter and am purging things besides paper! Knickknacks, miscellaneous items—by the garbage bag I am hauling out donations and giveaways. The other night I walked into one of my "de-cluttered" rooms and was amazed at how good the room felt. I had space to think, or even twirl in a circle if I wanted.

I have noticed that just as our surroundings get cluttered, our minds also get cluttered. I can testify that today's quote is true—whether it is applied to your physical surroundings or to uncluttering your mind.

Often we become our own obstacle—especially within our minds. We get wrapped up in something we can't change or that doesn't really matter. We exert hours of thinking over a situation that doesn't advance us any or help anyone else. We engage with negative people and let their negativity overshadow us. We make life more complicated than it needs to be. When we conduct "spring cleaning" of the mind and shed the thought patterns that don't bring us any benefit, life becomes simpler. Sometimes, instead of fighting an uphill battle, it is better to turn around, walk down the hill and find a better hill to climb.

Your Turn:

Where have you been making life more complicated than it needs to be? What can you do today to bring the focus back to a simpler way?

Today's Affirmation:

Each day, I focus on where I make a difference.

Reflection Questions

What battles are you fighting in your life? Are there any up-hill battles you might be better off walking away from?

March 30

"This is the beginning of a new day..."
—from a little orange slip of paper
in my daughter's take-home folder

Good morning! When my daughter was in fifth grade, I was emptying out her take-home folder and a little orange piece of paper fluttered to the ground. I picked up the small square and read it. Here is what was written:

This is the beginning of a new day. You have been given this day to use as you will. You can waste it or use it to your advantage. What you do today is important because you are exchanging a day of your life for it. When tomorrow comes, this day will be gone forever; in its place is something that you left behind... let it be something you're proud of.

I don't know where the piece of paper came from and I forgot to ask my daughter before she headed off for school. I guess where it came from doesn't matter as much as the message it carried: How blessed we are to have *this* new day. Let's make the most of it. Let's exchange a day of our lives toward building a legacy of hope and happiness.

Your Turn:
Take a moment to think about the wonderful gift of today. What can you do to make the most of it? When tomorrow comes, what gift will you have left with today?

Today's Affirmation:
Today I leave something behind, and it is something I am proud of.

 *March 31*

> *"It doesn't matter how slowly you go—so long as you do not stop."*
> —*Confucius*

Good morning! In a world in which time has become the master of many, Confucius's quote offers an important and simple reminder to us. As we reach and stretch and make positive changes in our lives, we need to report to our own internal time clock. Too often, we compare our progress to others.' Or we become negative coaches to ourselves, reprimanding ourselves for not doing more or accomplishing something sooner. This type of thinking usually leads to backward movement.

Remember, we are always moving. If we aren't moving forward, then we are moving backward. But let us not make the mistake of thinking we have to leap forward every day. It is more important to be consistent in our steps, no matter how small, than to leap forward and then stop. I have never seen someone make it by lurching toward success.

Your Turn:

Remember the story of the tortoise and the hare? Focus on consistent, measurable steps versus a sprint. Besides, we would all look funny if we were lurching toward success!

Today's Affirmation:

I consistently take measurable action to accomplish my goals.

Going Further

We are officially one-quarter of the way through the year. Stop and do a "goal check." Have you been taking consistent steps forward—regardless of the pace? Or, like 80 percent of people, did you abandon your goals before February's end? If you do not like your answer, use today's message to restart on your goal, making sure to set realistic, sustainable, and simple steps.

 *April 1*

"If at first you don't succeed, then skydiving definitely isn't for you."
—*Steven Wright*

Good morning! According to Kids Health (an organization of the Nemours foundation), the average American child laughs two hundred times per day, while adults only laugh about fifteen or eighteen times. A startling statistic, considering the adage: "Laughter is the best medicine." This famous saying now has basis in science! Studies have shown laughing helps:

- reduce stress
- lower blood pressure
- elevate mood
- boost immune system
- protect the heart
- encourage relaxation
- connect with others

A study published in the American College of Cardiology found that laughing increased blood flow by more than 20 percent, an effect similar to that of aerobic activity. The positive effect of laughing lasted for thirty to forty-five minutes. While I enjoy exercise, I love the idea of laughter giving me a similar benefit! I can't always find time to put on my running shoes throughout the day, but I *can* find time to laugh.

Your Turn:

Pay attention to how many times you laugh today and tomorrow. Don't try and change anything—just observe. Then make a concerted effort to add more laughter to your life. Notice the difference in how you feel physically and mentally.

Today's Affirmation:

I fill my life with laughter.

Inspirations: Need a laugh?

One of the quickest ways to laugh is to join in with someone else who is laughing. One of my favorite laugh visuals can be found at: http://www.youtube.com/watch?v=5P6UU6m3cqk.

Have kids? Visit Kids Health to learn more about encouraging your child's sense of humor. http://www.kidshealth.org/parent/growth/learning/child_humor.html.

April 2

"Isn't it just easier to be nice?"
—*Tracy*

Good morning! Tracy sent in this email along with her quote and it is a wonderful one to share with you. Tracy writes:

I work for a large bank where I am the branch manager. I am fortunate that I have a great staff and we have wonderful customers! So for the most part, I don't deal with too many complaints or angry people. But—on occasion I do, and I always say to my staff, "Isn't it just easier to be nice?"

Obviously, this goes for the people I work with, work for, customers I deal with, and people I see at other places.

I never understand why people don't say thank you or smile at other people. I don't get why people are rude or mean or negative. I love nice people and I don't care if it's my boss, my kids, or the drive-thru guy at McDonald's! I have found in my "all-knowing" thirty-one years that life is easier when you're a nice person.

I agree wholeheartedly with Tracy. In order to maintain personal happiness, we have to be nice, even when others aren't following the golden rule. The quickest way to diffuse a difficult situation is to handle it with genuine kindness and care. Often, when people get upset, or angry, or grumpy, all they want is to be "heard." Instead of hearing, many people lash back. Then you have two people trying to be heard. You can guess the result—no one is heard, because no one is listening.

Your Turn:

Today, don't miss an opportunity to be "nice." Smile at others, be genuine when you say "hello," and greet everyone with kindness.

Today's Affirmation:

I maximize every opportunity to be genuine and caring.

April 3

"We don't see things as they are.
We see things as we are"
—*Anaïs Nin*

Good morning! As I have had the privilege of working with more and more women, I have seen the truth of Anaïs' quote. Many women come to me wondering why they are having a disagreement, or feeling overcriticized, or wondering why some portion of their life just doesn't seem to be working.

When they look at their lives objectively, they think, "What do I have to complain about compared to so many others who are dealing with so much?" This type of self-comparison is not only useless, it is self-destructive. Everything is relative. One person's obstacle may be another person's inspiration. Why? Our collective thoughts and experiences go with us everywhere, and create the lens through which we see every event and hear every comment. We all have a different reality, because we have all lived a unique life.

We can't turn off this filter that we bring to life, or we would become robots. Instead, we must remember that as we face any event, we are facing it in the present, but we are often seeing it through our past. When we come to a difficult juncture or communication, it is important to anchor ourselves and to be aware of what past experiences are influencing our thoughts and opinion.

Let me give you an example. Let's pretend for a moment that you work for me. I come to you and say, "I am worried about this area of our business. I need you to focus on improving X, Y, and Z." What I have said is a very factual statement and a simple request. How you hear what I have said depends on your past experiences. If you are self-doubting, you might hear this: "I don't think you are doing a good enough job, and I really need you to ramp up your efforts." If you have had a boss who was unsupportive in the past, you might hear this: "Your work just isn't satisfactory. I don't think you can do it." Of course, neither of these statements are anywhere near what I said, but they could still be what you hear. When you hear a statement like that, you are likely to respond defensively. That would throw me off guard, because what I actually said wasn't anything to be defensive about. You can see how this could quickly escalate into a disagreement or misunderstanding.

Understanding that we bring this filter and lens to our interactions is the first step in pausing it so that we can truly hear what is being said to us.

Your Turn:

Today, make a concerted effort to hear what is being said to you. Hear the words without adding your own commentary. Watch how much more clear and effective your communications become with this tactic.

Today's Affirmation:

I stay present in the moment.

April 4

> *"It is better to light a candle than curse the darkness"*
> *—Chinese Proverb*

G ood morning! Jo says:

I like this quote, because "lighting a candle" is a simple, do-able action that makes a difference, and can be generalized to other situations where a simple doable action can make a difference.

I couldn't agree with Jo more. The other night after dinner, my husband and I were discussing various people and situations in our lives. In each situation, we could identify a simple "perspective change" that would change the situation itself. I asked him, "Why does human nature insist on making everything so complicated? Why do we look down instead of up? Why do we question ourselves, instead of asking questions about the situation?"

Your Turn:

Life becomes richer when we let go of the darkness and live by trusting in the light. Look up instead of down. Light a candle today in your own life. Instead of complaining or worrying about something that isn't right, take a step to make it right.

Today's Affirmation:

In times of darkness, I light a candle of light and trust.

Reflection Question

Where in your life have you been casting darkness through self-defeating actions or thoughts? Place a candle somewhere you will see it often as a reminder to cast light into these areas.

April 5

"After being bombarded with images and ideas of what a woman should be, a strong woman is one who can look at herself in the mirror and say, 'I prefer this.'"
—Doctoral student Erin Clair, as quoted in **What Makes a Strong Woman? 101 Insights from Some Remarkable Women** *by Helene Lerner*

Good *morning! I have been working on your programs and reading your* Good Morning *messages. Words cannot express my gratitude for the positive changes they are making in my life. I feel as if I am on the quest to remembering who I wanted to be when I grew up and who I want to be daily. At thirty-six, I would have thought I would have a clue but, as with many women in our culture, life as mother and wife took over and consumed all that I had hoped to be. Thanks for the prompts that are assisting me along this journey. I truly appreciate it.*

This was a powerful quote for me as I struggle daily to love the person I am right now, instead of waiting to love myself when I morph into the incredible woman that lurks beneath the layers of life. As a mother of daughters, it was also a powerful insight to a gift I hope to give them—that deep sense of self-worth and self-acceptance.—sent in by Tammy.

Tammy's kind note summarizes a challenge many women can relate to. While devoting time to mothering children and the daily demands of life, women may lose sight of mothering their own dreams, desires, and self-growth.

Through my work, I strive to help women meet the many commitments of life today without neglecting my "self." Learning to balance caring for others while still caring for ourselves will, in time, lead us to the place where, like the quote, we can say: "I prefer this."

Your Turn:

Take a moment to look in the mirror and affirm where you are today and the positive steps you have taken in your life. Carve out a half hour to focus on *you* and self-care.

Today's Affirmation:

I am proud of who I am and who I am becoming.

April 6

"The only way in which one human being can properly attempt to influence another is by encouraging him to think for himself, instead of endeavoring to instill ready-made opinions into his head."
—Leslie Stephen

Good morning! One of the things I always strive to do with my employees is to develop independent thinking on many levels. I am less interested in hearing my opinion repeated than I am in hearing their original opinions.

I have always been like this, in politics and the news as well. While I might watch a news show, I am not convinced or swayed by simple summaries or quick coverage. Instead, I investigate the topic on my own, getting information from many sources, forming my own opinion. And I apply this principle to child rearing as well. While there are certain values that I (and, I am sure, many parents) instill in their child, I am careful to instill what I feel are my "core values," and then to leave plenty of room for my daughter to create her own thoughts, opinions, and viewpoints of the world. Encouraging this independent thinking creates a natural curiosity about life.

Your Turn:

Today, observe how you are influenced by opinions and how you influence others. Ask more questions, do more research, develop your curiosity and curiosity for those you care about.

Today's Affirmation:

I form my own opinions, building a curiosity for life.

Reflection Question

Have you inherited any values from others that do not match your life? Sometimes we may blindly accept the values of others as our own (especially from parents or within intimate relationships).

April 7

"I only hope that we don't lose sight of one thing—that it was all started by a mouse."
—*Walt Disney*

Good morning! How I would have loved to have known or met Walt Disney! Every time I visit Orlando, I walk through the exhibit on his life and the story of his parks. For those who don't know, Mickey Mouse was born on a notepad while Walt was on a train from Manhattan to Hollywood. It was at a time when his business ventures were at their lowest ebb ever. Mickey Mouse became the catalyst for many great things in the life of Disney. Yet time and time again, Walt Disney would risk security for growth. He would "bet it all" on the faith he had in his vision—he would bet a lot on a mouse. He also said:

> Somehow I can't believe there are any heights that can't be scaled by a man who knows the secret of making dreams come true. This special secret, it seems to me, can be summarized in four Cs. They are Curiosity, Confidence, Courage, and Constancy, and the greatest of these is Confidence. When you believe a thing, believe it all the way, implicitly and unquestionably.

He walked his talk, living the four Cs time and time again. As we pursue our own dreams, let us remember the importance of:

- Curiosity: Ask questions, push the envelope, and dream big.

- Confidence: Believe in yourself and your vision, no matter what others think.

- Courage: Work through fear instead of being blocked by it.

- Constancy: Get up each day and do it again.

By living these four Cs, we can echo another of my favorite Disney quotes: "It's kind of fun to do the impossible."

Your Turn:

Write down these four Cs on a note card or sticky note and put it where you will see it daily. Work on applying these principles to your dreams on a daily basis.

Today's Affirmation:

I engage my dreams with curiosity, confidence, courage, and constancy.

April 8

"Feeling gratitude and not expressing it is like wrapping a present and not giving it."
—*William Arthur Ward*

Good morning! When we get caught up running on the treadmill of life, it is easy to forget to count our blessings. In her book *Simple Abundance*, Sarah Ban Breathnach introduces the Gratitude Journal, a special book for recording what you are grateful for each day. Using a journal to record daily gratitude can help us stay "in the moment" and recognize the countless blessings we each have.

However, the regular use of the Gratitude Journal is only the first step. The next step is to give outward thanks for our blessings. When we let someone know how they have helped us or influenced us, not only do we attract more "like behavior" in our lives, we also warm that person's heart. We encourage them to offer similar kindness to others. This is how the simple act of gratitude has the capacity to change the world.

Sometimes we forget to give thanks. We might think, "Oh, that person knows what she did was important." Or we get "too busy" to send a thank-you email, card, or phone call. When we behave in that way, we leave the cycle of gratitude incomplete. Perhaps the person who offered kindness was inspired to act kindly because of you. Your appreciation and thanks could be the catalyst in encouraging them to repeat the behavior. Remember that when we praise or appreciate a behavior, a person is more likely to repeat it.

Your Turn:

Who are several people who offered you kindness this past week or that you are grateful for? Take a moment to clearly thank three people who have made a difference in your life—or even your past week. As you complete your gratitude list each day, make sure to express "thanks" to them where you can.

Today's Affirmation:

I have a thankful heart and express my thanks to those who impact me.

Inspirations

Visit Sarah Ban Breathnach's website at http://www.simple-abundance.com/gratitude_journal.html for more ideas on how to use a Gratitude Journal.

April 9

"As long as one keeps searching, the answers come."
—*Joan Baez*

Good morning! Let's start this morning with a simple role-play question. You have lost your keys. What do you do? My guess is that you look for them. Now, let's say you look for ten minutes and can't find them. Do you quit looking and just decide never to use your car again? Or do you keep looking? (I am going to make another educated guess that you will keep looking.)

Why not treat your dreams and goals like your keys? Just because you don't discover them in ten minutes, don't give up. Your dreams are certainly more valuable than any car.

Your Turn:

Today, spend some time actively searching, and look for the next step toward your goals or dreams.

Today's Affirmation:

I continually move toward my dreams.

Reflection Questions

What dreams and goals have you short-changed?

It is estimated the average person spends over fifty hours each year looking for lost items. What might you find if you spent that time looking to make your dreams come true?

April 10

*"The pessimist sees the difficulty in every opportunity.
The optimist sees the opportunity in every difficulty."*
—**Winston Churchill**

Good morning! It should come as no surprise that the secret to living a rich, full, and happy life lies in the second sentence of this quote. Every time we face a difficulty we have two
choices: wilt or grow. It is that simple. We can complain about
the difficulty, analyze it, dislike it, think that it is unfair or unjust—and we might be right. But that doesn't matter. Whether
we are right or wrong, the difficulty remains. We can make the
difficulty a statue in our life by focusing on it, or we can make
the difficulty crumble, by growing and stepping past it.

This concept applies to all difficulties—not just the "little
things." My one and only sibling died suddenly when I was
twenty-three. He was my big brother and a father figure to me,
as my parents had divorced shortly after I was born and I did
not keep in regular contact with my father. Part of me wanted
to "wilt." Part of me wanted to give up, to curse what felt unjust
and unfair. We were a small family of three and now we were
a family of two and it didn't seem fair. Something within me,
though, refused to wilt.

I used that experience to create a book to help others, called
*I Wasn't Ready to Say Goodbye: Surviving, Coping and
Healing after the Sudden Death of a Loved One.* At the time
(2000), no such book was available. I coauthored the book
with a doctor I had known, Pamela D. Blair. Little did I know
when Caleb died that the United States would face the tragedy
and shock of 9/11. This book went on to become the best-
selling grief book on the market, and I received many letters,
calls, and emails from those who lost family and friends in
the terrorist attacks. Since then, I have continued to receive

many letters that have touched my heart. Does this make my brother's death "just" or "fair"? Of course not. But it does give it meaning and purpose. Instead of "wilting," my brother and I took this experience and used it to help thousands upon thousands of others.

That story is an example of being a true optimist. It isn't that we ignore or pretend that the bad doesn't exist, but when the bad comes to our door, we create something bigger that matters more. While we may lose loved ones, possessions, love, friends, physical abilities—there is one thing we never lose: hope.

Your Turn:

Where have you been seeing difficulty instead of opportunity? How would it feel to remove the stone statue of "difficulty" and replace it with fertile ground for hope to grow? What can you do today to begin crumbling that statue?

Today's Affirmation:

I greet each moment with hope.

April 11

> *"Life just is. You have to flow with it.*
> *Give yourself to the moment. Let it happen."*
> —*Governor Jerry Brown*

Good morning! I have found one of life's biggest challenges to be relinquishing control.

Several years ago, I finally came to the slow realization that the only person I can control is myself. There are many people

I want to help or influence, but ultimately, I can only give my personal best. Each person can then take it or leave it. I am not responsible for others' decisions or actions.

While relinquishing control is difficult, it is also extremely freeing. It's as if a weight lifts from your shoulders when you truly internalize the fact that you are only accountable for yourself. The less time you spend trying to control external circumstances, the more time you can spend giving yourself to the moment.

Your Turn:

In what ways are you trying to exert control in your life? How would it feel to relinquish that control?

Today's Affirmation:

I put my best out to the world, without the need to control what comes back.

April 12

> *"For every minute you are angry, you lose sixty seconds of happiness."*
> —*Ralph Waldo Emerson*

Good morning! I can't think of any better reason to confront and overcome anger, anxiety, fear, and other negative emotions than the reason Emerson offers. Surely each time we succumb to anger, we rob ourselves of happiness. In the end, the negative emotions we carry hurt ourselves the most. We move away from happiness and the very peace we are seeking.

Recently I had dinner with a friend I hadn't seen in a couple of years. It was great to catch up with her, but I was sad to learn that the years had not been kind to her. She had struggled with many obstacles and challenges, and she openly admitted that the zeal she once had was fading. She talked about how she was scared to trust, and how hard it was to open up. She asked me: "Brook... why should I take risks when so many things might go wrong?"

"But what happens when many things go right?" I replied. "You won't know if you don't open yourself up to the world." I continued to challenge her thinking by asking, "What's the worst that can happen? Perhaps you face another obstacle—but you already know you can conquer them. But what if the next thing destined to come your way is something wonderful?"

Your Turn:

When you find yourself facing a negative emotion today, read Emerson's quote. Do you want to lose even a minute of happiness?

Today's Affirmation:

I choose happiness.

Inspirations

Michael Anthony offers a free ninety-page e-book with ideas on how to increase and choose happiness. Check it out at www.howtobehappy.org.

April 13

"Some days there won't be a song in your heart. Sing anyway."
—*Emory Austin*

Good morning! Oh, the truth in Emory's statement... how I wish it wasn't so! But it is true—we have natural "highs" and "lows," and some days there isn't a song in our heart. So what do we do on those days? How do we embrace life and be positive on the days when the "spark" just isn't there? We do just as Emory suggests—we sing anyway. And we sing loud enough to wake up that spark.

One of the things cognitive therapy reveals is that when we consistently "act as if," we "become." Sometimes we have to force a behavior in order to do it consistently enough to internalize it. On our "down days" it is more important than ever to engage in behaviors that fight the negativity in our minds and the sadness in our souls.

You don't have to accept a mediocre day. You don't have to accept a mediocre life. In fact, I encourage you to accept nothing but the best. Sure, you will have days that start out "low." Fight back. Sing. In any given moment, you have the power to change your day. You have undoubtedly heard the quote "fake it until you make it." On those "low" days, shout out your affirmations. Write them over and over. Even if they don't feel sincere, keep saying them. Our words have power, and they have the power to transform the mediocre into the magnificent.

Your Turn:

Write this quote on the back of a business card and put it in your wallet. Let it serve as a reminder to find something to "sing" about each day.

Today's Affirmation:

I have the power to transform the mediocre into the magnificent.

 *April 14*

> *"I wish for 150 flowers in my bedroom…"*
> —*A five-year-old girl*

Good morning! Reader Sarah B. shared the following story I wanted to pass along.

Just wanted to share experience of hiking with friend and both sets of kids yesterday (beautiful here). Her five-year-old daughter was having so much fun running along picking dandelion heads and blowing wishes. I must have heard her easily make more than twenty-five very creative, spontaneous and heartfelt wishes: I wish to run like the wind; I wish for 150 flowers in my bedroom; I wish I could dance like Cinderella; I wish I could go to the woods each day to read… amazingly abundant wishes for a five-year-old—and I often found myself wishing with her. Children lead us so easily to that uninhibited joy. I thought I would challenge myself to come up with a list of twenty-five wishes today."

Your Turn:

Today begin your own wish list.

Today's Affirmation:

I wish for the wonderful.

April 15

> *"When problems arise don't get furious, get curious."*
> —*Author unknown*

Good morning! I have always been an advocate of asking questions. My friends will tell you that whenever I meet someone, I ask them so many questions they often think I am an attorney. I am not—but I *am* a knowledge-seeker. I love to learn about people, about places, about anything. I love to see how other people think, why things exist, and how they got there.

Today's quote stresses the importance of "questions" in our lives. I think one skill we could all benefit from is that of asking more questions. When something goes wrong, instead of getting upset, we could ask: How did this happen? Why did this happen? Did I contribute to it in any way? Is there something I could do differently? What are other ways this situation could have turned out? The questions are endless and they are much more productive than anger.

Your Turn:

Today, try to ask one hundred questions, either of yourself or of those around you. At the end of the day, evaluate how much you have learned by having a "questioning" attitude versus an "I already know the answer" attitude.

Today's Affirmation:

Each day I learn something new.

Going Further

Are there any areas you would like to learn more about? The internet offers many resources for satiating your curiosity. Stop by http://www.worldwidelearn.com/online-courses/continuing-education.htm for a comprehensive list of learning resources from math to crafts to CPR.

April 16

"For fast-acting relief, try slowing down."
—Lily Tomlin

Good morning! Medical research estimates as much as 90 percent of illness and disease is stress-related.

While we can't control all the events in our lives, we can manage our reactions to them. Here are some good ways to cope:

Take fifteen to twenty minutes a day for a "sanity break": Journal, meditate, visualize a peaceful place, or daydream.

Try to learn to accept things you can't change. Work to let go of the things you cannot change and focus on those you can.

Take a "response break": If you are feeling upset or angry, try to diffuse the situation and come back to it later. When possible, wait twenty-four hours before responding to a stressful event. A good night's sleep can make a big difference in how we perceive a stressful situation.

Exercise regularly. Do something you enjoy, like walking, swimming, jogging, golfing, walking a pet, tai chi, or cycling.

Spend less time with stressful people. Some people seem to be addicted to stress. Avoid negative and stressful social situations and people when possible.

Learn to say no. Don't promise too much. Give yourself enough time to get things done.

Your Turn:

April 16 is National Stress Awareness Day. How would you rate your stress level on a scale of one to ten? Implement some of the tips above to replace stress with sanity.

Today's Affirmation:

I control my responses and reactions to stressful situations.

Going Further

How stressed are you? Visit http://stresstest.net/ for a free and simple online stress test. When you complete the twenty-six questions the results display an overall score, satisfaction with life score, symptom distress score, and level of functioning score.

April 17

"Modern life is remarkable, but we're still human beings with basic human needs. We need real community. We need satisfying and compelling work. We need health, play, love, and companionship. A century of remarkable technological advances can't undo the millions of years of evolution that have made us who we are."
—*Moby (from my Starbucks cup… "The Way I See It #56")*

Good morning! First off today, I have to share with you the adventure of today's quote.

When I landed at the Milwaukee airport recently, my first stop before baggage claim (as always) was the coffee stand. Because it was a Starbucks, I did as I always do, and read the "As I see it…" quote they have branded on the cup. Later, on the drive back from the airport, my colleague and I stopped to grab some bottled water. She tried to throw away our two coffee cups to make room for the water in our drink holders.

She looked a bit confused when I grabbed the cup and yelled, "No, I need that!" She has learned not to question some of my silly behaviors—I think she just chalks them up to my creativity.

Then I got home and set my empty cup on the kitchen island. An hour or two later, I went to retrieve it to write today's message—but it was nowhere to be found.

I cornered my husband: "Where is the cup?" He also looked at me a bit strangely and then told me it was in the garbage. I rolled my eyes as if that was a crazy place to put an empty, coffee-stained, disposable cup. Fortunately, I was able to retrieve it.

As you can tell, I was rather attached to this quote! I love how it speaks so clearly to who we are when we strip away all the technology of daily life. Many of our technological advances, designed to make life easier, also take away from the core of the life we have known. Video games remove our children from nature; cell phones isolate us from those around us when a call comes in; email can be a great communication tool—but it can also become a way to avoid the phone. While the gifts of technology are great, we have to make sure they do not take away from our core needs and the core of who we are.

Your Turn:

Today, I challenge you to evaluate the technology and communications that you and your family use. Think of one way they detract rather than enhance your daily life, and then make a commitment to change.

Today's Affirmation:

Every day I communicate in a healthy way with those whom I care about.

 *April 18*

> *"The Constitution only guarantees the American people the right to pursue happiness. You have to catch it yourself."*
> —*Benjamin Franklin*

Good morning! Today we are going to start our morning with a simple role-play, a technique I like to use once in a while. Let's say that tonight for dinner you want to have homemade soup. You have a craving. Your family has a craving. Everyone wants soup. Unfortunately, you don't have a single ingredient needed to make the soup. What would you do? I will make a guess that you will go get the ingredients. Obviously, if you don't go get them, you'll never fulfill that homemade-soup craving.

Happiness is a craving we all have. But we can't sit and wait for it to come our way, just as the ingredients for a recipe won't magically appear. We have to make a conscious effort to go out and "catch happiness."

Many times throughout our day we are faced with something we want and we fulfill that want. We are thirsty—we go get something to drink. We are hungry—we go get something to eat. We want to write something down—we go get a pen. Happiness need not be any more complicated—if we want happiness, we must either go get it or create it where we are.

Your Turn:
Challenge yourself to create or catch happiness today.

Today's Affirmation:
I create happiness in my life.

April 19

> *"Most people would rather be certain they're miserable, than risk being happy."*
> —*Robert Anthony*

Good morning! This quote is very important, although it is a hard one to read and contemplate. Could it really be that some people would choose to be miserable over risking being happy? Look around. You'll see all the evidence you need to understand the truth of this quote.

Why is that, though? Why would someone choose to be miserable, or choose not to make positive changes? The answer is amazingly simple. Change is scary to many people. Positive change involves letting go of blame. Our problems and challenges can't be someone else's fault. We have to own them. We have to choose to move past them.

Why wouldn't we make the choice of taking a risk toward happiness? Well, what if we don't do it well? What if we don't have the willpower? What if we fail? While those are all valid questions, I encourage you to ask a more important question: If you try, and don't end up where you want to be, the worst place you'll be is back where you started. On the other hand, if you succeed (and I know you can), where will you end up?

Your Turn:

How have you used avoidance in your own life to escape taking responsibility for creating happiness? What would happen if you took the leap today and let avoidance and blame go?

Today's Affirmation:

I leap toward happiness.

Reflection Questions

The last two Good Morning inspirations have focused on happiness. Take a moment to reflect on these questions about your level of happiness with life.

- On a scale of 1 to 10, how happy would you rate your attitude yesterday and today?

- What are ten activities that make you happy?

- How often do you make time for these activities on a weekly basis?

- What might be holding you back from experiencing happiness?

- What steps can you take yet this month to add more happiness to your days?

April 20

> *"Every day is a birthday, every moment of it is new to us; we are born again, renewed for fresh work and endeavor."*
> —*Isaac Watts*

Good morning! Well, according to Isaac Watts, I guess a "Happy Birthday" is in order! Happy Birthday, everyone! In all seriousness, isn't this a hopeful quote, filled with the wonder of newness? Have you ever thought about why we are so happy when a baby is born? Or why we count down the seconds to a new year? These events speak of new opportunities, fresh starts, and hope.

This quote brings us to the very important realization that the same opportunity, newness, and hope resides in every day— in every moment. All we have to do is accept it. Today, you could make the biggest change of your life. There is no need to wait.

Your Turn:

When you look back at your life, what makes you say: "I wish I would have done this differently?" Embrace whatever your answer is. Then, today, take a step toward writing a different ending.

Today's Affirmation:

Every moment offers as much opportunity and hope as I choose to accept.

 *April 21*

> *"In order to be walked on, you have to be lying down."*
> —*Brian Weir*

Good morning! When we find ourselves worn down, anxious, or depressed, we have to get beyond the victim mentality and ask some basic questions. Are we standing tall? Are we thinking in healthy ways? Are we staying away from toxic people as much as possible?

When we hurt and feel pain, before pointing the finger at someone else, we have to point the finger at ourselves. How did we get to this place? What did we contribute to our current situation? As today's quote says, we have to be lying down in order to be walked on.

Taking responsibility is freeing in that we then have the power to control our destiny. However, it can also be scary, because blame is a security blanket that allows us to hide instead of heed messages of change. But the security blanket of blame wears quickly, has many holes, and will not protect us long-term. Responsibility and change are like a needle and thread—from them, we can sew a blanket big enough to cover ourselves and those we care about.

Your Turn:

In each situation, good or bad or in-between, be aware of your role and contribution. Learn your thought patterns (both good and bad). Awareness is the first step toward responsibility and change.

Today's Affirmation:

I release the need to blame from my life.

April 22

"There will always be times when you feel discouraged.
I too, have felt despair many times in my life, but
I do not keep a chair for it; I will not entertain it.
It is not allowed to eat from my plate."
—*Clarissa Pinkola Estes*

Good morning! I love the determination in Estes's words. The difference in our moods—from depression to elation—rests in the emotions we choose to entertain.

We will all feel many emotions each day. But it is up to us to choose which ones we allow to sit down at the table in our mind. Do we let the critical voice have a chair? The cheerleader? The doubt? The happiness?

Your Turn:

Draw a circle with five seats around it. What are the dominant emotions, thoughts, or feelings in your mind right now? Write down each one in one of the "seats" of your drawing. Then, make a big chair on your drawing. That is where you are sitting. Can you see how those other seats reflect how you feel today?

Today's Affirmation:

I only entertain empowering thoughts and emotions.

April 23

"Wherever there is a human being there
is an opportunity for kindness."
—Seneca

Good morning! Yesterday, we looked at the importance of compassion and care toward others. Today's quote offers yet another perspective for our care toward others.

Think about the past several days. Try to envision the faces of people that you saw, try to remember what they said, or what their facial expressions revealed about how they were feeling. Can you remember any of them vividly? Think not only of your immediate family and friends, but also of strangers that you encountered while shopping, walking, or doing errands.

Can you remember how you felt as you saw each of those people? Were you intimidated? Did you have a hard time recalling the faces of strangers because you were focused on something else? Were you judgmental of some of those you saw?

Imagine if we greeted each person we saw with the wisdom of Seneca. Each time we encounter another being, we have an opportunity to share kindness.

Your Turn:

Be aware of those you encounter today. Try to bring kindness or a smile to each person. Notice how sharing your own light warms your spirit and heart as well.

Today's Affirmation:

I greet each person with kindness and compassion.

April 24

"Only put off until tomorrow what you are willing
to die having left undone."
—**Pablo Picasso**

Good morning! As many of you already know, I love Picasso quotes and am always excited to stumble across a new gem. While we have all heard many versions of the message... "make every day count," or "today is all that matters," this quote seemed to sum that up in a fresh perspective for me.

When I first read it, I thought to myself: Is there anything to-day that I need to start or leave in process to make sure it is seen in the future? Anything so important I need to begin the process today? Is there any person I am thinking of getting together with, or calling, or sharing with, that I am planning to deal with "later?" Do all of those people know how I feel, or is there a call I need to make today? And what am I doing today that I could leave undone in order to make room for the things that I am not willing to leave undone?

Your Turn:

Reflect on today's quote. Do one more thing that truly mat-ters today than you would have had you not read today's Good Morning.

Today's Affirmation:

Each day, my focus is devoted to what truly matters.

Going Further

On a blank page in your journal or calendar, make a list of anything you have been putting off for another day. Whenever you have a spare moment, glance at this list and take action.

April 25

"When there's a hill to climb, don't think that waiting will make it smaller."
—*H. Jackson Brown*

Good morning! H. Jackson Brown certainly bursts a lot of bubbles with that quote—a few of my own included! I am unsure why, when something seems difficult, waiting seems to be a good idea. Somehow we convince ourselves that we will acquire tools or resources that will make the uphill climb easier. But life rarely works that way. The perfect time never comes. Instead, we usually acquire more fear about climbing the hill—and often we choose a different path—even though the climb itself was what we needed.

One thing I have learned to do, first in business, and now in my personal life, is to never put off the climb. No matter what the hill, take the first step.

The easiest comparison I can give you is the time I climbed Mount St. Helens. It looked really, really, really, *really* tall when I was at the base. But guess what? After that first step, it looked a tiny bit less tall. And after my first few steps, I knew I had made the commitment to see the adventure through. There was no turning around. After an hour of steps, its foreboding height dissipated all the more.

Your Turn:

When faced with a mountain or hill in your own life, don't turn around. Take the first step right away. By doing so, you make a commitment and, in one simple step, you have already decreased the amount of climb that is in front of you.

Today's Affirmation:

At the top of some of the hardest climbs in life are the best views.

April 26

"To be always doubting your ability to get what you long for is like trying to reach east by traveling west."
—*Charles Baudouin*

Good morning! I am convinced that one of the most common places we practice reverse psychology is on ourselves! In the past week, I was taking notes and here are some examples:

- The smoker who wants to quit and details her quitting plan over a cigarette.

- The woman who says she wants true love in her life, but stays in a relationship that is unfulfilling.

- The professional who wants to reach the top, but then watches the clock and never works a minute over forty hours per week.

- The parent who wants better communication with their children but doesn't have time to talk.

- The artist who feels a need to express herself but never carves out time for creativity.

I am sure you can add some to this list!

How silly we are to live these contradictions in our life and then wonder, "what is bothering me," or "why do I feel unfulfilled?"

I am not saying that I have never done this in my own life—I have! I know exactly what the problem is—I am not taking action steps that align with my desires. And I know there is only one way to fix it. Either scrap the desire (which is impossible with a true, core desire) or fix the action steps.

If we don't, we end up like today's quote—always traveling east while trying to get west or vice versa. Of course, I suppose if you travel east long enough, you'll eventually end up in the west—but what a bumpy, long, and indirect trip—and what a waste of time!

Your Turn:

Turn the spotlight on your own life. What true desire do you have where your actions directly contradict the desire? Who do you blame for it? What do you chalk it up to? How long has this been happening in your life? Can you see the freedom that comes from owning the responsibility and righting your action? Decide whether you have outgrown the desire or if your action steps are wrong. Then adjust accordingly.

Today's Affirmation:

I own all of my problems. I own all of my solutions.

April 27

"Whatever you can dream you can do, begin it;
boldness has genius, power and magic in it."
—Goethe

Good morning! Many times we immobilize ourselves by overthinking a situation. We analyze and ponder and weigh our options—but all we end up doing is creating a barrier toward action.

When we know in our heart that something is right (because it aligns with our core values), sometimes we have to just take a leap of faith. Interestingly, I have become quite good at this leap. And guess what? My wings have never failed me. There have been times where I was falling so fast I was convinced that I would hit the ground, but sure enough, those wings would come just in the nick of time.

I was talking with a friend about risk the other day. He commented that I seem to take a lot of risks without fear. When I reflected on our conversation later that evening, I realized that to me, *not* taking risks is what is scary. Being in that place where we eternally ponder what might happen is where I feel fear.

The reason that risk is not so scary to me is that I have tested my wings and I trust them. And it's amazing what happens the first time you "free-fall." As Goethe writes—"Boldness has genius, power and magic within it." When we remove the doubt and the questions and the "what ifs?" by jumping, we immediately move to the "what now?" state. And within that state we discover our own boldness, power, and genius that we can't find in any other place. It is there within each one of us. And the first time we meet those qualities within ourselves, our lives begin to change for the better.

Your Turn:

Is there something in your life you have been pondering that aligns with your core values? Instead of dancing on the edge, try jumping. Trust yourself. Commit to yourself. Find your wings.

Today's Affirmation:

Everything I need to be successful is already within me.

April 28

> *"Nothing in the world can take the*
> *place of perseverance."*
> —*Calvin Coolidge*

Good Morning! When I was seventeen, I was a sophomore in college at UW–Milwaukee. I worked full time five days per week at a Big Boy restaurant on Kilbourn Street in Milwaukee. I had Tuesdays and Thursdays off from work, and on those days I walked to campus where I fit in a full course load between 9:00 a.m. and 9:00 p.m. The employee break room at the restaurant was like many diner break rooms—kind of dark and cluttered. Amid the clutter was an old brown piece of wood with a fake-gold plaque mounted on it. The plaque read:

"Nothing in the world can take the place of perseverance. Talent will not; nothing is more common than unsuccessful men with talent. Genius will not; unrewarded genius is almost a proverb. Education will not; the world is full of educated derelicts. Persistence and determination alone are omnipotent."

—Calvin Coolidge

As a young teen, I know many people thought I would not

succeed in life. I even read the magazines that shared statistics of how "un-bright" my future looked. These people and the "accredited news magazines" relied on "facts," some of which included: being raised in a single-parent home (my dad left when I was eight months old), being in a small town, and being in "poverty" (while other people had more money, I dare you to find a house equal in love). These sources relied on statistics, I relied on heart.

The first time I read that quote, I remember deciding it needed to be polished and dusted. I carefully cleaned it, reading it a second time, and then gave it a more prominent position in the break room. I read that quote many times over during every break I had. While I may not have been raised with every advantage in the world, I was taught the biggest advantage of all: Nothing in the world can take the place of perseverance.

Your Turn:

Are there any areas of your life where you think "you can't" because statistically you don't have the best odds? How would embracing the idea "Nothing in the world can take the place of perseverance" change your actions and possibly your results?

Today's Affirmation:

Nothing in the world can take the place of perseverance. I persevere.

April 29

"If you hold back on life, life holds back on you."
—*Mary Morrissey*

Good morning! Have you ever had something you were yearning to say, but you suppressed it? Have you ever felt like you should spring into action, only to remain immobile? Have you felt the calling of your heart toward a dream—yet drowned the calling with doubt?

Mary rings the bell of truth quite simply today. "If you hold back on life; life holds back on you." While it is true that change, chance, and thin ice can be scary, they can also be exhilarating. Change and chance have the power to take us to new places. If we don't like some facet of where we are, it is time to jump on the raft of change and chance.

Your Turn:

In what areas of your life have you been holding back? You cannot reap the rewards of life without giving yourself fully. Take one action step today that will help squelch your hesitancy and move you forward to embrace life.

Today's Affirmation:

Where my dreams and future are concerned, I hold nothing back.

 *April 30*

Me: "I've had a long day, Sammy."
My then-ten-year-old: "Actually—all of your days are the
same, Mother. It is just your perception that is changing."

Good morning! A few years ago, I came home from my office and I was wiped out. The week had been hectic, and in additional to professional challenges, I had some emotional challenges, too. My daughter leapt out to greet me. She was not challenge-wrought. She was speaking excitedly, each sentence hitting a higher octave than the one before. Quickly, she rattled off an ambitious list of things she wanted to do in the few hours before bed.

"I've had a long day, Sammy."

She replied with the simple sentence I shared above. "Actually, all of your days are the same, Mother. It is just your perception that is changing."

As she skipped off toward the kitchen, I couldn't help but laugh to myself. My daughter seems to have inherited my interest in how people think, and what people think. And in this instance, her ten-year-old mind was very much on target. My day couldn't have been any longer than the one before, or the one to come next. My perception of what was within that day was overwhelming me—not the day itself.

Somehow, realizing that it is our perception of life, and not life itself, that troubles us makes it easier to climb to a better emotional place.

I quickly adapted my thinking. Instead of being "wiped out" by the day, I decided to appreciate all I had accomplished emotionally and professionally during it. (And to go to bed early and get a good night's sleep!)

Your Turn:

On your "tough days," appreciate all you have faced and accomplished. Reward yourself with a positive thought and a bit of extra self-attention and care.

Today's Affirmation:

I appreciate all life gives me each day.

May 1

> *"The name of the game is taking care of yourself, because*
> *you're going to live long enough to wish you had."*
> —*Grace Mirabella*

Good morning! Every Mother's Day marks the start of National Women's Health Week, which empowers women across the country to get healthy by taking action. The nationwide initiative, coordinated by the U.S. Department of Health and Human Services' Office on Women's Health (OWH), encourages women to make their health a top priority and take simple steps for a longer, healthier, and happier life. During the week, families, communities, businesses, government, health organizations and other groups work together to educate women about steps they can take to improve their physical and mental health, and prevent disease, like:

- Engaging in physical activity most days of the week
- Making healthy food choices
- Visiting a health care provider to receive regular check-ups and preventive screenings
- Avoiding risky behaviors, like smoking and not wearing a seat belt

This May, thousands of women across the country will embark on an eight-week physical activity challenge for better health. They will be part of the WOMAN Challenge—that is, Women and Girls Out Moving Across the Nation. The U.S. Department of Health and Human Services' Office on Women's Health coordinates this free eight-week challenge to encourage women and girls to walk 10,000 steps or get thirty minutes of moderate exercise every day. The WOMAN Challenge begins each Mother's Day.

Your Turn:

Celebrate National Women's Health week by joining the WOMAN Challenge, either as an individual or on a team. To register and receive your free tracking tools, visit http://www.womenshealth.gov/whw/about/womanchallenge.cfm.

Today's Affirmation:

I am ready to walk toward health.

Going Further

Join the hundreds of women who are taking the time to schedule at least one of the preventive health screenings recommended by their doctor or nurse within the next ninety days. Complete a checkup pledge and use the interactive online tool provided at http://www.womenshealth.gov/whw/pledge/ to learn about suggested preventative care.

 *May 2*

"Fall down seven times; stand up eight."
—Japanese Proverb

Good morning! All children have an ingrained optimism and determination. As they learn to walk on wobbly feet, they fall down many more times than seven, and stand up many more times than eight.

But as we grow older, we begin to lose that blind childhood faith in our ability to stand back up. We begin to worry that we might scrape a knee, or break a bone. We become content in sitting down, fallen instead of brushing ourselves off and trying again.

Today, I think we should remember that we all once held that blind childhood faith. We all fell and stood back up. We all knew how to believe in our abilities at one point in our lives.

Your Turn:

Is there somewhere in your life where you have become comfortable "sitting down?" Take a step today and stand up. Brush yourself off. The future is waiting—step toward it.

Today's Affirmation:

I may fall down seven times; but I will stand up eight.

May 3

> *Congratulations! Today is your day!*
> *You're off to great places!*
> *You're off and away!*
> *You have brains in your head,*
> *You have feet in your shoes*
> *You can steer yourself*
> *Any direction you choose."*
> —*Dr. Seuss*

Good morning! While many of us associate Dr. Seuss with childhood stories and rhymes, there is one book that we should all read as adults. The book is titled, *Oh, the Places You'll Go!* The story speaks directly to that child within us: that child who still wishes on stars and looks for four-leaf clovers in grass fields, the child who has boundless energy and limitless dreams. How that child is often lost as we grow older, listening to society's rules rather than our own hearts!

Your Turn:

Greet the day with childlike wonder. Let limits, barriers, and self-defeating thoughts drift away and be replaced by possibilities.

Today's Affirmation:

Today and every day, I choose a positive direction for my today and for my tomorrow.

Inspirations

Stop at your local library or your favorite bookstore and read *Oh, the Places You'll Go!* Embrace the message. You can also view the book online at: http://www.photohype. com/DrSeuss.htm.

May 4

"A hug is like a boomerang—you get it back right away."
—Bil Keane, Family Circus

Good morning! According to WebMD, schools of nursing began teaching their students about the value of the human touch decades ago, and 2006 research published in the professional journal *Psychological Science* has proven what the nurses knew all along: A human touch can soothe a lot of jittery nerves.

Psychologists, too, have noted the effects of human touch and healing, and an article in the fall 2005 issue of *Families, Systems & Health* discusses how many cultures have used this healing touch in healing ceremonies.

It's wondrous what a hug can do.

A hug can cheer you when you're blue.

A hug can say, "I love you so,"

Or, "Gee, I hate to see you go."

A hug is "Welcome back again!"

And "Great to see you!"

Or "Where've you been?"
A hug can soothe a small child's pain
And bring a rainbow after rain.
The hug! There's just no doubt about It,
We scarcely could survive without it.
A hug delights and warms and charms,
It must be why God gave us arms...
Hugs are great for fathers and mothers,
Sweet for sisters, swell for brothers.
And chances are some favorite aunts
Love them more than potted plants.
Kittens crave them. Puppies love them.
Heads of state are not above them.
A hug can break the language barrier.
And make the dullest day seem merrier.
No need to fret about the store of 'em.
The more you give, the more there are of 'em.
So stretch those arms without delay
And give someone a hug today!

—Author unknown

Your Turn:

The first full week of May is celebrated as National Hug Holiday Week. Celebrate by extending hugs to those to whom you are close.

Today's Affirmation:

I openly show affection to those close to me.

Going Further

Visit http://hugs4health.org/to learn more about National Hug Holiday Week.

May 5

"The big question is whether you are going to say a hearty "YES!" to your adventure."
—Joseph Campbell Brook's addendum:

"The big question is whether you are going to say a hearty "YES!" to your adventure
—day after day after day."

Good morning! We have all heard the clichés about being "high on life!" And how easy that is to do on a day when our stars align and our energy and goals flow almost effortlessly. It is easy to say "yes!" to our adventure on those smooth-flowing days. But we cannot get where we want to be by only yielding to the easy. To reach our goals, to be our own personal best, we must say "yes!" even on the tough days, the challenging days, the what-on-earth-am-I-doing-here-and-why days.

For those of you who have children or are close to a child, here is an interesting way to view today's message. Very often, we expect our children to "keep their chin up," or "be strong in the face of adversity." We place expectations on them to say "yes!" to life's adventure day-in and day-out. But what are we doing? Are we living "yes!" lives or "maybe" lives? Are we living the challenge?

Your Turn:

Stop and say a heartfelt "yes!" welcoming whatever lessons life brings today—whether they are lessons you welcome, or lessons you'd rather not learn.

Today's Affirmation:

Everything happens for a reason. Just believe.

May 6

> *"I am always doing things I can't do*
> *—that's how I get to do them."—Pablo Picasso*

Good morning! Picasso's quotes have always been some of my favorites. You can quickly see why he was such an innovative artist—he saw everything in a unique way, in a fresh frame, in a new light. Here is another of my Picasso favorites:

> "My mother said to me, 'If you become a soldier, you'll be a general; if you become a monk, you'll end up as the pope.' Instead, I became a painter and wound up as Picasso."

Both quotes share a common thread. Picasso was pushing past what others expected of him. Picasso was true to himself, instead of to the many voices that no doubt clouded his world.

Your Turn:

What if you were to listen to yourself? What would you hear? Take five minutes today and listen. Then tomorrow, follow through on at least one thing you heard during your self-reflection. (Want to really revolutionize your life? Do this exercise weekly, if not daily.)

Today's Affirmation:

I listen to and respect my inner voice.

May 7

> *"One hundred percent of the shots you don't take don't go in."*
> *—Wayne Gretzky*

Good morning! Many times we convince ourselves that it is easier not to try than to risk failing. However, when we challenge ourselves, we can also reach new levels that we couldn't reach without taking a chance.

Look at this famous figure:

Failed in business, 1831.

Defeated for legislature, 1832.

Second failure in business, 1833.

Defeated for speaker, 1838.

Defeated for elector, 1840.

Defeated for congress, 1843.

Defeated for congress again, 1848.

Defeated for senate, 1855.

Defeated for vice president, 1856.

Defeated for senate again, 1858.

Elected President of the United States of America, 1860.

What if Abraham Lincoln hadn't taken another "shot" as Wayne says? What if he had decided it was easier not to try? I wonder where we would be today. The road for Lincoln was twenty-nine years long. But he did not run out of gas, and he would not pull over, and he would not turn around.

Your Turn:

Never underestimate your own power. Take a risk. Take a chance. Life is yours to be lived. Are you really living life?

Today's Affirmation:

I find life's shots and I take them.

 *May 8*

> *"If you want to lift yourself up, lift up someone else."*
> *—Booker T. Washington*

Good morning! We all have seasons in our lives that are more challenging than others. Seasons in which more things seem to weigh on our shoulders, or our problems seem larger (or *are* larger!). When faced with such seasons, it is easy to fall into negative thinking, pessimism, or a general sense of the doldrums.

When I face these seasons personally, I have noticed that Booker's quote speaks to the simple truth of how to exit this turmoil. The quickest way to step out from under the weight of the world is to reach out to another and help him or her. We may feel like we have nothing to give when we are sad or hurting; but when we reach out we discover that not only do we have something to give—what we can give is unique, wanted, and needed.

Your Turn:

Are you down in the "doldrums" or feeling the weight of the world on your shoulders? Reach out to another.

Today's Affirmation:

I push past emotional resistance and lend a helping hand to others.

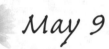

Inspirations

Read inspiring stories and learn how you can help others at www.helpothers.org.

May 9

> *"A rock pile ceases to be a rock pile the moment a single man contemplates it, bearing within him the image of a cathedral."*
> —Antoine de Saint-Exupery

Good morning! Sometimes in our lives, nothing needs to change except how we see the world around us. Problems can be conquered and moods can be altered when we "reframe" our world, take a new look, see with a fresh perspective.

Saint-Exupery's quote shows the value in a fresh perspective and open mind. When we look past the obvious, we have the ability to turn the mundane into the magical. Without fresh perspectives, we would likely have a lot more rock piles, and a lot fewer cathedrals.

Often we won't "take a new picture" because we are sure our vision is correct. But look at this example. You have two men: one sees a rock pile and the other sees a cathedral. Whose vision is correct? What camera would you rather hold?

Your Turn:

As you go about your daily life, remember that there are two sides to everything. Take a new picture. See the other side. You might fall in love with what you find there.

Today's Affirmation:

I let my preconceived notions go, and see the world from a fresh perspective.

Reflection Question

What preconceived notions do you have that might be creating rock piles in your life?

Use this as a checklist for approaching each notion with a fresh perspective.

May 10

> *"Your living is determined not so much by what life brings to you as by what you bring to life."*
> —*John Homer Miller*

Good morning! Optimism is a key that opens doors and opportunities. There is a story about a man who is locked in a room with a closed door. He is frustrated, negative, and miserable. "I'll never be able to get out of here with that door closed," he mumbles, while sitting and staring at the doorknob. He is so busy staring at the closed door that he never notices the open window.

Negativity causes people to focus only on what can't be, while missing all the avenues that can lead to opportunity and success. Optimism makes people more pleasant to be around, and an optimist is bound to enjoy life and live a fuller life than will a pessimist.

Sometimes our negativity is verbal and directed outward at society or others in our home. Other times we may say negative statements to ourselves like, "I look terrible today," or "I'll never accomplish what I want." These statements are harmful and eat away at our self-image.

Optimism, appreciation, faith, and belief are some of life's most important survival tools. We need to practice them and cherish them daily so we can pass them onto others.

Your Turn:

Be aware that negative statements often turn into negative outcomes. Look for the positive in situations and encourage your child to do the same.

Today's Affirmation:

Each day I demonstrate optimism, appreciation, faith, and belief.

May 11

"Our greatness lies not so much in being able to remake the world, as in being able to remake ourselves."
—*Mohandas K. Gandhi*

Good morning! I love the simple wisdom in this quote by Gandhi. Many times we try to remake the external world around us, forgetting that the place we have the most influence is in our own lives. Frustration comes from trying to change the external; greatness comes from remaking ourselves, our attitudes, and our reactions.

Your Turn:

This week, bring the focus back to *you*. What is something you can take action on that will improve yourself?

Today's Affirmation:

Each day, I improve.

Going Further

In what areas do you want to expand and learn? Visit http://www.docnmail.com/ for links to free online classes and learning resources spanning many interests.

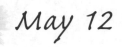 *May 12*

> *"A good book has no ending."*
> —*R.D. Cumming*

Good morning! Intrigued by the title, I bought the book *Eat, Pray, Love* when I first saw it on the shelf. Within several pages I fell in love with the book and began raving about it to everyone I know. It is one of the few books I have encountered that had me laughing out loud, nodding in recognition, and shedding a tear.

My daughter finds it amusing that the book has been sitting on my nightstand for months—unfinished. "I thought it is one of your favorite books of all time, Mom?"

"It is," I exclaimed, noting the bookmark tucked about fifty pages from the ending. "And I just don't want it to end!"

While I don't think that was exactly what R.D. Cumming had in mind with his quote, I have always been one to savor rich books. For me, truly captivating reads are hard to find, and when I am fortunate enough to come across one, it acts like a vacation, rejuvenating mind, body, and soul.

The American Association of Publishers founded Get Caught Reading month as a nationwide campaign to remind people of all ages how much fun it is to read. The reminder is well warranted, given an Associated Press poll revealing that, on average, only one out of four people read a book last year. Obviously, you are among this twenty-five percent—so thank you for choosing this book to invest your time in.

Your Turn:

Consider celebrating Get Caught Reading month by joining a book club, starting a book club, or trying a book from a new genre or new topic of interest.

Today's Affirmation:
I enrich my life through reading.

Inspirations

Looking for a good book? Although what makes a good book is largely subjective, here are a few lists you may want to browse for ideas:

Fiction:

http://www.time.com/time/2005/100books/the_complete_list.html

http://www.creativevisionbooks.com/booklist.shtml

http://www.nytimes.com/library/books/072098best-novels-list.html

http://www.nationalreview.com/100best/100_books.html

Romance books: http://www.theromancereader.com/top100.html

Adventure books: http://www.nationalgeographic.com/adventure/0404/adventure_books.html

Visit www.brooknoel.com to learn about the Make Today Matter book club and view my favorite book list.

May 13

> *"When we can no longer change a situation,*
> *we are challenged to change ourselves."*
> —*Victor Frankl*

Good morning! What wise words Victor shares with us. This reminds me of how often we try to hold on to a situation we cannot change—because we are scared of the challenge of changing ourselves.

But when we hold on to the outdated, the outgrown, the un-changeable, we slowly lose a piece of ourselves that needs to grow.

Your Turn:

Is there something in your life that you are holding on to that is unchangeable? Begin the gradual process of letting go and heeding the call of change.

Today's Affirmation:

I let go of the unchangeable and I change myself for the better.

Reflection Questions

What situations in your life are unchangeable? In what ways could you be challenged to change yourself? Choose one area and write out a plan for change.

 # May 14

> *"When it is obvious that the goals cannot be reached,*
> *don't adjust the goals, adjust the action steps."*
> —*Confucius*

Good morning! Sometimes our goals seem to fall into place without a huge effort on our part. At other times, reaching our goals isn't so easy. What is important during those "non-easy" times is not to abandon or change our goals, but rather to change the action steps we are taking to move toward them. I love the saying, "If you keep doing what you have always been doing, you will keep getting what you have always been getting." If what you have been doing isn't taking you closer to your dreams, it is time to reevaluate—not the dream or goal itself, but the steps you are taking.

Your Turn:

How are you coming on achieving your goals? Can you feel forward movement and progress? Take a moment today to evaluate your progress. If you haven't moved closer, adjust your action steps.

Today's Affirmation:

I will never abandon my heartfelt goals and dreams.

I persevere, adjusting my steps for success.

Inspirations

Motivational guru Zig Ziglar provides a Goal Setting Blueprint to help people transform goals into reality. Visit http://www.about-goal-setting.com/ to read these seven articles:

The Goal Setting Blueprint

Step 1—Intense Desire: Rocket Fuel For When You Set Goals!

Step 2—Writing Goals Down Ties Them Up!

Step 3—To Reach Goals: Bypass Resistance & Gather Assistance.

Step 4—Goal Planning: Use Deadlines As Lifelines.

Step 5—Goal Objectives: Looking Ahead To Get Ahead With Planning.

Step 6—When Reaching Goals Use Mental Pictures: Put An MGM Studio In Your Head!

Step 7—Achieving Goals: The Remaining 90%—Sheer Persistence.

May 15

"You yourself, as much as anybody in the entire universe, deserve your love and affection."
—Buddha

Good morning! How easy it is to love another, and how hard it can be to love ourselves. We are often our own worst critics, holding ourselves to standards that no one else would ever consider doing. A few years ago, I learned an exercise from a therapist. It involved treating my failures, weaknesses, and shortcomings as I would those of my daughter. What a revelation that was! I would never say the things to my child that I often say to myself when I make a mistake. While I nurture and respect her, I often treated myself much differently.

Your Turn:

Instead of criticizing your shortcomings and holding yourself to unrealistic standards, ask yourself how you would treat a friend who made a similar mistake, or had a similar shortcoming. Offer yourself the same kindness, for: "You yourself, as much as anybody in the entire universe, deserve your love and affection."

Today's Affirmation:

I, just as much as anybody else in the universe, deserve love and affection.

 *May 16*

"Believe in your dreams and they may come true;
believe in yourself and they will come true"
—Author unknown

Good morning! No matter how wonderful or well-thought-out our dreams are, without inherent self-belief, we risk the chance of truly accomplishing them. However, when we respect ourselves and believe that our dreams can come true, we leave nothing to chance. Self-belief and self-love can move mountains.

Your Turn:

Do you truly believe in yourself, or do you believe in your dreams? Take a moment to reflect on the difference. Commit to self-belief and self-love and watch how that step can turn dreams into reality.

Today's Affirmation:

I believe in myself. I am worthwhile. I am worth loving. From this belief, my dreams have fertile ground.

Going Further

If you are having a hard time having faith in yourself and your ability to reach your goals, or to build the life you desire, check out the valuable tips and articles at the website of Mayo Clinic.

Self-Esteem Check:

http://www.mayoclinic.com/health/self-esteem/MH00128

Self-Esteem Boost:

http://www.mayoclinic.com/health/self-esteem/MH00129

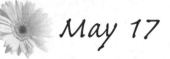 # May 17

"This is my wish for you: comfort on difficult days, smiles when sadness intrudes, rainbows to follow the clouds, laughter to kiss your lips, sunsets to warm your heart, hugs when spirits sag, beauty for your eyes to see, friendships to brighten your being, faith so that you can believe, confidence for when you doubt, courage to know yourself, patience to accept the truth, Love to complete your life."
—Author unknown

Good morning! I discovered this quote the day before my daughter started middle school and it captures exactly what I wish for her—and for all those I care about in life—including you, one of my cherished readers. Life is what we make of it, and when we are surrounded by a community of caring people, we have the ability to continue to enhance our lives and grow.

Your Turn:

Read this quote and think about all the people you care about. Perhaps you might print a copy or two, tuck them in handwritten cards, and send to friends in the mail. Or put this in your child's lunch bag as they start school. When we reach out and share our support with one another, we strengthen the platform upon which happiness is built.

Today's Affirmation:

When faced with doubt, I find confidence. When faced with loneliness, I seek out and give love and support.

May 18

"Too often we underestimate the power of a touch, a smile, a kind word, a listening ear, an honest compliment, or the smallest act of caring, all of which have the potential to turn a life around."
—*Leo F. Buscaglia*

Good morning! As I was traveling recently, I gave up my seat to a family who wanted to sit together. I ended up sitting next to two friends who have been friends for over forty years and were giddy with excitement for their upcoming vacation. The experience reminded me of today's quote and how life has a funny way of reminding you of how a simple hello can turn any day into one to remember.

Have you seen the movie (or read the book) *The Five People You Meet in Heaven*? I strongly suggest reading the book. To me, one of the most fascinating concepts in it was how we can have a *dramatic* influence on each other's lives—and, often, we don't even know it.

Without giving away the crux of the story, the main character meets five people on whom he had a dramatic impact during his lifetime. Interestingly, he didn't even know the name of some of the individuals.

About a year ago, I received a call from a young publisher. She had entered into the field and was realizing great success after meeting me at a seminar. Another time, I received a very touching email, spurred by a simple gesture that I wouldn't have thought twice about making. It turned out that this gesture had been a lifeline at a very trying time for this person.

Many of us long to give back to the world but believe we lack time or resources to do so. This quote and these experiences help me remember that giving back often takes little or no time if we are open to the possibilities.

Your Turn:

As you go throughout your day, remember that all the things you *do* and all the things you *don't* do have a major impact on those around you. What legacy are you going to create today?

Today's Affirmation:

Today, I recognize each opportunity to act with caring and kindness. I live (and will leave) a legacy of love.

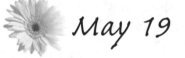 *May 19*

> *"The hardest thing in life is to know which bridge to cross and which to burn"*
> *—David Russel*

Good morning! While we all know that sometimes it is important to push ourselves forward, and sometimes it is important to let go, knowing when to do each isn't always easy. It is at these times that we need to learn to recognize and hear that little voice inside of us that intuitively knows where we need to go, and will not lead us astray. However, when we go years without listening to that voice, she can become very hard to hear. Like all skills, we must practice listening and respecting to that inner voice. We must heed it and honor it, and she will return to being a guiding force in our lives. When we listen to her, and we connect regularly with God, we have a light post in our lives to help guide our way.

Your Turn:

As you face decisions today, even small ones, practice listening to that little inner voice. Quiet your mind and let your heart speak. Continue to practice this listening skill to help you lead a healthy life of wise choices.

Today's Affirmation:

I take the time to quiet my mind and listen to my heart.

Inspirations

Journaling can be a great way to get in touch with your inner voice and discover your authentic self. My favorite journaling-prompt website is http://journalingprompts.com Hover over any day of the year for a prompt. You may also want to stop by www.brooknoel.com to learn about our Discovery Club. The Discovery Club offers written and visual journaling ideas for self-discovery.

May 20

> *"Trust yourself. You know what you want and need."*
> —*Brook Noel"*

Good morning! It isn't that uncommon anymore for people to have problems trusting one another. As we move through childhood and our hectic lives, many of us have had our trust betrayed one too many times. While the fact that many of us have a hard time trusting is sad, it becomes even sadder when we stop trusting ourselves. When life experiences sway us to stop listening to that inner voice that knows where we need to go, we step past the betrayals others have done to us and betray ourselves instead.

Your Turn:

When was the last time you listened to what *you* had to say? Find some quiet time to do so today. If the idea makes you uncomfortable, it is all the more important that you do it. Start with just a few minutes and try to work up to ten. Don't worry about what you are focusing on or thinking about, just concentrate on listening. Excluding God, no one knows you better—your wants, your needs—than you do. Give yourself the space needed for your heart to tell your mind the answers during life's tough moments.

Today's Affirmation:

I listen to myself. I respect myself. I trust myself.

 *May 21*

> *"If you want to make good use of your time, you've got to know what's most important and then give it all you've got."*
> —*Lee Iacocca*

Good morning! While we would all love to be a superparent, the reality is that few of us will ever measure up—and nor should we, since superparent is as fictional as Superman. I see many parents who are stressed and overwhelmed with trying to "do it all" in work, family, and home life, yet they don't take steps to reconcile this overzealous aim.

Take a moment to admit to yourself that you will never be able to do it all. You won't be able to raise a perfect child; you won't have the energy to battle every battle; you won't have the knowledge to make every right decision. That's all right. If you try to win every battle with your child, you will only create a more stressed "you" who will not be able to meet the needs of your child as effectively. Instead of trying to "do it all," choose what is important to you and let the rest go.

My mother gave up the battle of trying to have me keep a clean room. I was always creative, messy, and disorganized as a child. (My husband might argue that I still possess these qualities.) At first she would ask me to clean my room, then she would tell me to, then finally I would do it. Within four hours, it would be back to its more normal, unruly state. Eventually, she decided there wasn't much harm if my room was messy, as long as nothing was growing within the four walls— and I kept my door shut.

I know another mother who lets her three-year-old draw on her windows with candles. Her child loves it and they've discovered that Windex is a quick artwork eraser. When Samantha was little, I let her color in her books.

While these may not seem like "major" battles, the important thing is that we are admitting to ourselves we can't do everything—-and "everything" isn't important. Instead of spreading our focus over many areas and giving them all cursory coverage, we can focus on what really matters and loosen up about everything else.

Your Turn:

What have you been holding on to tightly that doesn't really matter in the grand scheme of things? Let go of the minor so you have more energy to focus on the major.

Today's Affirmation:

I focus on what matters.

 *May 22*

> *"Do the best you can with what you know and*
> *when you know better, do better."*
> —*Rhonda Miga*

Good morning! This inspiration comes from Rhonda Miga, who was a reader for several years before becoming part of the motivational team behind my online community. Rhonda wrote:

I attended a workshop for parents of children with special needs and discovered this quote. I find I often say it to myself: some days I am hard on myself because I do not feel I am doing all I can for my son who has autism, or I question my parenting skills for my daughter, or a countless number of other situations where I question myself.

However, when I think of this quote, it helps me to realize every day is a learning opportunity. I am not expected to KNOW how to do everything right, but the situations I experience each day help me to "know better, and therefore, do better."

When I have a moment where I belittle myself for not doing better, I say this quote to myself and realize that I just had a learning experience that will enable me to do better tomorrow.

By the way: I just ordered new checks and they had a place to put a favorite quote. I was limited to a certain number of letters, so the quote I added to my checks is: Something great WILL happen today!

Your Turn:

Today, follow Rhonda's advice: When you have a moment where you belittle yourself for not doing better, say this quote to yourself and realize that you just had a learning experience that will enable you to do better tomorrow.

Today's Affirmation:

I do not make mistakes; I just have different types of learning experiences.

 May 23

"Life isn't about finding yourself—life is about creating yourself."
—George Bernard Shaw

Good morning! How many books and shows have you seen that are all about "finding your true self?" I think the reason there are so many shows and books on this topic is because that is a quest with no result. No matter how high or low we look, we will never "find ourselves." Life is our blank canvas. We must create our "self."

Your Turn:

View your life as a blank canvas today. Live in color.

Today's Affirmation:

Each day, I add to the creation of my own unique and wonderful story.

Inspirations

Artella is food for the eye, mind, and soul and a great example of living "life in color." Whether you visit to find creative projects and ideas, or to browse for inspiration, this is definitely a site worth the click www.artellawordsan-dart.com.

May 24

"What you think, you become."
—**Mohandas Gandhi**

Good morning! Today we are going to do a simple "emotional self-check." If you were to embrace the Gandhi quote, and then look at your life yesterday—and how you thought—what would you become?

Your Turn:

Remember that each day we have the choice to think our own thoughts. Keep using your affirmations to inspire you and keep your thoughts on track. Try this simple self-check once a week as a way to measure your progress.

Today's Affirmation:

I think only positive, encouraging, loving thoughts.

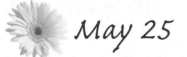

Inspirations

Need an extra dose of daily affirmation? Stop by these affirmation sites offering a new affirmation each day.

http://www.affirmationplanet.com/

http://www.louisehay.com/affirmation.php

May 25

"When we do face difficult times, we need to remember that circumstances don't make a person, they reveal a person."
—*Richard Carlson, PhD*

Good morning! How easy it can be to simply throw up our hands when faced with difficult or trying times. It can be easy to put on that "poor me" hat and figure we are another victim of circumstance.

While we may feel those emotions temporarily, we cannot hold on to them or they will make us into victims.

Instead, follow Richard's words. Let the difficult times reveal who you are, the talents you possess, your strength, your courage.

Your Turn:

Have you felt you are a victim of circumstance in an area of your life? Choose not to be the victim. Choose to let this trying time reveal a step that you can take toward the stronger, courageous, true you.

Today's Affirmation:

Each difficult time is a step that I take to build my true self.

 *May 26*

> *"Why compare yourself with others? No one in the entire world can do a better job of being you than you."*
> —*Author unknown*

Good morning! I love this quote. How much time do you spend comparing yourself to others? Perhaps measuring your success, health, willpower, determination, wealth, and beauty? Let me ask you this: What good can that possibly do? We cannot know the exact circumstances of anyone else's life. We cannot understand their shoes, for we have not walked in them. And at the end of the day, "No one in the entire world can do a better job of being you than you."

Your Turn:

As you find yourself comparing yourself to others, reread this quote. The world would certainly be boring if we were all clones of one another. Do not relish other's successes or envy their efforts. Instead, relish who you are and your unique offerings to our world.

Today's Affirmation:

I do not compare myself to others.

There is a beauty and uniqueness that only I can offer the world.

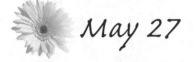 ## May 27

"I recognize that winning is not everything,
but the effort to win is."
—*Zig Ziglar*

Good morning! When Rosemary sent in this quote, she also included the following Ziglar excerpt.

To utilize the ability you have, you must start by getting rid of any loser's limp you might have. A typical Loser's Limp is, "I'm not a born salesman, or a born doctor, lawyer, artist, architect, engineer, etc. (Brook's side note: or cook, or housekeeper, or _____ .)

I would like to emphasize this point. In my travels, I have picked up newspapers from the rural villages of Australia to the bulging metropolises of North America and Europe. I've read where many women have given birth to boys and girls, but thus far I have never read where a woman has given birth to a salesman, or a doctor, lawyer, artist, engineer, etc. However I do read where doctors, lawyers, salesmen, etc., die. Since they are not "born" but they do "die," obviously, somewhere between birth and death, by choice and by training they become what they wish to become.—Zig Ziglar

It is so easy to forget that we have the power to choose and the power to be part of the design of our lives. First we must decide and dream about what we wish to become, then we must begin our journey, and follow it step-by-step, regardless of obstacles or blocks along the way.

Your Turn:

Where have you been giving up power and choice in your life? What do you want to become? Take a moment today to reflect and decide on what you want to become. Realize you can live the dream... the only person that can ever stop you is you.

Today's Affirmation:

I exercise my power and choice to live my dreams.

 *May 28*

> *"To achieve great things, two things are needed: a plan, and not quite enough time."*
> —*Leonard Bernstein*

Good morning! I love this quote because it holds an absolute truth that we often forget. So many times when we long to achieve greatness, we think we have to wait for "the right time." But the right time never comes. Life doesn't offer clear plateaus without something pulling us one direction or another.

Andy Warhol said, "They say that time changes things, but you actually have to change them yourself." It is when we commit with a solid plan even though we don't have quite enough time that we propel ourselves to action. When we give up the myth of that "perfect time," we propel ourselves toward action.

Your Turn:

How has the myth of the perfect time held you back from achieving your goals? Repeat the quote above several times—let the myth go to propel yourself forward.

Today's Affirmation:

Any time is the perfect time for change.

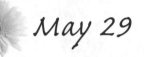

May 29

"Praise does not say you are perfect. It says I admire you and what you have accomplished and what I know you will go on to do. Praise is the food of the soul."
—*Wayne Dyer*

Good morning! So often when we are given a compliment, we brush it off or have problems absorbing the kind words of others. We may be able to give such compliments, but absorbing them is another matter indeed. What I like about today's quote is that it removes that pressure of perfection. When someone compliments you, they don't think you are perfect— no one is that naive. It means that they admire you or something you have done. Don't shortchange yourself by deflecting kind words. We live in a world where not enough kind words are said—so absorb each one that comes your way.

Your Turn:

Today, absorb with a simple "thank you" each compliment that comes your way. And while you're at it—offer sincere praise to at least three others throughout the day.

Today's Affirmation:

I am worth each compliment I receive and I accept them with grace.

See January 24 for additional ideas for sharing and collecting compliments.

May 30

> *"Both optimists and pessimists contribute to our society. The optimist invents the airplane, the pessimist the parachute."*
> —*Author unknown*

Good morning! I was talking with a friend recently and she had one of those wonderful "a-ha" moments. She explained that she considered herself an optimist and wanted to be an optimist. Yet as we spoke, I noticed that she continually snuck in little jabs at herself no matter what area of her life we were discussing. This had become so habitual that she didn't realize how frequently she was doing it. She worried that her life was careening out of control and she couldn't figure out how to stop it. Yet if she wanted the best, and was willing to aim for the best, and considered herself an optimist at heart—how could everything seem so "lost?"

There are definite optimists in life. There are also definite pessimists. There is another group of people, a large group, that I will nickname "poptimists." "Poptimists" are optimists at heart—yet their level of disbelief forces them to "pop" their hope as soon as they create it. They are so convinced that nothing will work, because very few things have, that each ray of hope also carries a shadow of doubt. Yet they aren't pessimists—because they haven't given up. They still know how to hope.

If we use today's quote to visualize a "poptimist," a poptimist would be wearing a parachute while sitting in the airplane. She doesn't want to get off the plane really, because she knows there has to be something better. Yet, she isn't willing to let go of her safety net and disbelief long enough to truly enjoy the scenery that is visible from the plane. Her vision is constantly hampered by her parachute.

The biggest challenge for the poptimist is letting go. A poptimist must learn to trust themselves and trust in life. You can't truly experience the journey if you are constantly waiting for the "other shoe to drop." This would be like trying to enjoy a Sunday drive with the parking brake on. We can't move forward, when we doubt the steps ahead of us.

Your Turn:

Are you an optimist, pessimist, or poptimist? If you relate to the idea of "poptimism," make an effort to put down your parachute so you can fully enjoy life. Suspend your disbelief for an hour, and talk nicely to yourself. Then challenge yourself to do it for two hours, then three, then a day, until you embrace a shadowless heart of hope.

Today's Affirmation:

I let go of doubt and disbelief, knowing that I deserve the best and can create the best.

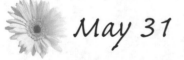 *May 31*

> *"We do not learn only from great minds; we learn from everyone, if we only observe and inquire."*
> —*C.A. Doxiadis*

Good morning! I am a lifelong learner. I attribute that trait to my success in achieving my personal and professional dreams. I am known for asking 1,000 questions and always seeking to learn, inquire, and absorb.

Each day, we are offered many chances to learn. They aren't always obvious. But if we pay attention, we can become life-learners very quickly. Perhaps a coworker or friend handles a problem in an effective way. When we truly observe, we can adapt that method in our own life. Or perhaps their resolution isn't that productive—and there is plenty to learn from that model as well.

When we are out shopping and see how a salesperson relates to a customer, we can learn the value of a helping hand and a smile. Likewise, if he or she isn't pleasant, we can learn how important and influential a missing smile can be.

Life is our greatest teacher. There is always a lesson to be learned. Even when things are trying and difficult and we can't seem to make sense of the "fog," there is a lesson to be had. We often resist learning when we are in a "dark place." But perhaps that is the time we need to observe, inquire, and learn all the more. I know my greatest lessons have come at the times I really wanted to resist learning. It is when we actively learn from both good and bad that we enrich our lives on a different level.

Your Turn:

Set a goal of learning something from as many people as you can today.

Today's Affirmation:

I am a life-learner, and every day that I harvest a new lesson enriches my life.

 *June 1*

"It is by 'spending' oneself that one becomes rich."
—*Sarah Bernhardt*

Good morning! I cannot imagine truer words. Being rich is not a matter of having money. It's a matter of experiencing life, enjoying the moment, involving yourself with your children, family, and friends; it's committing to a cause of great importance to you, learning new ideas, keeping an involved and educated mind, feeling with all your heart—those are the riches that are measured by a full life—not the ones you "take to the bank."

Your Turn:

Take a moment to reflect on the true "riches" in your life. What makes you happy? What are you passionate about? Make sure and take time today and every day for the true riches in your life.

Today's Affirmation:

I invest time and passion daily in the "true riches" in my life.

Reflection Question

What riches exist in your life? Begin compiling a list in your journal. Challenge yourself to list fifty riches over the course of June.

 # June 2

"Time is amazingly forgiving. No matter how much time you've wasted in the past, you still have an entire today. Success depends upon using it wisely —by planning and setting priorities."
—*Denis Waitely*

Good morning! How wonderful to realize that today is "ours"—no matter what yesterday held. When we greet each morning with that willingness to use the day wisely, plan, and set priorities, we can achieve our full potential. Make a list of three priorities for the day—three things you can do to make today matter. Then complete that list to make today count.

Your Turn:

Today, forgive yourself for past days that weren't all they could be. Take a moment and revisit your priorities, dreams, and aspirations. Commit to using today, and every possible day, wisely.

Today's Affirmation:

Regardless of yesterday, I choose to use today wisely.

Going Further

Visit www.brooknoelstudio.com for a printable "Three-Step Action List" where you can record three priorities to make every day matter.

June 3

"Call it a clan, call it a network, call it a tribe, call it a family. Whatever you call it, whoever you are, you need one."
—*Jane Howard*

Good morning! I think Jane Howard is trying to express just how important our family is to each of us, and how each of us in turn is important to our family. Let's not waste a day by not making our family first and foremost in our thoughts, energies, and joys. Tonight at dinnertime, let's share our day and rejoice in the specialness each one of us brings to our family's dinner table. If you haven't planned a meal ahead, why not order in pizza and play a board game together?

Your Turn:

Today, keep your family first and foremost in your thoughts. Share a laugh, a compliment, a touch.

Today's Affirmation:

Each day I value every member of my family (and my inner circle) and take the opportunity to tell them so.

Going Further

Looking for ideas for family time? Visit http://www.families withpurpose.com/family-fun-ideas.html.

 *June 4*

"The best way to predict your future is to create it."
—*Peter Drucker*

Good morning! Worrying has definitely reached epidemic proportions. As technology offers access to more and more information, it also brings more and more things to worry about! Sometimes we worry about something we have influence over—but more often than not we worry about things that are well beyond our control.

While we may not like the way worry feels, it has become a "safety net" for many. Let's say that one of your dreams is to take up hiking. Well, push a few keys on an Internet search and you can quickly find a hundred reasons never to hike. You can find more than a hundred justifiable reasons to make it excusable to save that goal for a rainy day. What if you slip and you get this ankle problem newly discovered by a researcher on the other side of the world? What if you forget a whistle and you are attacked by a bear? (Maybe there aren't any bears in your area—but what if, like one website shows, bears are moving and one moves to your neck of the woods?)

When we worry, we come up with very creative (and often crazy) scenarios to feed our worry. Worry allows us a justifiable way to avoid taking a risk. If we don't take a chance, we can't fall or fail.

My challenge to you is to put worry in its place. While it may not be easy to give up worrying completely, at least balance it out. Think of a scale and place all the worry on one side of the scale. Now, on the other side, place positive reasons that combat worry. In our hiking example, while I won't be eaten by a bear if I stay home, I also would never have stood above the clouds like I did one day on Mount St. Helens. Our worry is almost always something with very low probability—yet if we succumb to worry, we exclude the joy of possibility.

Your Turn:

What is something you have been worrying about? Put it on a scale and then balance it out with positive thoughts and benefits. Don't let worry steer your life, because odds are that if you do, you won't go anywhere. Which brings us back to today's quote. You control the creation of your future. Don't let worry be your primary building tool.

Today's Affirmation:

I do not let worry block the path of beauty and growth.

 *June 5*

> *"Keep your love of nature, for that is the true way*
> *to understand art more and more."*
> —*Vincent Van Gogh*

Good morning! When my husband and I lived in the Pacific Northwest, we discovered a wonderful remedy for the overstressed and overwhelmed family (or our overstressed and overwhelmed selves!). Both of us had grown up in scenic Wisconsin but had never paid much attention to the beautiful offerings that nature bestowed. When we moved to Washington, we sought out exploration opportunities. One of our first stops was an REI store, where we picked up a book on hiking in the area. Soon we visited Mount St. Helens, Multnomah Falls, and other notables of nature.

We moved back to Wisconsin when our daughter was three. While we weren't able to walk for miles as a family once we got back home, we continued to regularly go outside, away from answering machines, phones, and demands, and enjoy some of the more simple pleasures of our planet. Nature helps people to connect and rejuvenate—whether alone or within a group.

Here are a few ideas for exploring nature around you:

Take a nightly walk. The benefits of incorporating regular exercise are obvious, but a nightly walk also serves as a wonderful way to unwind and wish on a star!

Start a routine of a weekly hike. Each weekend, take an adventure hike.

Nature walks. Use walks to encourage the interest of nature in young children. Use field guides to identify plants, leaves, bugs, birds, and animals.

Portraits of nature. Use your walk to photograph your surroundings. Let children take pictures of a regular path, to document the different seasons of the year.

Your Turn:

Whether it is one of the above ideas or one of your own, choose a way to connect with nature this week!

Today's Affirmation:

I take the time to see and enjoy the beauty outside.

Inspirations: Hit the trail...

The first Saturday of each June marks National Trails Day, sponsored by the American Hiking Society. Since 1993, National Trails Day has grown to inspire many thousands of people to enjoy trails on the same day nationwide. Learn more about the event, register a hike in your area, or find local trails by visiting www.americanhiking.org.

June 6

"Those who have found tranquility are calm and pleasant to be with."
—Zen saying, excerpted from A
Thousand Paths to Tranquility

Good morning! Since our day is greatly dependent on how we begin our mornings, give yourself some extra time to calmly organize for your day. I know this can be hard. I am not a morning person. If it was up to me, life would start around 11:00 a.m. But, it isn't up to me, so if you can't beat them, join them.

I bound out of bed every day by 5:30 or 6:00 and give myself thirty or sixty minutes to center, sort, and get in the right mindset to face the day. I do some positive reading, I put on my makeup, I write my affirmations, take a look outside, I say a quick prayer. I don't oversleep very often, but when I do and don't have this "centered time," my day looks more like "A Thousands Paths to Chaos" than the quote above from *A Thousand Paths to Tranquility.*

For those of you with school-age children, try to get in this habit now, before the start of the school year. It will be much easier to wake up your children with a smile and a compliment if you have had that cup of coffee and a chance to center yourself. Morning should be a pleasant time, not a mad dash and scramble to get everyone directed down their path for the day. Everyone will feel so much better, all the day through, by getting a confident and calming send-off first thing in the morning.

Your Turn:

Find fifteen to thirty minutes of time for YOU in the morning. Tune out daily demands and pressures and tune into the positive. Consider reading a positive passage from a book, writing affirmations or reading them aloud, or writing in a journal. Give yourself some "soul food" to begin your day.

Today's Affirmation:

I care for myself and in turn care better for others when I give myself morning reflective time.

Inspirations

Ready to relax? If you need some help destressing or relaxing, visit these sites for step-by-step how-to plans.

How to Relax Your Body http://www.lessonsforliving.com/how.htm.

How to Relax: http://www.wikihow.com/Relax.

How to Relax at Your Desk: http://panicdisorder.about.com/cs/shrelaxation/ht/relaxdesk.htm.

June 7

*"No matter what you've done for yourself or for humanity, if
you can't look back on having given love and attention to
your own family, what have you really accomplished...?"*
—Lee Iacocca, automobile manufacturing executive

Good morning! Take Lee Iacocca's words to heart and turn
today into a day to express love and appreciation for your family
and close friends.

Say "I love you" out loud, rather than just thinking it. When
given the chance, be an attentive listener, putting down your
magazine or turning off the TV and/or computer screen while
someone is talking to you. Make time to sit down and engage
in conversation—actual sentences back and forth—not grunts
and nods as you, or they, dash out the door or look back over
a shoulder. Make eye contact. Tell a joke. Make yourself, and
those around you, laugh. Have fun. Be a kid again. Lighten up!
Give yourself a compliment, or two, or three.

Your Turn:

Today, start saying "I love you" and expressing appreciation to
your friends and family members as the most important job
and priority on earth. After all—it very well may be.

Today's Affirmation:

I take advantage of every opportunity to express appreciation
and love to those I care for.

Going Further

June marks National Home Safety Month. An annual check to make sure our homes are safe is a wonderful opportunity to care for family members. Visit http://www.homesafety-council.org/resource_center/rc_hsmchecklist_p001_pdf.html for a downloadable checklist and walk-through to keep your home safe.

June 8

> *"It matters not what a person is born,*
> *but who they choose to be."*
> —*J. K. Rowling*

Good morning! I really enjoyed stumbling across this quote, especially given the author. For those who don't know, J.K. Rowling is the author of the Harry Potter series. She is an inspiration to those who chose to follow her dreams. A single parent receiving financial assistance from the state, Joanne pursued her writing dream in every spare moment she had. And of course, the rest is history, as she continues to set publishing record after publishing record.

Your Turn:

Is there a piece of your life that you feel predestined to live out? Did you grow up in a family without money and thus feel that financial security is not within your reach? Did adults around you discourage your dreams until you forgot how to dream them? Take the words of J.K. to heart—choose to be more.

Today's Affirmation:

Each day I choose to be all I can be.

 *June 9*

> *"If you ask me what I came to do in this world,*
> *I will answer you: 'I am here to live out loud.'"*
> —*Emile Zola*

Good morning! This quote has always resonated with me. I actually found it on an inspirational wall calendar my mother gave me about five years ago. I placed a photo of me doing a running leap and breaking a board in karate and mounted it over the photo on the calendar. I then framed it and look at it often as an inspiration of what I can do when I set my mind to it.

Karate has always interested me. When I was little, I remember envying other kids who were enrolled in lessons at a young age and earned their various belts. I liked the idea of being able to protect myself. When my daughter was five, I took her to a local karate studio, wanting her to have the experience that I hadn't. The Master of the studio talked me in to giving it a whirl. I fell in love with the discipline.

Your Turn:

What hidden dreams or goals or childhood ambitions do you have? Why not pursue them? Why not live out loud? Pick up a paintbrush, join a karate or jazz-dancing class. It is never too late to pursue a childhood dream, unless we allow it to be.

Today's Affirmation:

I pursue my ambitions, treating them with as much importance as I do those of my family members.

Inspirations

Looking for motivation and ideas on how to step outside of your comfort zone into a more daring life? I fell in love with the book *You Can Do It!: The Merit Badge Book for Grown-Up Girls* on first sight. Author Lauren Catuzzi Grandcolas was an experienced sales and marketing professional pregnant with her first child and embarking on a writing career when she died on United Flight 93 on 9/11. Her husband, family, and publisher rallied together to complete this incredible 512-page book, which encourages middle-aged women to do the things they have always dreamed of doing. Divided into categories like "Dare," "Create," and "Learn," the book is patterned after a Girl Scouts badge program offering unique challenges for women.

Learn about the book and view sample badges at http://www.amazon.com/exec/obidos/ASIN/0811846350/ref=nosim/divatribe-20.

 *June 10*

"Don't be afraid to give up the good for the great."
—**Kenny Rogers**

Good morning! Often, as we change, we hit plateaus. Sometimes the plateaus aren't ones that we like, and other times they are very comfortable. We have made a step forward, a big step, and we enjoy and reap the benefits of our hard work. And we should. We deserve it. However, we can't confuse a plateau with a stepping stone. It only becomes a plateau when we refuse to let it spiral us upward to something more. As Kenny says, we cannot be "afraid to give up the good for the great."

Your Turn:

Take a moment to pat yourself on the back for the positive strides you have taken. Let those steps be a demonstration of the willpower and strength you have within you. Then, dedicate yourself to stepping up to the next level.

Today's Affirmation:

I let go of the good and inherit the great.

Reflection Questions

Where are you at a plateau in your life?

Are there any plateaus that could be used as stepping stones to move from good to great?

# *June 11*

> *"Perseverance is the hard work you do after you get*
> *tired of doing the hard work you already did."*
> **—Unknown**

Good morning! In 2003 I was chosen as one of the forty most influential businesspeople under age forty by the *Business Journal*. There was a newspaper supplement that featured a 300-word interview with each of us. The gist of the interview was, "What is your key to success?" The bold headline below my name read: "coffee, perseverance and faith." I have always believed that perseverance is a vital component to realizing success in any aspect of life. Those who reach their goals and their dreams refuse to give up. There are many stories that illustrate this point: the story of Edison's many "failures" prior to successful inventions; Colonel Sanders knocking on 620 doors before finding an investor at door 621. When we believe in our venture and ourselves, we refuse to settle for less than we deserve.

Your Turn:

What drives you? Is it being the best mom you can be? The best wife? Do you have an unrealized dream of writing a book, winning a competition, or starting a business? What is your passion? Take a moment to evaluate what is most important to you. Then persevere, and allow that dream to become a reality.

Today's Affirmation:

I persevere until I reach the dreams closest to my heart.

Going Further

Visit www.brooknoelstudio.com for information on my Values e-book that walks you step-by-step through defining your values and creating a Vision Statement for your life — a key tool for persevering toward your goals.

June 12

*"Excellence is caring more than others think is wise;
risking more than others think is safe; dreaming
more than others think is practical; and expecting
more than others think is possible."*
—Author unknown

Good morning! I fell in love with this quote the first time I saw it many years ago. While going through a difficult period in my life, I found it on an inspirational poster with a photo of a soaring eagle. It resonated with me, because it matched my core beliefs—even though those core beliefs often required walking up to the precipice of life and taking uncalculated risks. Yet I knew that these were principles I had to live by in order to experience all that life would offer me. I never wanted to miss a chance, even though they required falling down and getting many a bruise.

Last night, I was reflecting on what a full life means to me. I believe one key is to "greet each moment with a sense of appreciation instead of expectation." I believe we pass another milestone when our fears become inspirations instead of deterrents in achieving our full potential. Learning to take risks, and enjoying that sense of adventure—no matter what the end result, is another key. When we can appreciate our own cour-age, despite the result, we see—and, more importantly—*take* the opportunities life so often presents. That statement leads me back to a quote I saw on a card when I was only fourteen. I bought the card and have it still. The outside of the card fea-tures a small sailboat on an ocean night. Below the photo is the simple text: "One cannot discover new lands without los-ing sight of the shore."

To me, this quote speaks volumes about change. So many of us want to realize change, but we are unwilling to "cast away" the lines that tie us to our old habits. We try to reach the "other side of the ocean" while leaving those ties around us. That is an impossible journey. We must be willing to throw off the ties and set sail toward our dreams.

Your Turn:

Review today's quote and think about what it means to you. How can you practice excellence in your life? And what about change? Are you trying to change while still holding on to the past? If so, make a concerted effort to cast away the lines and see where the wonderful journey of life will take you.

Today's Affirmation:

Each day, I sail toward and realize the great gifts of this life.

June 13

A woman was waiting at an airport one night

With several long hours before her flight.

She hunted for a book in the airport shop

Bought a bag of cookies and found a place to drop.

She was engrossed in her book but happened to see

That the man beside her as bold as could be

Grabbed a cookie or two from the bag between

Which she tried to ignore to avoid a scene.

She munched cookies and watched the clock

As this gutsy cookie thief diminished her stock.

She was getting more irritated as the minutes ticked by

Thinking "If I wasn't so nice I'd blacken his eye."

With each cookie she took he took one too

And when only one was left she wondered what he'd do.

With a smile on his face and a nervous laugh

He took the last cookie and broke it in half.

He offered her half as he ate the other

She snatched it from him and thought: "Oh brother.

This guy has some nerve and he's also rude

Why, he didn't even show any gratitude"

She had never known when she had been so galled

And sighed with relief when her flight was called.

She gathered her belongings and headed for the gate

Refusing to look back at the thieving ingrate.

She boarded the plane and sank in her seat

Then sought her book which was almost complete.

As she reached in her baggage she gasped with surprise.

There was her bag of cookies in front of her eyes.

"If mine are here" she moaned with despair,

"Then the others were his and he tried to share."

"Too late to apologize," she realized with grief,

That she was the rude one, the ingrate, the thief.

—*Author unknown*

Good morning! I ran across this poem the other day and thought it spoke volumes about our relationships with others and those around us. How often do we automatically assume the worst, half-mindedly think negative thoughts, nonchalantly cast the blame on the other person, "pass the buck," shirk responsibility, make excuses, call the glass half-empty instead of half-full, or just become oblivious to the truth or our surroundings altogether.

Why not make today a day to become kinder, gentler, more understanding and giving, less critical or judgmental, a little more patient, a little more nurturing, a little more insightful, and, above all, positive in thought and energetic in learning and living? Add a lightness, and a politeness, into your step and embrace today.

Your Turn:

Make that positive first step to connect, really connect, with the world around you—be it a relative, a friend, a stranger in need, a pet, the person behind the checkout counter at your grocery store: whomever or whatever—reconnect!

Today's Affirmation:

I assume and expect the best at every turn.

June 14

> *"Nothing can stop the man with the right mental attitude from achieving his goal; nothing on earth can help the man with the wrong mental attitude."*
> —*Thomas Jefferson*

Good morning! Take a quick attitude "temperature" check. How is your attitude this morning? Are you ready to have a great day?

As we work to make our days consistently brighter, we learn the "tools" it takes for us to have a great day. Each of us has triggers that help us to make the most of our day. Our triggers might include getting up on time, having a healthy breakfast, or having time to write an affirmation or read a positive book. Think through the tasks you normally do that help get your day off to a good start.

Your Turn:

Think about your "good days," "medium days," and "average days." Which days are most enjoyable and productive for you?

Odds are, it is the good days that help you make progress toward creating the life you desire. The first key ingredient to a good day is the right mental attitude. Likewise, the major component in reaching a goal (as today's quote states) is the right mental attitude. Realize that taking the time to program yourself for a great day with a great attitude is important. It is never something to be neglected.

Today's Affirmation:

I make sure that, each day, prior to leaving my home or interacting with others, I have a great mental attitude.

 *June 15*

"Destiny is no matter of chance. It is a matter of choice: it is not a thing to be waited for, it is a thing to be achieved."
—*William Jennings Bryan*

Good morning! I had an interesting conversation about accomplishment with an old friend yesterday. He was asking how I had managed to get where I am today, despite many obstacles, hindrances, and setbacks that might detour, in his words, most people.

I had never really thought about my life in those terms, so my answer was short and basic. "What's the alternative?" I know now, and I've always known, that I would never be happy if I let circumstance win. I have dreams, ambitions, and goals that are more important than the obstacles that come my way. My devotion to my dreams is unwavering.

Your Turn:

Destiny is indeed a choice. If you choose not to create your destiny, you are making the choice to "default" and let the world create it for you. Take today's quote to heart and don't wait for the world to "roll your way." Instead, take steps to make the life you want happen.

Today's Affirmation:

Each day I take a step toward the destiny I desire.

June 16

> *"We all live in suspense, from day to day, from hour to hour; in other words, we are the hero of our own story."*
> —*Mary McCarthy*

Good morning! My best friend shared this quote with me and I was very moved by the words. We truly are the heroes of our own story. There is very little else to say—except one simple question:

Are you living like the hero in your life? Or are you living like the victim?

Your Turn:

You are in control of your story. What are you going to choose to live? Remember that those around you (including your children) emulate you. So are you the hero? Are you the victim? Are you somewhere in between? Today is a great day to change, isn't it? There is nothing holding you back from being a hero today.

Today's Affirmation:

Each day, I choose to be a hero instead of a victim.

June 17

> *"I have found that if you love life, life will love you back."*
> —*Arthur Rubenstein*

Good morning! Have you figured out the importance of "Good Mornings" and why we do them? I'll give you a clue... read the above quote again.

When we put out good thoughts and good feelings, we feel better and they return to us. The old saying, "What goes around comes around," holds true. However, that means that if we put out negativity, anger, and fear, they will "come around" as well.

Life is too important to leave to chance. Saying an affirmation and a positive good morning allows us to take the wheel and put our best foot forward each day. If you slip into negative thinking patterns during your day, you're not alone! We all do from time to time. Keep some of your favorite quotes handy and read/write a few extra affirmations during those days.

Your Turn:

If you haven't been saying heartfelt good mornings to everyone, consistently, start. If you haven't been saying and writing your affirmation, start. Reread the tips in the introduction for effectively using the Today's Affirmation at the end of each inspiration. You can only reap the results this can offer by diving in. What do you have to lose?

Today's Affirmation:
I embrace life, always putting my best foot forward.

June 18

> *"Every day in every way I'm getting better and better."*
> —*Emile Coue*

Good morning! This would be a wonderful quote to add to the routine of how we start our day. What I love most about this is that it reminds us that each day matters, each day we can improve, and each day we can get closer to our goals.

Some days we might take giant strides. Other days or weeks, we might have interruptions, but if we keep our emotions focused, and we keep practicing the pillars of the challenge, we still get better and better.

Your Turn:
Add this quote to your affirmations for a week. Say it bright and early each morning. Say it throughout the day when you need a pick-me-up.

Today's Affirmation:
Every day in every way I'm getting better and better.

 *June 19*

> *"You can have anything you want if you will give up the belief that you can't have it."*
> —Dr. Robert Anthony

Good morning! Do you truly believe you can have the things that you desire most in your life? If you don't truly believe you can have what you desire, you will not achieve your desires. The law of attraction is always at work. We attract that which we think about. If we think we cannot have something, we write our own ending and make it so. Likewise, when we give up limiting beliefs, we can turn the page and write a new story.

Giving up limiting beliefs isn't easy. At some point, our limiting beliefs probably served a purpose. Perhaps they kept us safe from an adult that could hurt us with words or might, or they protected us from other children in school. When we carry these beliefs into adulthood, there comes a time when we have to "lay them to rest" if we truly want to reach our full potential.

To lay a limiting belief to rest, we must first be very conscious of the belief. We have to be able to articulate the current negative belief and then the new belief we want to lay in its place. Every time the negative belief or pattern emerges, replace it with the new belief. It is best to do this aloud, in the mirror, or by writing down our belief, rather than just thinking it.

Your Turn:

Identify at least three self-limiting beliefs. Articulate each limiting belief in a single sentence. Next, write a positive statement to counteract the limiting belief. Each time you catch yourself engaging in negative thought, turn to a blank page in your journal and write your positive belief until the negative feeling disappears.

Today's Affirmation:

I shed limiting and negative beliefs, and put positive and supportive thoughts in their place.

 *June 20*

"There can be no happiness if the things we believe in are different from the things we do."
—*Freya Stark*

Good morning! I love to create tools to help women discover the delta of what makes us happy—where we want to be—versus where we actually are. In today's society, we have become experts at being busy, but we are often busy doing things that don't matter or don't match what we believe in.

Your Turn:

Answer quick: What are the three things you believe in most strongly? If you can't answer within sixty seconds, consider spending some time reflecting on the values that shape your life. If you could answer within a minute, your guiding values are clear. Now, take a look at your day today, and make sure the things you are doing match what you believe in. (At least as much as humanly possible.) And don't forget—if family is on your "important" list, doing laundry counts as something you believe in. It is part of running your family.

Today's Affirmation:

I consistently complete action items that match my beliefs.

Going Further

If you are struggling to define your values, consider investigating my e-book workbook *Values: A Compass for Contentment.* The workbook takes you step-by-step through narrowing down a list of values from 295 to five, and provides exercises and ideas to help you live in tune with these values. You can learn more at www.brooknoelstudio.com.

June 21

> *"The more light you allow within you, the brighter the world you live in will be."*
> —Shakti Gawain

Good morning! A simple sentence can have so much power behind it. I have always loved the work of Shakti Gawain. I was fortunate to stumble across her book *Creative Visualization* when I was only fourteen years old. That book taught me the power of my own thinking and how to use affirmations to improve the quality of my life (and eliminate self-destructive habits). The concept here is simple: Each day, we have the power to choose how much light we let in and how much light we cast around us. We let light in by "feeding the soul," through good deeds, kindness, and prayer.

Your Turn:

Imagine that you have a "Spiritual Bank Account." Each time you pray, do an act of kindness or practice positive self-reflection, a deposit is made into that register. That balance determines the light within you and thus the light you can shine onto others. How does your account look? If it is looking like things might "bounce," grab your short-term to-do list and make some plans to fix it.

Today's Affirmation:

Today, I renew my commitment to refuel and reenergize so that I may have more light within to cast onto the world around me.

Inspirations

This is the perfect time to let the light in, given that June 21 or 22 is the summer solstice. The word solstice comes from the Latin word *sol*, meaning sun, and *stice*, to stand still. On this day the sun will reach its highest point in the sky, creating the longest day of the year.

Take some time to stand still today and let the light in.

June 22

"Some pursue happiness—others create it."
—*Author unknown*

"It is not easy to find happiness in ourselves, and it is not possible to find it elsewhere."
—*Agnes Repplier*

Good morning! Pursuing happiness is a difficult battle. Happiness is fleeting if we chase it. When we learn what makes us happy, we can create our own happiness instead of relying on something external (or something out of our control).

Your Turn:

Do you know what makes you happy? Start a list in your journal or daily planner and record the moments that bring you happiness and pleasure. Once you have identified your "happiness stimuli" you can work to create more of such stimuli in your life.

Today's Affirmation:

Each day, I create happiness and joy.

Inspirations

Need some happiness help? According to the *Journal of Personality and Social Psychology*, published by the American Psychological Association (APA), at the top of the list of needs that appear to bring happiness are autonomy (feeling that your activities are self-chosen and self-endorsed), competence (feeling that you are effective in your activities), relatedness (feeling a sense of closeness with others), and self-esteem. At the bottom of the list are popularity, money, and luxury. Stop in at http://www.thingstobehappyabout.com/ to find a list of things to be happy about every day of the year.

 *June 23*

"Be kind, for everyone you meet is fighting a hard battle."
—*Plato*

Good morning! I once listened to a speaker who shared a story I will never forget. He was at a restaurant working on a speech. He had hoped to have some quiet time to reflect and prepare. Shortly after he arrived, a family was seated about three tables away. The children were behaving badly. They were stomping forks and knives on the table, pulling at each other, and making a general ruckus. The speaker couldn't understand how this father could let his children behave like that... or why he would take such misbehaving children out in public.

He tried to be patient, but after twenty minutes of the noise, he asked his waitress to ask the family to quiet down if possible. The father then stood up and walked over to the speaker. The next words changed the speaker's outlook forever.

"I am sorry, sir," he said in a kind, sincere, and sad voice. "The children just lost their mother two days ago, and I just haven't been able to get them to settle down since. I thought getting a good meal in them would help." He and the speaker went on to exchange a few lines and parted on good terms. Of course, the speaker wasn't "wrong" for wanting his private time to prepare and reflect. Nor was the father "wrong" for taking his children out for a meal. But, we often think in terms of "right and wrong," when in reality every story has different angles—sometimes many different angles. Looking at these angles is great exercise for the mind.

Your Turn:

We all have habitual tendencies that allow us to believe some-thing about a given situation, whether it is right or not. Try to stop worrying about right and wrong. Instead, exercise your mind and come up with as many reasons for different situa-tions as you can—explore all the angles.

Today's Affirmation:

I do not concern myself with right and wrong. I do concern myself with understanding.

 *June 24*

"The best years of your life are the ones in which you decide your problems are your own. You do not blame them on your mother, the ecology, or the president. You realize that you control your own destiny."
—*Albert Ellis*

Good morning! One of the most freeing moments in my life was when I truly understood that every problem in my life was just that: *my* problem. While others might play a part in it, the problem couldn't exist or be *my* problem if I wasn't involved! It sounds quite simple, but we so often blame our problems on everyone else—or some circumstance beyond our control. We often do this when our problems are big and scary, as we don't know how to face them. The great news is that when we take ownership of a problem, we also inherit the power to problem-solve. Instead of waiting at someone else's mercy to fix things, we can take control and fix things ourselves.

Your Turn:

Are you taking responsibility for the problems in your life, or are you still blaming them on others and waiting for a magic solution? Man-made solutions will make you stronger than magic solutions. Choose a problem and take ownership of it. Then, begin to brainstorm how you can move forward. And don't just brainstorm: *act.* If you need help, do this in a group to explore new ways of seeing the problem, fresh ideas, etc. Odds are, everyone has a problem or two that could benefit from a fresh point of view.

Today's Affirmation:

I am a professional problem-solver.

 *June 25*

Do more than exist: live.

Do more than touch: feel.

Do more than look: observe.

Do more than hear: listen.

Do more than listen: understand.

Do more than think: reflect.

Do more that just talk: say something
—Author unknown

Good morning! What wonderful guidelines this quote offers for truly living our life! What else can I add?

Your Turn:

Read this quote several times. Which lines speak to you most? Make a concerted effort to practice at least two of these philosophies today.

Today's Affirmation:

Choose whichever lines speak to you most and write them as an affirmation. Example: I reflect and speak with meaning. I listen intently. I look beyond the obvious and observe life.

 *June 26*

> *"Dreams come a size too big so that we can grow into them."*
> —*Josie Bissett*

Good morning! Today, I want you to... Stop. Take a deep breath. For the next two minutes, we are going to be doing something that might be a bit foreign—*relaxing!* (Don't just read this—do it!) Close your eyes and take another deep breath. Now exhale. Imagine you are *breathing in* all things good and wonderful and *exhaling* all your stress and troubles.

Your Turn:

Once you are relaxed, take a moment to reflect on this question: "What dream do you hold in your heart?"

Today's Affirmation:

"I will reach any dream I set my mind and heart to."

June 27

> *"Get up and dance, get up and smile, get up and drink*
> *to the days that are gone in the shortest while."*
> —*Simon Fowler*

Good morning! Isn't that a wonderful, yet bittersweet, quote? It reminds us that what is all around us won't last forever. Yet in the same breath, it also reminds us to dance and smile and celebrate.

What will you do today to celebrate the fact that you are here? To celebrate what you have that is good in your life?

Your Turn:

We don't need a party to celebrate—each day is a present waiting to be unwrapped. What is one thing you could do today to "celebrate" and show your appreciation for all that you have? Remember that gratitude for the things we love brings more of those things. Likewise, complaining about what we don't have brings more lack.

What story would you rather live in? What choices will you make today to support that story?

Today's Affirmation:

Every day I embrace and celebrate the precious gift of life.

 *June 28*

> *"It's not what you do once in a while, it's what you do day in and day out that makes the difference."*
> —*Jenny Craig*

Good morning! Oh, if only it was what we did "once in a while," how easy life would be! If I could eat well one day and have it last a month, or think positively one day and have it resonate for a year... but alas, that isn't how life works. Life makes us learn and learn again those skills we want to instill and embrace. But as another one of my favorite quotes states, "Anything worth trying is worth trying at least ten times."

It is always perseverance that separates the "men from the boys" or the "women from the gals." It is consistent effort, day after day, that eventually becomes habitual.

In two days, we begin the second half of the year. Do you need to restart or recommit? Are you a "once in a whiler" or a "day-in and day-outer"?

Your Turn:

What do you want from life? Make a decision today and then accept nothing less. If you have stumbled, dust yourself off and restart. Celebrate June 30 as a second New Year's Eve, and recommit to your goals.

Today's Affirmation:

I don't settle. I expect and accept greatness from myself.

June 29

"We are what we repeatedly do. Excellence,
then, is not an act, but a habit."
—Aristotle

Good morning! There is so much truth in this simple quote. Think about your day yesterday: What did you do? What did you practice—excellence? Kindness? Negativity? As you live life, remember that if you keep doing what you have always done, you will keep getting what you have always gotten. If you seek new results in your life, you must change what you are doing.

Your Turn:

Today, practice what you want to see in your life, whether it is kindness, excellence, beauty, or all of the above.

Today's Affirmation:

Today and every day, I practice and attract the qualities of change I want to create in my life.

Going Further

What qualities and characteristics do you want to be present in your life? Generosity? Grace? Kindness? Friendliness? Patience? Challenge yourself to create a journal list of fifty qualities you would like to fill your days. Post this where you will see it often and read through it. Watch how the awareness of what you want in your life serves as a guidepost for creating it.

June 30

> *"Just because you bought the ticket doesn't*
> *mean you have to stay for the second act."*
> *—Author unknown (from a print*
> *hanging on my wall)*

Good morning! When I realized that tomorrow marks the official start of the second half of the calendar year, I knew just the quote I needed to dig up and share with you. I nodded in recognition when I first read this quote. It resonated with how often we start something and commit our time to it, and then realize that the activity isn't fulfilling our purpose or goals in the way we had hoped. Or perhaps we have filled our calendars with activities that keep us busy but do not take us any closer to the life we truly desire.

At least once each season it is valuable to step back and look at our activities and commitments. If they are not leading us to a more fulfilling and rich life, then we would be wise to change paths. As the quote says, "We don't have to stay for the second act." Our time is valuable. Our energy is valuable. Our lives are valuable.

Your Turn:

Reflect on your current activities and commitments. Are they leading you toward a more fulfilling and rich life? Think about ways to minimize the activities that don't reward you, and make space for activities that are more rewarding.

Today's Affirmation:

I spend my time wisely.

Reflection Questions

What goals did I set at the New Year?

What goals have I outgrown?

What goals have I added?

What goals will I revise?

What have I learned in the first half of the year that can help me maximize the six remaining months?

July 1

"A smile can happen in a flash, but the
memory can last a lifetime!"
—Author unknown

Good morning! Today's inspiration comes from Tammy K., who writes:

I have this saying on a little sign at the office I work in, right next to my in-box and the candy dish, which coworkers visit daily. It is a nice reminder for all of us to be humble, caring and loving. And to maybe let people know that it's okay to feel good about smiling and how much that smile might mean to someone else.

Of all the ways to make today matter, being joyous and caring in our words and actions is one of the best. No matter what our mood, the way we behave, think, and act will spread to others—

thus each of us, each day, has an impact on the entire world around us. When we are negative or down, that spreads to others. When we are positive, smiling, and hopeful, that spreads to others. As we enter each day, let us remember the important role we each play and the effect we each have on one another.

Your Turn:

Challenge yourself to try and spread five smiles each day this month.

Today's Affirmation:

Each day, I focus on being the best " me" I can be, and on giving that gift to others.

 *July 2*

> *"Let him that would move the world first move himself."*
> —*Socrates*

Good morning! Nancy sent in this quote with the following note:

I like this quote because it shows that nothing has really changed in thousands of years—even Socrates saw our human tendency to think about what others can do better... rather than do it ourselves.

Nancy and Socrates have both touched on one of the biggest challenges we face in moving forward toward our heart's desires: the human tendency to wait for someone else to make a change first. While we might talk a good game, do our actions match our voices?

Studies have shown that the most successful business owners have worked in each area of their businesses. In other words, they haven't asked anyone to do something they are not willing (or have not done) themselves. We can apply this principle of success in our own lives. Before we ask others to do something for us, before we go out and change the world, let us first ask the best from ourselves and transform ourselves into the best people we can be.

Your Turn:

Pay attention to how much energy you spend thinking about solutions for others or the way things "could" or "should" be. Realize this time steals from the time available to take positive action in your life. Redirect your energy inward, instead of outward.

Today's Affirmation:

Each day, I am improving my life.

July 3

> *"Thoughts are energy. And you can make your world or break your world by your own thinking."*
> —*Susan L. Taylor, journalist*

Good morning! For those of you who have sincerely practiced one or more of the Good Morning routines, you have likely noticed that a chipper Good Morning has a drastic influence on your morning, and therefore the rest of your day. Just as we say that breakfast is the most important physical component of a day, I feel that a "Good Morning" is the most important emotional component of our day. It also shows how positive thinking (even when it is difficult to do or done halfheartedly) has the power to change how we feel and impact those around us. Don't let that attitude fade away after your "Good Morning," though. Make a consistent effort to keep your positive energy flowing throughout the day.

Your Turn:

Say several "Good Mornings" today! Each time you eat, say Good Morning afterward to remind yourself of the power of positive thinking. If you think a negative thought, talk back to it! Research has shown that it takes twenty-seven positive thoughts to counteract the power of one negative thought. Today, keep talking and thinking positive thoughts until you tip the scale to a positive mind-set for the majority of the day.

Today's Affirmation:

I am a positive person, spreading positive and hopeful energy to all I come into contact with.

July 4

"And so, my fellow Americans: ask not what your country can do for you—ask what you can do for your country."
—*John F. Kennedy*

Good morning! In JFK's famous speech, he shared: "Let every nation know, whether it wishes us well or ill, that we shall pay any price, bear any burden, meet any hardship, support any friend, oppose any foe, in order to assure the survival and the success of liberty."

What is on your agenda for today? A picnic, family gathering, or day at the lake? While millions of us celebrate a national holiday and look forward to a day off from work, many of America's one and a half million troops on active duty will not. It only takes a moment to share words of support and thanks to our troops. Visit the Department of Defense website, www.americasupportsyou.mil and follow the link on the home page to email your support.

Your Turn:

During your celebrations take time to remember the important history of this day and to thank those who are defending our freedom.

Today's Affirmation:

I celebrate and appreciate independence.

Inspirations

- Watch JFK's inaugural speech online at www.youtube.com/watch?v=xE0iPY7XGBo&feature=related

- Find history, a link to the Declaration of Independence, quizzes, recipes, e-cards and more at the Holiday Spot. www.theholidayspot.com/july4/

- If you have children visit familyfun.go.com/arts-and-crafts/season/minisite/4th-of-july-main/ for printables, craft ideas, recipes, decorations, and many other creative celebration ideas.

July 5

> *"Grab a chance and you won't be sorry*
> *for a might-have-been."*
> *—A. Ransome, writer and novelist*

Good morning! If only "should haves" and "could haves" were franchises—how rich many of us would be! How many times have you looked back and thought... "If only..."; or, "I wish I had..." Here's the good news—you have the power to eliminate the need for the majority of "should haves" and "could haves" from your life by seizing the changes that come your way.

Begin each day by creating a Three Step Action List. Let this list reflect three things you can complete in a single day that align with your priorities. How long they take is not important, as long as they align with life priorities. Today, cross off each item on this list as you move toward the life you desire. As you continue this practice, I think you will be amazed at what a difference one day can make.

Your Turn:

Create a Three Step Action List for the day that aligns with your most important personal goals. Continue this practice daily, committing to crossing off these three items to make today matter.

Today's Affirmation:

Each day, I am guided by my priorities. I live in the present, moving toward my goals.

July 6

"We don't need to increase our goods nearly as much as we need to scale down our wants. Not wanting something is as good as possessing it."
—*Donald Horban*

Good morning! How much time and energy do you spend trying to attain something, whether emotionally or physically, which you believe you need in order to be happier, more fulfilled or make life easier? Common examples of where we get caught up in the "chase" include:

Believing we need someone's approval.

Believing the next "planner" will organize our lives (instead of organizing it ourselves).

Believing that some better-than-Botox cream will make us beautiful.

Believing that our child needs a specific brand item or toy to be happy.

Believing that we are responsible for fixing problems beyond our control.

Believing that we are responsible for someone else's happiness.

If I were to stockpile all the time and energy I have put into endeavors like these in the past, surely I could take the next month off—maybe even two months! How freeing it can be to realize that maybe we don't "need" everything we think we do—instead, what we need to do is scale back on perceived needs.

Your Turn:

Create a list of things you have spent time and energy on that you felt you "needed." What needs can you scale back on so that you can enjoy today more?

Today's Affirmation:

My energy and time are spent only on life's true needs.

Going Further

Pace Consulting has great tips for scaling back and analyzing needs. Read through the ideas at http://www.getmore-done.com/tips7.html and make a list of those you could implement to bring more peace to your days.

July 7

"The sculptor produces the beautiful statue by chipping away such parts of the marble block as are not needed—it is a process of elimination."
—Elbert Hubbard

Good morning! Think about the journey of self-improvement you have taken. How many times have you succumbed to adding a new system, tool, approach, mission statement, goal? Consumer-culture has taught us to look externally for solutions to our problems instead of internally, and that the next "tool" could be the "magic cure" for all of our woes.

Yet, when we look externally time and time again, all we do is add to the confusion of trying to decode our path. We have to wade through all its tools and systems. Today's quote reminds me that often our answers are internal. Instead of adding on, we should focus our energies on looking within, chipping away at the pieces that don't work, until we find our "core."

Your Turn:

We are all the sculptors of our own lives. What type of sculpture are you creating?

Today's Affirmation:

Daily I look within, reflecting and honing my purpose.

 *July 8*

> *"Time is free, but it's priceless. You can't own it, but you can use it. You can't keep it, but you can spend it. Once you've lost it you can never get it back."*
> —*Harvey MacKay*

Good morning! Our time is more valuable than money. Our time is the one thing money can't buy. If only we would protect and cherish our time as we would a winning lottery ticket. One of my mentors is a very successful CEO, who has gone through vigorous, top-notch, elite training programs. When I asked him for advice, he shared that the single most important thing a person can do is to recognize their core competencies. He explained that there are things in this world that ONLY Brook can do. He stressed that I needed to spend 90 percent of my time "in that zone." He also explained that there are many things Brook can do, but that can also be done by others. He shared that one of the biggest mistakes we make is not being true to our core competencies, and spending too much time doing things that other people can also do.

Sometimes we do this because we think "our way is the best way," or because we are scared to let go. But each time we veer from our core competencies, we also veer from our core mission.

Your Turn:

What are your core competencies? What tasks do you need to "let go" so you can spend more time "in the zone?"

Today's Affirmation:

I value and cherish my time—always spending it wisely.

July 9

"How wonderful it is that nobody need wait a single moment before starting to improve the world."
—*Anne Frank*

Good morning! The fact that you are reading this shows your commitment to improving your surroundings and the world around you. The best part about changing our lives, and the world, for the better, is that we don't have to wait until tomorrow to start. Today, many opportunities will come your way to make a difference.

Will you seize them and take the opportunity to reach out to someone? To make someone smile or laugh instead of shrugging your shoulders? The magic of living is right here, right now. Seize the day.

Your Turn:
Remind yourself constantly today to "make a difference." Keep a smile on your face; truly listen instead of just nodding your head; make eye contact—connect.

Today's Affirmation:
Today I seize every opportunity to improve my world.

Going Further
Visit www.networkforgood.org to find opportunities to volunteer and make a difference.

July 10

> *"It isn't how hard you kick—but how you kick."*
> —*Samantha Noel*

Good morning! A few years ago, my daughter enrolled in a day-camp program about archaeology, through the Milwaukee Public Museum. As part of the day-camp, they had group activities and group sports.

During the camp week, I had been out of town for five days, so upon my return we went out for a "girls' night" to catch up. She was detailing the camp and the different students and the daily structure of the program.

Sammy is a wonderful child, although she is not naturally athletic. However, she has learned that even with sports, part of it is natural talent but part of it is what you do with what you have. With that mentality, she has learned to excel. It was difficult for her, because she had to survive being the last person picked, and use confidence and positive reinforcement to overcome the opinions of others and shine anyway.

In this particular camp, there was a girl who was also not naturally athletic and who was very nervous about the group sport activities. During kickball, she would often miss the ball completely or just punt a few feet. She seemed to be constantly "out," without ever making it to base.

Sammy pulled her aside and said, "You don't have to be naturally good at sports or super-athletic to be a good player. It isn't about kicking the ball hard or with force, but with confidence. Bring confidence to your kick and the ball will respond." (This is literally how she talks, in case you were wondering: She has a vocabulary and way of saying things that blows adults away. In fact, while I was gone I asked her during a phone conversation why she was upset, as she sounded bothered, and she said, "Mother, I am upset about multiple issues.")

Back to our kickball story—this girl went up to kick and took Sammy's advice. She kicked the ball hard enough to make it all the way to second base. Then she ran with confidence on the subsequent teammate kicks and made it to home plate for her first time.

Your Turn:

Where in your life have you been thinking you need some "secret to success" or special talent to achieve the results you desire? Try following a child's advice. Approach your goal with confidence—you will be pleasantly surprised at the result. Use confidence and positive reinforcement to overcome the opinions of others and shine anyway... then make it to "home plate" for the goal of your choice.

Today's Affirmation:

I approach my actions and goals with confidence.

 *July 11*

"If you have time to whine and complain about something, then you have the time to do something about it."
—*Anthony J. D'Angelo*

Good morning! I don't know about you, but I have made a few observations. (1) A lot of people like to complain—they almost seem addicted to complaining, chaos, or negativity. (2) Often we are too busy to just "stop" and be thankful!

Thanksgiving has always been one of my favorite holidays, with its absence of stressors like presents and high expectations. It reminds us all to STOP and celebrate what we have instead of what we want.

I think many of us could benefit from a few more "Thanksgivings" throughout the year. In our home, we began celebrating the twentieth of each month (chosen at random) as Thankfulness day. Then we even prepare a special dinner and spend our time thinking of all we are grateful. Sammy and I take turns being the designated "journal keeper," writing down each gratitude, who said it, and the date. Then, on Thanksgiving Day, we share our "Family Gratitude Journal."

Your Turn:

Whether you are a family of one or 100, designate one night a month to celebrating thankfulness. I have found when I anticipate recording items I am thankful for I appreciate more and more each day. We tend to find what we look for—begin looking for life's blessings.

Today's Affirmation:

I am thankful for today.

July 12

"In my experience, there is only one motivation, and that is desire. No reasons or principle contain it or stand against it."
—*Jane Smiley*

Good morning! I have long been a believer in the type of "desire" Jane refers to in this quote. Desire can move mountains, help us stand after falling for the hundredth time, and it can perform miracles and get us through our darkest times. When we truly desire something with our body, mind, and soul, there is no indecision or moments of inaction—every step becomes a part of the journey toward our goal.

Life doesn't offer us a smooth path. Instead, it offers us mountains and valleys, cold and warm phases: life "seasons" us. Yet, heart-born desire propels us forward through all of life's seasons and allows us to move with purpose.

Your Turn:

What fills you with the type of desire that can move mountains? Devote more of your time to this desire and passion, and nurture it.

Today's Affirmation:

I nurture my passions.

Going Further

Summer has a way of passing by in the blink of an eye. Take some time today to reflect on your personal or family goals for the summer. Choose one passion to nurture and schedule it on your calendar today.

July 13

"You must have the courage to do the thing you think you cannot do."
—*Anne Morrow-Lindburgh*

Good morning! Sometimes the best encouragement and inspiration can come from our peers. This quote was submitted by a very courageous reader—it had been on her refrigerator for a very long time. One night, when her abusive husband was occupied in the bathroom, she took her two children and went out the front door. She drove all night to a different state. This admirable woman found the courage to do something she likely didn't think she could do. This quote defines what true courage is. Courage is the ability to stretch past our perceived limitations, take a chance, dance on the edge, and believe we will not fall.

Your Turn:

Where in your life can you hear the call of courage? What have you discounted, avoided, or left uncompleted because of fear? Commit to live courageously today.

Today's Affirmation:

My strength and courage are more powerful than my fears.

 *July 14*

> *"The key is not to prioritize what's on your schedule, but to schedule your priorities."*
> —*Stephen Covey*

Good morning! Have you ever taken a hard look at your to-do list? It can be an interesting and revealing exercise. Many of us feel guilt when we don't accomplish those items we have labeled as "to-dos." But before feeling guilt, perhaps it is time to look at your to-do list in a new light. When we have items that remain incomplete on our list, that doesn't necessarily mean we suffer from procrastination. Sometimes the undone tasks can offer insightful clues as to where we are in this season of life, and help us define our priorities.

Have you ever had someone ask you how you feel, only to respond: "fine"? Or have you had someone ask you what you want to do, and you find it hard to make a decision? In the process of self-discovery, sometimes it is easier to figure out who we are not, instead of who we are.

Our incomplete tasks can give us clues about what is and is not important to us at this season of our life. If a task stays on our list long enough, it simply isn't a priority for us right now. Perhaps it is a priority to someone else in our life, or it is something we "think we should do."

Your Turn:

Take a look at your to-do list. Practice the art of self-discovery by uncovering things that are not important to you at this season in your life. Analyze your to-dos and let the ones that are not a priority go.

Today's Affirmation:

I let my priorities guide my actions.

 *July 15*

> *"The first step to getting the things you want out of life is this: decide what you want."*
> —*Ben Stein*

Good morning! Over the past few months, I have been very intrigued with the notion of creating the "ideal day." I have been going through many shifts in my life; my company has moved our offices, my schedule and commitments continue to change and unfold. Like many of you, my life doesn't really contain a formula for a "typical day." It is constantly in flux.

But I became intrigued with the concept of building my own ideal day. If it were up to me (and it is up to us!) what would my day look like? How would it start? What activities would I make sure to include? What steps would I take toward my goals? Who would I spend my time with? In essence: If I could build my life (which I can) what blocks would I choose to use as my foundation?

Interestingly, if we don't ask ourselves these questions, we get whatever blocks are tossed in our path and make the most of them. When we take an active and aware interest in constructing our days, our weeks, our months, we move closer to our ideal.

Your Turn:

Today spend some time doing a self-interview of your desires during this season of your life.

Today's Affirmation:

I choose what I create in my life.

Reflection Question

What would your ideal day look like? Describe it in detail from start to finish. Include how it would begin, activities, actions, who you would spend your time with, and how it would end.

 *July 16*

> *"The key to success: do only one thing at a time*
> *—and give it everything you've got."*
> —*Brook Noel*

Good morning! Do only one thing at a time: don't laugh—
I really mean it! I know this concept might seem difficult to
grasp and I understand the skepticism. Just as I was born complicated, I was also born a multitasker. I am naturally one of
those people who have eighteen different programs or windows open on my computer. I am reading (or writing) multiple
books at a time. I can't even buy one pet at a time! I acquired
two cats that were brothers, and two golden retrievers that
were sisters.

However, I had to come to terms with the fact that doing
multiple things at one time didn't make me more efficient:
It just made me more stressed. It led me to falsely believe
I could do more with little time. Yet when I embraced the
concept of doing one thing at a time and began *focusing* on
one thing at a time, something amazing happened. Suddenly
I didn't feel so rushed—I didn't feel everything was "urgent."
I didn't feel like I was on a treadmill. Instead, I felt centered
and in control. I was able to do my best, because I wasn't being distracted and divided by multiple tasks, but instead was
focused on a single purpose.

This was true at work and also at play. Try watching a movie
while paying bills or folding laundry, instead of just watching
the movie. Try playing a game with your child, rather than playing a game while also fixing dinner. Which way offers more
peace, more enjoyment, more magic in the moment? When
we cram a single moment with multiple activities, we might get
more done, but we can only do so by sacrificing the magic of
the moment.

Your Turn:

Today, instead of cramming a lot into each moment, slow down and focus on enjoying one moment at a time—and giving it all you've got!

Today's Affirmation:

I am focused and centered in the moment.

July 17

> *"Do not be afraid of going slowly; be afraid only of standing still."*
> —*Chinese Proverb*

Good morning! One of the phrases that I am always saying in our office is "forward movement." I am always pleased with the day if we have made "forward movement" in our projects. Sometimes that forward movement doesn't look like it matches our plan or our goal—but it's forward movement all the same. Nothing feels as good as moving in the right direction—and nothing feels as uncomfortable as moving in the wrong direction or standing still.

Your Turn:

Each day, look at your priority list and focus on "forward movement." Forward movement, consistently practiced, is how a dream finds a foundation.

Today's Affirmation:

Each day I take a step forward, a step toward, my dreams.

July 18

> *"There are some things you learn best in calm, and some in storm."*
> —*Willa Cather*

Good morning! How nice it would be if we could learn all of life's lessons in calm. However, many times during the "calm" we are not receptive students. Things are going smoothly, and we become comfortable or content in that smoothness.

When our lives are "shuffled up" a bit, or our emotions are uncomfortable for us, or we have a gnawing ache inside—then we become open to the question of "why..."; we become open to life's lessons.

When I reflect on my own life, I have noticed that when I felt things were "falling apart," it was actually often life nudging me in a new direction. The discomfort and "storm" only stayed for as long as I resisted the lesson.

Your Turn:

Reflect on the times you have realized the most change in your life. Were they during the "calm" or the "storm"? If you are facing a physical, emotional, or spiritual "storm" right now, what lesson might be waiting for you?

Today's Affirmation:

I face the storms of life with an open heart and open mind.

Reflection Questions

What storms have you faced in your life, and what lessons did they carry?

Are you currently in the calm or the storm? If in the storm-time take some time to reflect and write about possible new directions that could be on the horizon.

July 19

> *"People are just about as happy as they*
> *make up their minds to be."*
> —*Abraham Lincoln*

Good morning! Recently my daughter had her second band concert. Her band teacher likes to highlight each student throughout the course of the concert and often chooses "rounds" so that each student, or a small group of students, can play eight to sixteen measures of a song.

The band as a whole had made wonderful progress since their first concert, when they had only had their instruments a few months. That was an enjoyable—but often squeaky—evening. The second concert, four months after the first, featured wonderful sounds and some great jazz and blues favorites.

During the small-group playing, I noticed that my daughter had a very strong tone to her instrument. There weren't any squeaks, there were no mistakes and her playing was smooth and deliberate in her few short measures. Many children did well (all did better than I would have done!) but some did not play as loud or as confidently in front of the packed auditorium.

On the way home I asked Samantha what helped her do so well. She said, "I know I have practiced and know the music as well as I ever will. So I don't focus on that or what will happen next. Instead I focus on positive things. I think about the neat birthday banner the kids at school put on my locker. I think about our vacation."

"Do you think about those things while you play?" I asked, intrigued by her explanation.

"Nope. I think about positive things right before I start each song. When I play I only think about letting the positive out."

I smiled as I continued driving. Our kids often have so many words of wisdom when we are curious enough to ask and slow down long enough to listen.

Your Turn:

Where in your life has uncertainty hampered your ability to do and be your best? Release the grip of uncertainty by preparing, planning, and then "letting the positive out."

Today's Affirmation:

Today I focus on "letting the positive out."

July 20

> *"Only those who do nothing at all make no mistakes*
> *… but that would be a mistake."*
> —*Author unknown*

Good morning! When I woke up I was thinking about how many of us become addicted to right and wrong. As children, we learn limits and boundaries, and life is often spelled out simply as right or wrong. Our tests in school are graded right and wrong, not leaving a lot of room for gray. We know that the kids with the A and B average are doing something "right." We know classmates with lower averages are doing something "wrong."

We take this simplistic thinking into our adult lives. We often make decisions based on what is right or wrong. But how much of life is really that clear? Life certainly would be simple if it worked that way, but more often than not, unless we are taking a test, it doesn't. Often we don't take a chance or try something new or share an opinion in fear of being wrong. While not sharing certainly allows us the safety of never being wrong, it doesn't by default make us right.

Your Turn:

What role does "right and wrong thinking" play in your own life? Do you shy away from situations for fear of being wrong? Reflect on how such behavior might be limiting your life.

Today's Affirmation:

I am open, sharing, and courageous regarding issues I care about.

July 21

"The longer I live, the more I realize the impact of attitude on life. Attitude to me is more important than facts. It is more important than the past, than education, than money, than circumstances, than failures, than success, than what other people think, say or do. It is more important than appearance, gift, or skill. It will make or break a company... a church... a home.

The remarkable thing is we have a choice every day regarding the attitude we will embrace for that day. We cannot change our past... The only thing we can do is play on the string we have, and that is our attitude.

I am convinced that life is ten percent what happens to me and ninety percent how I react to it. And so it is with you... we are in charge of our attitudes."
—*Charles Swindoll*

Good morning! A good attitude has been proven to be the single most important asset in developing our full potential. How is your attitude? If your life does not reflect what you desire, instead of looking outward, look inward—beginning with an attitude check.

Your Turn:

Complete an attitude check by rereading today's quote and then reflecting on the past thirty days. How did you react to trying circumstances or stressful circumstances? How was your attitude? Can you see how changing your attitude would have made the situation different? Keep that in mind as you move forward this week.

Today's Affirmation:

I choose healthy, supportive, and nourishing reactions.

July 22

*"Nothing splendid has ever been achieved except
by those who dared believe that something
inside of them was superior to circumstances."*
—*Bruce Barton, American congressman (1886–1967)*

Good morning! As you read today's quote, what comes to mind? Do you have a strong belief in yourself? For many of us, the answer might be "no." Perhaps we have tried and failed one too many times—and our self-belief waivers. Perhaps we too often compare ourselves to others and, instead of recognizing our unique value, we see only the missing pieces.

Here is the good news: That is your choice. And if that is your choice, then you have the ability to choose otherwise.

The most effective way to develop self-belief (or self-confidence) is through taking action steps that demonstrate that we believe that we are worthwhile. Reading the Good Morning inspirations, writing the affirmations (you are writing them, right?), and implementing the "Your Turn" exercises are one example of a step you can take to develop your self-belief.

Your Turn:

Make a list of ten things that are wonderful about you. Keep this in a place where you will see it often. Add to it regularly. (Side note: I don't create these exercises for fun—I have created them because they work. Are you working them?)

Today's Affirmation:

I am a wonderful person filled with one-of-a-kind value, worth, and love.

Going Further

Celebrating a person's unique qualities is a great way to build self-esteem. At one of my staff meetings, I asked each employee to type up three qualities they admired about each staff member. These lists were anonymous and collected in employee envelopes I created. At the next meeting I gave each employee their "Quality Collection." The office atmosphere was electric that day. Consider duplicating this exercise in your workplace, with friends, or with family.

July 23

> *"The happiness of your life depends on the quality of your thoughts."*
> —*Marcus A. Antoninus*

Good morning! Being responsible is one of our most important personal duties. Responsibility makes the difference between the medium and the magnificent. Unfortunately, much of the world has developed a "victim mentality," in which it's easier to blame others than to take responsibility. When we learn that we are responsible for our actions, thoughts, goals, and futures, we can begin to lay a path toward greatness. If we are stuck in the victim mentality, then we always leave our fate at the hands of others.

Self-management expert Carol Gerber Allred, PhD, author of *Positive Actions for Living*, offers this insight into self-management:

Whether we realize it or not, we are all managers responsible for our own resources. Every one of us has resources of time, energy, talents, money, possessions, thoughts, actions and feelings that we need to manage. We feel good about ourselves when we manage our resources well.

Here are a few fundamentals to review about self-responsibility:

We are responsible for our own actions. No matter who tries to sway us or encourage us, in the end we are completely responsible for everything that we do. When acting out in any form, know that you are responsible for the positive or negative outcome that results from your action.

Blame need not exist. Blaming another person is a seed of the victim mentality. Blame allows people to avoid taking responsibility and action. When we are productive and responsible, there isn't any issue of blame.

Give up the guilt. By being responsible, we are bound to make decisions that won't always be the "best" or "correct." That's all right. It's better to make mistakes and learn than it is to blame and stall.

Your Turn:

Take some time to think about the role of responsibility in your life. Are you responsible? If the answer is No, think about the areas where responsibility lacks. Choose a strategy to try and reinstate responsibility.

Your Affirmation:

I am responsible for my life, my choices, and my thoughts.

July 24

"Courage is not the absence of fear, but rather the judgment that something else is more important than fear."
—*Ambrose Redmoon*

Good morning! We often admire others we see as "courageous." We admire their drive, their spirit, and their commitment. It is easy to wish we could live without fear and with such devotion.

I love this quote because I think it speaks an important message about truth and courage. People are not courageous because they do not feel fear: People are courageous because they have found something that is more important than their fear. They have found something that awakens their heart, mind, and spirit. This "something" changes their perspective. The "something" becomes large, so their fear becomes small.

When we don't have an important "something" in our lives—one that awakens mind, body, and soul—fear will be overwhelming.

Your Turn:

What drives you? What awakens your heart, mind, and soul so that your destination becomes more important than your fear?

Today's Affirmation:

I am courageous.

Reflection Questions

When in your life have you experienced courage?

When have you experienced fear?

What was the instigator of these experiences?

Is there any area of your life calling you to develop your courage and move past fear?

July 25

> *"How far you go in life depends on your being tender with the young, compassionate with the aged, sympathetic with the striving and tolerant of the weak and the strong. Because someday in life you will have been all of these."*
> —*George Washington Carver*

Good morning! I love the simple and compassionate wisdom in these words. If, each day, each of us could strive to be understanding instead of being judgmental, and supportive rather than selfish, what a different world we would live in.

The choices aren't difficult, and they often don't take more time or energy: They are simply a matter of making that choice. The right choice always leaves us feeling better about our world and ourselves.

Your Turn:

When our lives move at a hectic and fast pace, it is easy to forget that we always have a choice. As you go throughout your day, strive to be aware of the choices you make and to choose compassion, support, and tenderness.

Today's Affirmation:

I am compassionate, supportive, and tender to those around me.

Reflection Questions

What area of your life could benefit from more tenderness?

Who in your life could use your support

Are there any life areas where you might practice increased compassion?

 *July 26*

> *"Your current safe boundaries were once unknown frontiers."*
> —*Author unknown*

Good morning! This is a quote to make us think, isn't it? Often, we pull back from change out of fear. We are comfortable with where we are, and establishing new habits and routines is so difficult. Or, even if we aren't comfortable, change can be scary and seem so hard.

But this quote offers an interesting perspective. What we now know to be "safe" was once unknown. We made it to this place, and that is evidence that we have all the strength and stamina needed to make it to the next place.

Your Turn:

Let your accomplishments to date be evidence of your strength and stamina to make the next step forward in your life.

Today's Affirmation:

I already possess the strength and stamina to achieve my dreams.

 *July 27*

"See the beauty in everything."
—from my daughter's fortune cookie

Good morning! In 2005 I was completing a twenty-six-city tour, and events often came up last minute. One Thursday I received a last-minute call that I was needed in Miami that weekend. (Not exactly a hop, skip, or jump from Wisconsin.) I had already made plans with my daughter and knew she would be disappointed if we could not spend time together, so I decided to take her with me. We flew to Miami on Friday, did an appearance on Saturday morning, and then flew to Orlando. We spent Sunday at Disney World and flew back Monday just in time to attend her mandatory band concert that evening.

I have to confess, I was a bit worried about how the trip would turn out. Without direct flights, the flight days last eight hours or so, and we flew three out of the four days we were gone. Much of the days were spent waiting in lines, waiting for transportation, waiting for events... and patience has never been one of my virtues, so I couldn't expect my then-ten-year-old to inherit it from my side of the family!

Despite my trepidation, we began our journey. And I was pleasantly surprised at my daughter's incredible behavior, thoughtfulness, patience, and kindness throughout the entire trip. (She may very well have behaved better than I did!) Although we were up until two o'clock in the morning every night and going on very little sleep, her spirit soared. It wasn't just during the "fun stuff" that she was so happy, but during the waiting and logistical problems and delayed flights and everything else. Ninety percent of our time was spent working versus vacationing.

On the plane ride home, I asked her what her good mood was accredited to. She pulled this fortune from her pocket: "See the beauty in everything." She told me that all of life is fun and joyful when you try that.

I chuckled to myself. Isn't that what we are all trying to do as we challenge life? It is a lot easier to do on the good days, than it is on the days where we wait in lines or when plans go askew. But maybe I (and maybe you) can inherit something from this youthful wisdom—a reminder to see the beauty in everything.

As I faded off to sleep on the plane, with that thought fresh in my mind, I felt a soft blanket being spread over me and tucked under my chin. I opened my eyes ever so slightly to see my daughter carefully covering me with her blanket, a smile on her face.

Your Turn:

Write down Samantha's fortune on several index cards. "See

the beauty in everything." Put one in your wallet, one by your computer, on by your mirror, one in your car. Practice seeing beauty every day.

Today's Affirmation:

I see the beauty in everything.

 *July 28*

> *"Life is like riding in a taxi. Whether you are going anywhere or not, the meter keeps ticking."*
> —*John C. Maxwell*

Good morning! Recently, I was reading a little book on time management and the following statistics, presented by John C. Maxwell, seemed quite enlightening:

If for five days a week, for fifty weeks, we streamlined:

Five minutes from our morning routine

Ten minutes from our settling into work

Five minutes of idle conversation and distractions

And a daily ten-minute reduction in our lunches and break times...

We would gain 125 hours of time in a year!! Maxwell reminds us that that is the equivalent of three forty-hour weeks to use for anything we want—and we can double that time by watching thirty fewer minutes of television every day!

Your Turn:

When was the last time you didn't have enough time? Is there anything above you can implement? If not, what can you change? Time won't change: We have to change how we use our time. What minutes are escaping you each day that are yours to reclaim if you put your mind to it?

Today's Affirmation:

I invest my time wisely.

Going Further

If you find you're constantly seeking more time, complete a time inventory by tracking how you spend your time for a week. This exercise reveals many opportunities to reclaim our time.

July 29

> *"The longevity of our soul lies not only in the hands of God, but in how we are remembered."*
> —*Wendy Louise… a.k.a. my mom*

Good morning! Today is a special and bittersweet day for my family. On this day in 1970, my brother was born. We lost him tragically in October of 1997, from a fatal reaction to a bee sting. While every day without someone you love is hard, certain days are even harder—birthdays, anniversaries, etc. A bit later today I am heading down to my mom's house and we are going to have a slumber party and surely share laughs and tears.

Despite the sadness that radiates during this time of year, there are many joyful memories. It also serves as a reminder of how the world can change overnight—and there is no time like today to challenge life.

Your Turn:

Today, I ask you to share with me in celebrating my brother's life. If today, each of us takes just a moment to let go of all of life's minutia and spend some quality time with someone we love, I am sure Caleb will look down and smile. That is the birthday gift I would like to give him today... I hope you will partake in the party.

Today's Affirmation:

Today, I let go of life's little stressors and instead engage in life's true joy.

Going Further

What little stressors have been on your mind during July? Make a list and attach it to your August calendar. Resolve to let go of these little things so you can experience more of what matters.

July 30

> *"Of course there is no formula for success except,*
> *perhaps, an unconditional acceptance*
> *of life and what it brings."*
> —Arthur Rubenstein

Good morning! Throughout this book I share what I have found to be formulas for successful living. Each formula I have shared has contained, in essence, *intent—action—belief— faith—and then letting life happen.* Reread today's quote several times and really absorb what the words mean. Remove "success" and try "peace" or "happiness" or "contentment" or "joy" in its place.

When I seek success in something, I first focus on what I want and why I want it. When I know that it matches my mission of helping women create more positive lives, I then make an action plan. After all that homework is done, I believe with my heart and soul that nothing will stand in my way from realizing the vision. And then I do something else that many people forget to do when chasing a dream: I let it go.

It might seem odd to let a dream or vision go, especially right after we take our first action steps. And, I don't mean that I literally let it go and never think of it again. It means that I have faith and trust in the mystery of miracles and life. When we hold on to what we want very tightly, we don't give it room to grow into what it might be. Instead, we mold it and twist it to match only what we can see and believe. Yet life often has wonderful things in store for us that we may not yet be able to envision or believe. We have to let go of our limited scope of seeing a result in order to let life meet us halfway—to transform a goal into a vision.

Your Turn:

Where in your life is letting go the next step to moving forward?

Today's Affirmation:

I let go and trust.

 *July 31*

> *"I am an optimist. It does not seem too much use being anything else."*
> —*Winston Churchill*

Good morning! I laughed when I came across this quote. Winston has a very good point, doesn't he? We know what happens to the pessimists—they live a sad, pessimistic life. Since we can choose whether to be optimistic or pessimistic about any single situation in life, what use does pessimism serve? We have all chosen pessimism from time to time. We know what it looks like: We feel bad about ourselves or the situation at hand. I don't know about you, but that doesn't sound like much fun to me!

Likewise, we know what optimism feels like when we ask ourselves creative questions, use creative thinking, and look for the good that rests somewhere (although sometimes it is hard to find) in every situation.

If I asked you this question—would you rather I give you $500 or have you owe me $500?—which would you choose? My guess is that the choice is obvious and quick. You would choose to take $500. Optimism gives to our lives, pessimism takes away and leaves us bankrupt. The choice should be as simple as the money question example.

Your Turn:

Today, find the silver lining in each encounter that comes your way.

Today's Affirmation:

I am optimistic.

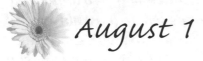 *August 1*

> *"Live your best life now."*
> *—the title of a Joel Osteen book*

Good morning! As we enter a new month, it is the perfect time to revisit the progress we are making toward achieving our goals. Often life has the ability to get in the way of the goals we want to achieve in life. We get sidetracked, or discouraged, or we hit a plateau. But we must remember: We don't have to stay there. We are in control of our own story. What will your August chapter hold?

Your Turn:

At the start of August, review your goals. If you have not been using the three-step action list diligently, begin today. What do you want to accomplish by the end of August? By the end of this year? Write your goals down. Research shows that writing your goals down increases your odds of success by over 70 percent. Make a commitment to yourself to step forward each day this month. You are worth it.

Today's Affirmation:

Each day I take a step forward toward reaching my goals.

 *August 2*

> *"Success is to laugh often and much... to appreciate beauty... to give of one's self. To have played and laughed with enthusiasm and sung with exultation."*
> —*Ralph Waldo Emerson*

Good morning! Have you ever noticed how elusive happiness can be? When we chase it, it is like our shadow—it cannot be caught. We can't mix together a few ingredients and instantly create happiness. We *can* decide that we won't be derailed by negativity—but that alone won't create happiness.

As I have made this journey of self-discovery with thousands of women, I have found it interesting how many people want to chase happiness down. They don't realize that all the elements of happiness are already here. Looking for them somewhere else won't bring them any closer than they already are. Trying to accomplish lengthy to-do lists and tasks before one feels happiness is a crazy expectation that we put on ourselves.

Why do we want to complete those lengthy to-do lists, anyway? Usually the answer is so we can have a more balanced, happier life. How ironic is it, then, to be a slave to these to-dos and schedules, to the point of giving up happiness today? Do we somehow honestly think that the happiness will be "better" later?

We need happiness every day because that is what inspires and motivates us in other areas of our lives. We can't work the equation backward. "Once I accomplish this, this, and this—then I'll be happy and content." It doesn't work that way. Happiness has to be at our roots—at our core—it isn't something we produce through accomplishment. When we put off realizing happiness, the harder it will be to find when it does come our way.

Simply put, many of us have made happiness more complicated than it needs to be. Ironically, we have added happiness to our list of things we need "to do." But this is life, and our to-do lists will be ever-evolving, because we aren't done until we are done living. So—do you want happiness to be on your list for another day? Or do you want to grab it now, and live it today? You won't find happiness anywhere else except right here, and right now. Happiness needs "the moment" in order to live.

Your Turn:

How have you complicated happiness in your life? What do you feel you have to "get done first"? What rules have you added to this simple emotion? Happiness only needs the moment to live—that is its oxygen. How can you remove the barriers to happiness you have imposed and let it grow in your daily life?

Today's Affirmation:

The only place where happiness exists is in the moment. I recognize and embrace the simple gift of happiness that only requires that I be present to enjoy it.

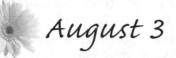

August 3

"I live by this credo: have a little laugh at life and look around you for happiness instead of sadness. Laughter had always brought me out of unhappy situations. Even in your darkest moment, you usually can find something to laugh about if you try hard enough."
—*Red Skelton*

Good morning! We all have days that test our ability to remain upbeat and positive. We all have days where it seems that every little thing is out to wear us down. Often, these days come after several days or weeks of "up time," where we are busy creating the life we desire.

Some people view these days as the world saying, "I told you so." They use these days as an excuse to let their dreams and hopes go.

I think that these days come for a different reason. I think these days are a great opportunity to improve ourselves. While I used to get down on these days too, I had to learn to treat them with the same respect that I did the "good days." Surely, these days must have a purpose. When I approached these days with that attitude, I quickly uncovered their purpose.

These days don't intend to bring a dark cloud to live on our doorstep. These days come to challenge us to see something new—to remember how to laugh—to remember what is good. These days ground us and challenge us to explore our core values for the simple and delightful daily rewards of life.

The path of life is never smooth. These "cloudy" days will come and go. We can't hide from these days and wait for a better one. There simply isn't enough time in life to waste a single day.

Your Turn:

When a "cloudy day" comes your way, embrace it. Use it as a catalyst to find something to laugh about or someone to laugh with. Turn back to life's simple joys—a child's smile, a phone call, a serene walk. While what is going on externally can be either sunny or cloudy, only we control whether our reaction to the situations around us will be sunny or cloudy.

Today's Affirmation:

I used life's stormy days to strengthen my umbrella.

 *August 4*

> *"To speak gratitude is courteous and pleasant, to enact gratitude is generous and noble, but to live gratitude is to touch Heaven."*
> *—Johannes A. Gaertner*

Good morning!

I am grateful for the inspiration you send me each morning. You do a wonderful job with your writing. Thank you for helping me start my day with a smile. That is the first "great" thing that happens, which helps lead to more great things throughout the day!

Yvette's note brought a smile to my face and warmth to my heart. The reason it touched me so much is that Yvette goes beyond reading the message. Instead, she "lives" the morning messages.

With our hectic and crazy lives, it is so easy to read this little morning note and think, "Wow, that's me. I should really do that." But several hours later we may have forgotten what we read.

Your Turn:

Think back to the morning messages that really resonated with you. Did you bookmark them? Scan back through them using the "Your Turn" challenges to go beyond reading, and start living the changes that will improve your life.

Today's Affirmation:

When I discover a way to positively improve my life, I implement the idea and maintain it until it becomes a habit.

Inspirations

Express your gratitude for children by joining in the celebration of National KidsDay, the first Sunday of each August. National KidsDay was created to encourage adults to spend meaningful time with America's children, and to celebrate their value. Visit www.kidsday.net for simple ideas to celebrate.

 # *August 5*

"If you had a friend who talked to you like you sometimes talk to yourself, would you continue to hang around with that person?"
—*Rob Bremer, speaker*

Good morning! On a scale of one to ten, how would you rate yourself on this statement: "I am a good friend." Most of us rate ourselves highly; we pride ourselves on being reliable and supportive.

Next question, on a scale of one to ten: how would you rate yourself on this statement: "I am a good friend to myself."

Many of us stumble on question two. We demand things of ourselves that we would not demand of others. We criticize ourselves with harsh words that we would never say to a friend. While we forgive our friends' shortcomings, we belittle ourselves for our own shortcomings. Just as we build friends up, we knock ourselves down.

How wonderfully our lives would change if we would treat ourselves with the same kindness, thoughtfulness, encouragement, and forgiveness we show our friends.

Your Turn:

Today, each time you have a thought directed toward yourself, ask—is this a thought I would share with a friend in the same situation? If the answer is no, replace it with the type of kindness and encouragement you would show to a friend. When we learn to be better friends to ourselves, we in turn become better friends to others.

Today's Affirmation:

I treat myself with kindness, respect, and encouragement, just as I would my best friend.

Going Further

Every August 5 marks International Friendship day. Sometime today, call a friend you haven't visited with in a while and schedule a time to meet for coffee, take a walk, or enjoy a meal.

August 6

"Try not to do too many things at once. Know what you want, the number-one thing today and tomorrow. Persevere and get it done."
—George Allen

Good morning! Allen reminds us of the power of focus and intent with this quote. Stop for a moment and look at your to-do list for the day. How many goals or projects are you chasing?

Imagine you are at a carnival. Your goal at the carnival is to gather as much candy and as many prizes as possible by winning the little carnival games. What would your strategy be? I would likely look at the games, choose which ones I was best at, start with those, and then work my way to the other games. What I wouldn't do is try to play all the games at one time, running around the carnival like a madwoman.

However, in our lives, we often run around bouncing between a zillion goals and to-dos, trying to "get it all done." What we often overlook is that spreading our energy and focus from task to task in a manic manner isn't effective. We mustn't confuse busyness with effectiveness. We are effective when we choose our primary focus points and attend to them, and *then* move on to the next item.

Your Turn:

What items do you need to focus on today above all others? Write down three and commit to them above all others.

Today's Affirmation:

I focus and succeed.

Going Further

The first week in August is National Simplify Your Life Week, a week to get organized and declutter for a more stress-free lifestyle. Ohio State University Extension suggests that you do something each day of that week to reduce the stress in your life and start enjoying life more. Here's a day-by-day list of suggestions—be creative and come up with some of your own!

Day 1: Make romance an important part of your daily life by identifying what your partner considers to be romantic. Spotlight ideas for new romantic adventures.

Day 2: Read *Life Is Too Short* or *Life's Little Relaxation Book* for some super ideas on how to start savoring life—it's not as hard as you think.

Day 3: Get soaked! Put a eucalyptus branch (you can find them cheap at a florist) under the faucet as the bath fills. The warm water will release a super-relaxing scent. Enjoy!

Day 4: Keep an artificial long-stemmed rose on your desk, dashboard, or kitchen counter to remind yourself to stop and smell the roses.

Day 5: Think of something that would be a total waste of your time. Then do it!

Day 6: Put on your favorite music, then sing and dance.

Day 7: Get out of your rut: eat breakfast in the evening, turn the TV off, start a new hobby

August 7

"If someone is too tired to give you a smile, leave one of your own, because no one needs a smile as much as those who have none to give."
—Author unknown

Good morning! The past few days we have been focusing on how our thinking and choices affect our days. But what happens when we run into someone else who is unpleasant, or rude, or impatient? How do we cope with that? The cliché "kill them with kindness" exists for a reason. When we are kind to each other, we kill that seed of anger or distrust or unhappiness that caused someone to act out negatively in the first place. We are all conditioned by what we know. The more kindness and happiness we experience, the kinder and happier we become. Think about it this way: Each time you meet someone who is grumpy, tired, or sad, you have the option of leaving either a seed of happiness or a seed of indifference or negativity. Whatever seed you leave will be part of this person's conditioning for all of time (even if it is someone you have only met for a nanosecond). What is best for that person? What is best for you? Amazingly, the answer is the same—leaving a seed of hope, or happiness, or a smile (as in today's quote) is the best for all. It reminds us of the fact that what is all around us won't last forever. Yet, in the same breath, it reminds us to dance and smile and celebrate.

Your Turn:
Try to sow ten seeds of kindness today, or share ten smiles.

Today's Affirmation:
I radiate happiness and kindness to all those I come into contact with.

August 8

"Too often we get distracted by what's outside our control. The door to the past has been shut and the key thrown away. And you can't do anything about tomorrow; it is yet to come. However, tomorrow is determined by what you do today. So make today a masterpiece."
—John Wooden, UCLA's Hall of Fame basketball coach

Good morning! I have an interesting challenge for you to try today—or on the next Monday. (Don't try it on the weekend or while you're off during the holiday—try it on a day that is "representative" of your normal day.)

Here's how it works. Every two hours, take a five-minute break. Write down how much time (percentage-wise... a rough estimate is fine) you spent:

1. Thinking, fretting, or regretting the past.

2. Worrying or thinking about the future.

3. Worrying about something that is happening today, or something outside of your control.

4. Taking positive, forward action today or enjoying the moment.

Print that little challenge and tape it to your planner on your next "representative day" so that you don't forget.

Why is this important? Well, this simple "math problem" equals the amount of contentment and happiness you are creating in your life. If you spend 80 percent of your waking hours on the top three items, you should only expect to reach 20 percent of your "happiness level." If you spend 50 percent of your time on the top three items, you can reach 50 percent of your happiness level for that specific day.

Your Turn:

When we wonder why we feel stressed, anxious, overwhelmed, depressed, or hopeless, this is a good practice to revisit. This "calculation" holds our answer. Make a concerted effort to redirect yourself to making a positive, forward action when you catch yourself engaging in the top three thought patterns. Our goal should be to be taking positive, forward action at least 90 percent of the time.

Today's Affirmation:

I let go of the past, I am not anxious about tomorrow...

Instead, I trust in today, and enjoy today, living life to the fullest.

August 9

> *"A man becomes what he thinks about all day long."*
> —*Ralph Waldo Emerson*

Good morning! This quote goes nicely with the challenge of yesterday's Good Morning and the quote we featured from UCLA basketball coach John Wooden. This Emerson quote offers a quick and easy way to "step into the moment" and double check our thinking. Read this quote at the end of your day. At midnight, instead of turning into a pumpkin like the Cinderella story, what would you turn into based on your thoughts?

Ask yourself that question each day for the next month as part of your nightly reflection. Write down your answers. This will quickly give you an "insider look" at where your life is headed. You certainly don't need a crystal ball, all you need is to evaluate and observe your thoughts.

Your Turn:

Challenge yourself to write a different, positive ending to each day of your life.

Today's Affirmation:

My thoughts represent where I want to go in life and how I want to feel... and where I want to be and how I want to feel today.

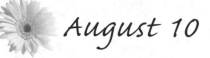

August 10

"Life is like an ever-shifting kaleidoscope—a slight change, and all patterns alter."
—*Sharon Salzberg*

Good morning! What slight changes have you made for yourself lately? Think about how a happier you reflects into the fabric of your family, creating a happier kaleidoscope of day-to-day living experiences for all! The change can be as little as always, always, *always* leaving your car keys in the same place every evening when you come home, so that you can find them right away every morning when you need them! Or the change can be as big as updating your family mission statement, with a new goal, a new plan, or a rejuvenated addendum.

Your Turn:

Choose one of the ideas above, or one of your own, to put your "kaleidoscope" in positive motion.

Today's Affirmation:

I realize that a little change in actions or thoughts can shift my world for the better.

August 11

"Between whatever happens to me and my response to it is a space. In that space is my freedom and power to choose my response. And in my response lies my growth and happiness."
—**Stephen Covey**

Good morning! Kyrsti wrote this quote on an index card after reading *The Seven Habits of Highly Effective People* and she reads it every day. She writes: *It has had a big impact on my life. I knew that if I could cultivate the habit of being patient within this "space" after an event or words spoken to me, I would be able to get to a response that would promote less stress and more happiness.*

This concept is one that we need to think about on a daily basis. While we can't control everything that goes on around us (nor is it worth our energy to try!) we can control how we react in that "space." And how we react will directly impact our day, our week, our month—our life.

When we choose anger, gossip, negativity, or getting defensive, we build walls in our lives that keep out the "bad"—but those same walls also keep out the good and the wonder of life.

Your Turn:

Today, notice the "space" where you have the choice to respond. Think about how your choice will influence your life. Respond in a way that promotes understanding, caring, and personal peace. You'll feel much better about the situation at hand—and your life will reflect it.

Today's Affirmation:

I choose to respond to external events in a caring, understanding, and peaceful way.

 *August 12*

> *"You may have to fight a battle more than once to win it."*
> —*Margaret Thatcher*

Good morning! I love Thatcher's quote, because it reminds me that things rarely go as planned the first time around, regardless of whether the challenge is about personal change, career, family, our homes, or some other area.

In a society that places emphasis on perfection, we often don't give ourselves enough leeway to "find our answers." Instead, when we make a plan and it doesn't work, we jump ship, forgetting the wisdom in Thatcher's words: "You may have to fight a battle more than once to win it."

Each time we go through an experience, even if it doesn't turn out as we planned, we gain knowledge for the next time around. That knowledge is what builds success. Success and happiness aren't built by "getting lucky on the first try," but by the wisdom gained from standing back up and trying again after we fail.

Your Turn:

What area of your life is calling you to get back up and try again?

Today's Affirmation:
Just as much joy can be found in the second or third attempt as the first.

> ## *Reflection Question*
> What battles are worth fighting for in your life?

August 13

> *"Life is not measured by the number of breaths we take,*
> *but by the moments that take our breath away!"*
> —*Author unknown*

Good morning! This quote from Cathi arrived at a perfect time for me—it was one of those "unexpected blessings." I received it just after learning that a close friend of my brother and myself had passed away over the weekend. He was in his thirties and his death was sudden and unexpected. My brother passed away suddenly in 1997. Throughout the years, I have learned to find the "blessing in tragedy" by focusing on the gifts he left behind, instead of the moments we do not have together anymore.

One of the greatest gifts we can find in tragedy is awareness. We learn the value of a moment—of a second. We learn not to take any moment for granted, because each moment is special. I wanted to create a Good Morning in memory of Todd—as a reminder to value what we have—*today*—while we have it. I couldn't seem to find the right words this morning. Then this unexpected email came from Cathi... and I'll let her tell you the rest.

I may have heard or seen this quote before, but if I did, it really didn't have meaning for me until my brother passed away unexpectedly last November. My sister and I put together picture boards for his memorial and purchased some vellum sheets used in scrapbooking to add quotes to his boards.

The above quote was on one of the sheets. Russell was only forty-five, so we felt he was much too young to die—he hadn't taken enough breaths in his life. But as we looked through his pictures to select those that would go on the boards, we found many in which he was in nature and the scenery around him would take your breath away: sitting on a cliff overlooking the Rocky Mountains; precariously standing on a rock pile overlooking a beautiful valley; sitting among the fall leaves. We could see that even though his life was cut short, he had had many beautiful moments that took his breath away.

Now this quote has more meaning—it reminds me to pay attention to those moments that take my breath away. It may be as simple as the beauty of a snowflake, the sparkle of dew on the grass, the smile of a child, a ray of sunshine peaking through the clouds, etc. In fact, my "something great" from yesterday was that as I reviewed a video I had taken last week of the clouds and sky, I found that I had captured three gorgeous rays of sunshine shooting out of a cloud. As I paused the video and captured the pictures frame by frame, I ended up with thirty beautiful pictures of the rays that hadn't been visible with the naked eye. While some people may not think this is anything special, it took my breath away and made me smile—and as I shared the pictures with my family, they had similar reactions. I've included one of the pictures with this note.

Similar to the "something great is going to happen" quote, this one has an impact by reminding us to be aware of and acknowledge all the beauty and greatness around us.

Your Turn:

Today, practice awareness of the moment. Don't take anything for granted. Celebrate today and all of the people in your life.

Today's Affirmation:

I celebrate life.

 August 14

"Opportunity is an Attitude"
—Wendy Louise

Good morning! How many times do you catch yourself saying, "If only I had the opportunity to_____ I would _____." Well, really, we do have that opportunity, right here! Right now! Knocking at our door! at this very moment! We only have to recognize it.

Opportunities are really just situations waiting for our attitude to attach itself to the particular situation we are in—waiting for our recognition, waiting to be invited into our realm of possibility, waiting for our positive and creative energy. We have two choices: We can view a situation as an opportunity and move forward with control and a positive outcome; or we can react as if it were a setback and spiral out of control and backward. I know which scenario I'd rather pick, and I bet you do too.

Your Turn:

Today, try to turn every situation into an opportunity, no matter what, with a positive and strong attitude that yields a successful outcome.

Today's Affirmation:
I create and attract opportunity.

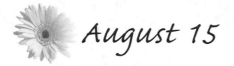 *August 15*

*"Women need real moments of solitude and self-reflection
to balance out how much of ourselves we give away."*
—Barbara De Angelis

Good morning! I received a note from a reader with this message:

I came to an epiphany that being peacefully connected to that inner authentic self centers me and directs me in how to be the best woman, mother, and wife I can be. Spending that time to sit, listen, and center is invaluable!

August 15 is celebrated as Relaxation Day. Holiday Insights offers these top ten ideas to enjoy on *Relaxation Day:*

- Do nothing today.
- Go to a spa.
- Go fishing.
- Play a round of golf (caution: not always relaxing).
- Lounge around in a hammock.
- Take a bubble bath.
- Spend the day at the beach.
- Go to the movies.
- Do a little gardening (no heavy-duty work, though).
- Have a picnic in the park.

Your Turn:

This week, schedule three ten-minute times to do nothing but center yourself quietly. Play some soft music and let yourself get lost in it. Observe your breathing, your body. Let a moment of simplicity envelop you and refresh your spirit.

Today's Affirmation:

I celebrate silence.

Inspirations

Need some relaxation help? You'll find it at http://www.how-to-meditate.org/.

August 16

> *"People who look through keyholes are apt to get the idea that most things are keyhole shaped.*
> —*Author unknown*

Good morning! I have always found it interesting that what one person perceives to be very stressful can be motivational to someone else. Stress seems to be fairly subjective, controlled largely by perception.

The other day I was talking to my best friend about stress. My work pile seemed so overwhelming that I didn't even know where to begin, and I felt like I would never get out from under. On that particular day, I hadn't had much sleep and had yet to put a healthy morsel in my mouth. Two days later, that same work pile (which had actually grown in size) didn't seem so intimidating! The stressor hadn't changed, but my attitude toward it had—primarily because of my self-care.

Your Turn:

What stressor are you facing in your life from lack of self-care? Give yourself a "good nurturing" and then see how they look the next day.

Today's Affirmation:

I replace stress with self-care.

Going Further

Here is another stress-buster. Grab your to-do list and highlight the three most stressful items on it. Many times stress is a natural resistance to something we just don't want to do. Evaluate why that item is on your to-do list. Could it be delegated to someone else? Scratched off completely? If it must be completed, can you find a way to do it less often?

August 17

"People must remind each other that it can be done, and it must be done. We must keep up each other's courage. In that way, we are enormously strong."
—*Vincent van Gogh*

Good morning! I love "I CAN" people. Much of my business success and personal contentment rests in forming a network of stable and consistent "I CAN" colleagues and friends. When we associate with people who inspire and encourage, we catapult ourselves forward. Likewise, when we associate with people who doubt and discourage us, we quickly stall or move backward.

I have carefully chosen my close friends and current employees, each of whom reflects the "I CAN" attitude. We also have the "I CAN" attitude in our home. When I travel or go out for a day of shopping or errands, I am often astounded by the amount of negativity and discouragement in the world. I wonder why people would choose to spend time in such a place when instead they could create positive and encouraging surroundings. We all have our share of negative people that we have to deal with. We may also treat ourselves negatively. But as adult women, we also have the right to shape our futures by proactively choosing whom we spend our time with.

This beautiful quote is so powerful because it reminds us how important our words of encouragement can be to one another. It is our encouragement that creates strength and positive action.

Your Turn:

Who do you need to give encouragement to today? Who can you help to be strong through positive words? Likewise, who encourages you? What can you do to spend more time with those people? Who discourages you? What steps can you take to spend less time with those who doubt and discourage?

Today's Affirmation:

Each day I encourage and support those around me through word and action.

 August 18

> *"Opportunity dances with those who are*
> *ready on the dance floor."*
> —*H. Jackson Brown Jr.*

Good morning! I have always felt that one of the best things I have going for me is my eternal quest to learn more. As we move through life, we keep our minds fresh and our souls young when we strive to continually learn and improve.

The options available today for learning are endless. We can learn online, through videos, books, local colleges, art stores, correspondence courses... I can't think of any group that demonstrates personal growth better than those who go back to school late in life. A young friend of mind recently graduated from college and received her degree, right after an eighty-two-year-old classmate, who had just completed her B.A. At her graduation party, this eighty-two-year-old still hadn't quite decided what she was going to do with her life.

Personal growth allows us to experience new and exciting parts of this world and also shows our children how to be open to new experiences, more options, and a diverse opportunity.

Your Turn:

Every year, make a goal for yourself in the area of personal growth. Perhaps it will be to take a new class, learn a new skill, research a home-based business, or read a certain number of books. Whatever goal works for you is fine, as long as it pulls you past old boundaries.

Today's Affirmation:

Every year, I challenge myself to learn something new.

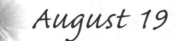

Inspirations

Take a moment today to enjoy this positive reflection
greatday.com/cgi-bin/jsenter.pl?2000r05JPyf3

August 19

> *"The butterfly counts not months but moments, and has time enough."*
> —*Rabindranath Tagore*

Good morning! So often we chase the elusive concept of "more time." While we chase and run and hunt down more time, we lose the time we have now. This quote by Tagore reminds me that we can't save and stockpile our time and put it away for a rainy day. All we have now is this moment, and if we grasp it fully, it is enough.

Many of us know this intellectually but have a hard time putting it into practice. When we see tragedy in the world, we remember how valuable time really is. When we learn that someone has lost a loved one, for a moment or two we truly appreciate those around us. But time and days speed up again, until the moments become months that are so often missed.

This is why the gratitude journal is so important. Each day, hunt down the moments that are gifts, and write them down. Don't let them pass you by because you forgot to open your eyes. Each day brings thousands of moments that will never come again. Only you can decide if you will turn moments into memories, or just let them pass by.

Your Turn:

What "checks" can you put in place to stay centered and aware throughout the day? Every time the clock hits :00, could you stop and just check to make sure you are present in the moment? Think of a self-check that would work for you and then implement it.

Today's Affirmation:

I embrace the magical moments of today.

Going Further

Here are a couple of ideas for finding more magical moments in daily life:

Set out a glass jar with colored slips of papers. Encourage family members to write down magical moments and then share when the jar is full.

Each night at dinner or each morning at breakfast, have each family member share a magical moment from the past twenty-four hours.

August 20

"If you haven't the strength to impose your own terms upon life, you must accept the terms it offers you."
—*T.S. Eliot*

Good morning! During a twenty-six-city tour I was returning from a television appearance in Minneapolis and chatting with a colleague. We were discussing fatigue and stress. We both agreed that the weeks in which we thought about all we needed to accomplish on our to-do lists, but did very little, were weeks that often left us fatigued.

However, we also noticed that during the weeks in which we charged ahead and took action, instead of thinking about all that needed to be done, we were much more invigorated and less fatigued.

I think part of this ties into the quote offered by T.S. Eliot. When we are strong and we move forward, when we impose our terms upon life, we gain momentum, energy, and additional strength. When we sit back and just analyze the terms life has offered us, it is easy to lose momentum.

Your Turn:

Give yourself a quick and honest assessment. How much time do you spend thinking about all that you need to do? How much time do you actually spend moving ahead and taking action? How do you feel while engaging in both of those activities? Brainstorm some ideas for moving forward and implementing your terms for what you want to accomplish in your life. Then—most importantly—take action.

Today's Affirmation:

I do not settle for less than I deserve. I am not immobilized or overwhelmed by life's challenges. I seize the day and move forward, greeting life and all it offers with open arms.

 *August 21*

> *"A child's life is like a piece of paper on which every person leaves a mark."*
> —*Chinese Proverb*

Good morning! I chose this quote because today is my mother's birthday. Happy birthday, Mom! I was extremely blessed throughout childhood to have a loving, caring, tender mother who left many wonderful "marks" on my childhood. My mother is a beacon of strength, wisdom, and determination. A single parent since I was eight months old, she worked very hard to give me and my brother a wonderful childhood filled with tender moments and memories. Beyond that, she instilled in me the knowledge and complete belief that I can do anything I set out to do.

I remember expressing my fear that we would not be able to afford for me to go to college. She simply looked at me and said, "Of course we can; we will just sell the house." A complex problem was solved by one woman's conviction to raise her children as she wished she had been raised.

Your Turn:

What mark will you leave for your children or the youngsters around you? Remember that when we don't make a choice, life often chooses for us.

Today's Affirmation:

I love, encourage, and empower my children through word and deed each day.

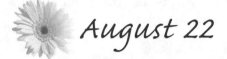 *August 22*

> *"One's real life is often the life that one does not lead."*
> —*Oscar Wilde*

Good morning! I stumbled across some quotes from Oscar Wilde, and was struck once again by how easily he captures some of life's truths in a simple sentence. When I read this quote, it reminded me of a circle of men or women, sharing stories about all they could have done, could have been, could have seen—sharing their stories of regrets.

Options are comforting. Without options, we feel trapped and vulnerable. When we generate options and possibilities, we free our spirit. When we open ourselves to options and possibilities, the world brings them to our door. But there is an inherent danger in this as well. While options and possibilities are comforting, actually taking advantage of an option or possibility can leave us anxious and full of fear. So we have a choice. Do we take that step, or do we turn away from the very options and possibilities that we seek?

Many people seek opportunity and options. They wait for them. They watch them come—and they watch them go. And someday they will remember those options with regret in their voice. But at least they were safe. They did not stumble, they did not fall, and they were not bruised.

And then there are other people—there are many fewer of them, but they exist nonetheless. These people seek out options. They wait for them. They watch them come, and they hold their breath, and they jump. And it is exhilarating, no matter whether they land on their feet or on their head. Because when you believe and jump, you learn the true meaning of faith. You learn to trust in life and the process, instead of yourself and your mind. And once you reach that place... your options and possibilities are limitless.

Your Turn:

Think about your life and the options, dreams, and possibilities you have sought out. Have you hunted for something, only to retreat when it landed on your doorstep? We can only learn and become more by going to a place we don't know—where we have room to *become*. Columbus couldn't have discovered the new world if he only looked in his backyard. Where are your options taking you? What land are you being called to discover? What will you do about it? Will you live your story, or will you tell a story of regret?

Today's Affirmation:

I step outside of my comfort zone and into life.

August 23

"One of the most helpful images to have of yourself in your family is that of a trim tab—the small rudder that moves the big rudder and eventually changes the entire direction of the plan."
—Stephen R. Covey

Good morning! It seems that society is filled with people who love to ponder. We think about doing one thing or another, weigh the pros and cons, and then continue to think some more. Examine for a moment the common notion of getting in shape by following a workout schedule. First, we think about joining a gym. Then we think about the pros and cons— cost versus benefits of commitment. Then we think, maybe we're better off just getting an exercise machine. Then we turn on Oprah and she is praising the benefits of walking, and we think, "Oh maybe we'll just do that." Then we think about if we will have the "stick-to-itiveness" to do it alone, or if we should get an exercise partner... and the beat goes on.

What does all this thinking allow us to avoid? It allows us to avoid taking action. It allows us to continue to live in the comfort of the familiar and avoid change.

Simply making the decision to invest in our goals is one of the best forward steps we can take. Webster's dictionary defines "decide" as follows: "(1) a: to arrive at a solution that ends uncertainty or dispute about < what to do> b: to select as a course of action—(2): to bring to a definite end synonym DE-TERMINE, SETTLE, RULE, RESOLVE."

This definition eliminates the pondering and moves us toward our end goal. Take action and decide. Instead of resting in the comforts of noncommitment, take hold of today and resolve to reach your goal!

Your Turn:

Today, make a real decision to bring a new result into your life.

Today's Affirmation:

I move forward in the right direction without hesitation. I commit.

Going Further

With back-to-school time around the corner, take some time to prepare now to eliminate morning madness and keep your morning routine balanced.

Chart Your Way to Success: Create a checklist for each family member and tuck it into a plastic sleeve. List out *everything* that needs to be done before school: i.e., eat breakfast, lunch money, pack homework. Let children enjoy the feeling of success that comes with marking each item "done" with a dry-erase marker.

Wake-Up Call: Don't wait for that first Monday to begin getting up early! Adapt your new wake-up time for the whole family one week prior to school starting.

Gooooood Morning Family!: Start each day like Ty from *Extreme Home Makeover.* Wish a sincere "good morning" to all (even if family members look at you funny). Just as breakfast is the most important meal for our physical needs, a sincere good morning is the best emotional breakfast.

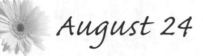

August 24

"You have to have confidence in your ability, and then be tough enough to follow through."
—*Rosalynn Smith Carter*

Good morning! Envisioning the target of a goal is a great tool while implementing new ideas into your personal improvement plan. It's so easy to read about a good idea, or see some great new technique on television and think, "That describes me! I should do that!" We plan to take a new approach to an old problem, but when the opportunity arises, we quickly find ourselves choosing the familiar—even if it isn't working.

Change requires energy. Yet, today's world doesn't often leave us with an overflow of energy. To help choose change instead of the familiar, envision the result of the goal you are working toward. Imagine yourself or your life as you want it to be—then choose a route or implement a new technique that will help to move you toward that goal.

Your Turn:

Take a moment and close your eyes. Envision your goal. As you go through the ups and downs of choosing new patterns over old, recall this image to offer encouragement on your journey.

Today's Affirmation:

I envision where I want to go—and then I go there! CHARGE!

 *August 25*

"A good home must be made, not bought."
—*Joyce Maynard*

Good morning! When I started touring and traveling to many different cities and hotels, I was amazed at how dramatically my mood might change depending on the room. Some hotels were so warm and inviting that I was ready to move in. Other rooms were dark and uninviting, and if I wasn't careful, my mood would shift downward quickly. After noticing this, I realized how large a part our physical surroundings play in supporting or hindering our attitude on a daily basis.

Fortunately, it doesn't take a million-dollar makeover budget or the help of a designer to beautify our surroundings. Simple steps can dramatically shift the mood of any room.

COLOR: Do the walls represent the room? If your house has all-white walls, consider toying with color. Painting a room is the quickest way to give it a fresh look. Stenciling is another option for those who don't want to brave a full paint job. If you want to keep your white walls, are there prints or paintings that could be added to give the room a new tone? Color can also be changed in more subtle ways—adding throw pillows, for example.

DECORATIONS: What elements could be added to change the tone of the room? How about a small water fountain in a room where you like to relax? These can now be found very inexpensively at discount stores like Target, or Wal-Mart. Would an arrangement of candles or dried flowers add to the room's tranquility?

FOLIAGE: What about plants? Plants brighten and bring relaxation to any room. If you have a bad history with plants, don't despair. Go to your local garden center and explain that you want a very durable plant for someone without a "green thumb." Knowledgeable garden center employees can help you pick a plant that will work for you.

WORDS: Add words to a room for a quick theme. Print off some of your favorite quotes and frame them or place them in colorful picture frames.

Keep an eye out for ideas in magazines. Often, one simple change can set a new tone.

Your Turn:

Today, choose one room to focus on and select a beautifying strategy from above (or choose one of your own).

Today's Affirmation:

I enhance my surroundings through care and beauty.

Going Further

Consider making a "Home Beauty Book." Use a three-ring binder and create a tab for each room of your home. Add pictures and ideas to each category as you come across them. Each month choose a tab (a room) to work on.

August 26

*"I never failed once. My invention just happened
to be a 2,000 step process."*
—*Thomas Edison*

Good morning! I am so glad Thomas Edison kept going, aren't you? What is something in your life that you have given up on or aren't pursuing as avidly as you might because it seems too hard or unattainable? What if, like Edison's, your goal is a 2,000 step process? What if, instead of thinking of your goal as unattainable, you realized how many of those 2,000 steps you have already taken?

Your Turn:

Ask yourself where you have given up or been detoured by the idea of failure. Embrace Edison's quote and restart and rejuvenate your goal.

Today's Affirmation:

Failure does not exist, unless I choose to let it.

Inspirations

Thinking today's message is just positive-rhetoric? Visit gloryinlife.com/motivational-inspirational/16-most-inspiring-famous-failures/ for sixteen examples of famous "failures," among them Marilyn Monroe, Walt Disney, Michael Jordan, and Steven Spielberg.

August 27

"Let us rise up and be thankful, for if we didn't learn a lot today, at least we learned a little, and if we didn't learn a little, at least we didn't get sick, and if we got sick, at least we didn't die; so, let us all be thankful."
—*Buddha*

Good morning! What are you grateful for? What little things bring a smile to your face? What ordinary occurrences make you deliriously happy? Take a moment to rediscover the everyday subtleties that make you happiest. What cute thing has your child done lately? Who phoned after you had them on your mind... Did a late summer flower just bloom?

Your Turn:

Today, "light up" your thoughts by making an extra-long gratitude list. Keep a sheet of paper with you all day and try to write down at least fifty things by the end of the day. Whenever negativity surfaces or life gets you down—this is one of the quickest cures.

Today's Affirmation:

I am observant and grateful for life's many gifts.

 *August 28*

"Life is really simple, but we insist on making it complicated."
—**Confucius**

Good morning! Every year in the small town where my mother, brother, and I grew up (about five hours north of where I live presently), a water ski barefoot tournament is held in honor of my brother's memory (he was an INCREDIBLE barefoot water skier—one of the best there is).

This heavily wooded little town holds about six hundred people year-round and thousands in the summer. Its main attraction is a chain of nine lakes connected by channels. If you have a boat or love the water, this is the place to be.

Life moves at a slower pace there—or maybe life goes at the pace it should and we just move faster elsewhere. There aren't any drive-through fast-food options for over twenty-five miles, so you actually have to plan what you are going to do for meals. Stores still close at 4:00 and 5:00 p.m., so commitments don't eat into the nighttime hours. There isn't a gym or fitness center for miles, so you'll see many people swimming in the lake, walking, jogging, or biking. Hotels don't have high-speed Internet and there isn't a Best Buy to grab a new computer game to keep a young one busy.

Going up north reminds me to go with the flow. My friend Sara was with me on last year's visit and our hotel did not have a hair dryer, shampoo, or Internet. We arrived with forty-eight hours to help complete a long list of duties for the ski tournament. Our cell phones were out-of-area in many places; and every task required at least forty miles of driving round trip.

We realized we had a choice. We could "go with the flow" or become stressed because of what we needed to do, yet couldn't get done due to the "inefficiencies" of missing items and the traveling distances required for tasks. After washing my hair with a 1/8-inch thick bar of hotel soap, Sara and I connected for the daily duties. We both held the same attitude of going with the flow and letting the days unfold versus trying to create a certain day. For both of us, this made a big difference in our ability to enjoy and cherish the many moments that were to come.

Your Turn:

Start your day with good intentions and a solid plan of action, but when things go awry or off-plan, don't miss the gifts the day might have in store because you are so busy trying to push the day back into something that it just isn't.

Today's Affirmation:

I let life happen.

Reflection Questions

How often do you get stressed versus going with the flow?

Where in your life do you focus on things outside of your control?

How often do you try to create a certain memory or day versus letting the day unfold and bring its gifts to you?

August 29

"Your preoccupation should be on doing what you do as well as you can."
—*Jay Leno*

Good morning! One night I was tossing and turning, as I often do when trying to fall asleep. Sammy, who was nine at the time, had been sitting in a bean bag in my room reading a book. She must have noticed because she said, "What are you doing, Momma?"

"Trying to sleep. I often have a hard time falling asleep though, my mind just keeps spinning."

"Well, just turn it off," Sammy stated simply.

"How do I do that?"

"You just do," she said matter-of-factly. "You think about nothing. If you believe that you can think about nothing and turn your mind off, then you can. That's what I do."

I think she could tell that I wasn't convinced. "Come on, try it," she said. "Is your mind clear now?"

I paused for a moment. "Yes, it's clear, Sammy."

"Okay, so don't think about anything."

A moment later: "Are you thinking about anything?"

"I am thinking that I am thinking nothing."

Sammy laughed. "Okay, try this. Imagine a night sky with beautiful stars. Just look up at the stars in your mind and get lost in them." I did as she instructed, keeping my focus on the stars and their patterns.

"Are you thinking anything now, Momma?"

Well, actually, she had to tell me after I woke up that she had even asked that question—I had already fallen asleep.

That night Sammy reminded me how what we set our mind to is often what we create in our lives. I had convinced myself I would toss and turn and Sammy changed my focus.

Your Turn:

Where are you tossing and turning in your own life because you have set your mind to "I can't?" Today, choose one area that is being penalized by an "I can't" attitude and change your view to "I CAN!"

Today's Affirmation:

I can accomplish anything I set my mind to doing.

August 30

> *"That some achieve great success is proof*
> *to all that others can achieve it as well."*
> —*Abraham Lincoln*

Good morning! There are two ways to look at those whom you think are successful—whether they are friends or those you hear of on the news. One is to feel a sense of unjustness or jealousy: "Why not me?" "Why can't I accomplish that?"

The more productive way is to realize that this person is living proof that success is attainable. If they can do it, you can, too!

Your Turn:

Today and every day, look for those people who are success-ful and realize they are living proof that the same success and happiness is available to you. Cheer on everyone you meet in their unique journey toward their dreams.

Today's Affirmation:

Each day I take a step toward success and am inspired by the successes of others.

August 31

> *"Only as high as I reach can I grow, only as far as I seek can I go, only as deep as I look can I see, only as much as I dream can I be."*
> —*Karen Ravn*

Good morning! Karen truly captured a truth of life with this quote. Our limits are set by our thoughts. When we expand our thinking about how we see the world, we expand our opportu-nities within the world.

Your Turn:

How far do you reach? How far do you seek? How deep do you look? How high do you dream? Answer each question care-fully and honestly. Is there room to grow—to seek further, look deeper, reach further, and dream higher? Commit to at least one of these four concepts and incorporate the practice into your daily life.

Today's Affirmation:

I reach for the stars, I seek the truth, I look beyond the surface, I dream beyond the stars.

 *September 1*

> *"When the root is planted deep, there is no reason to fear the wind."*
> —*Chinese Proverb*

Good morning! As we start a new month, take a moment to analyze how deep your devotion to change is planted. Are you looking for a quick solution, or are you committed to making lasting change? My work in the self-improvement field has always focused on lasting change. I strive to create programs for those who have tried enough "quick fixes" to realize that they are in a long and endless spiral with little result.

But change is tough. Today and every day, it is important to review your reasons for change—and to affirm how important your changes are to you and your family. This is "the root." When that root is planted deeply, the occasional stumbling block or pothole will not deter you from achieving your goal.

Your Turn:

If you haven't yet listed out your reasons for embracing change, do so today. If you have, take a moment to review them.

Today's Affirmation:

I embrace change... and everything that comes with it.

September 2

> *"To do or not to do? That is the question."*
> —*My friend Sara*

Good morning! My friend and I were discussing how "to-do lists" often become "to-don't" lists, because people do not use them effectively. I think the concept of a "to-don't" list is quite interesting. We don't intentionally wish our "to-dos" to become "to-don'ts," but if they are managed ineffectively, that is often what happens.

I think all of us could benefit from taking the concept of a "to-don't" list one step further. As you make your action plan for the day or the week, also create a "to-don't" list.

Here are some examples of what might be on that list:

- I won't overcommit my time.
- I won't sacrifice my self-care time.
- I won't let someone else bring me down.
- I won't spend any more time than absolutely necessary with negative people.
- I won't engage in negative self-talk.
- I won't let a challenge or obstacle stop me.
- I won't overspend.
- I won't say "I can't."

Your Turn:

Think of three things you "won't do" and create your own "to-don't" list.

Today's Affirmation:

I shape my life by the things I choose to do and not do.

September 3

> *"Choose your rut carefully: you'll be in it for the next ten miles."*
> —*road sign in upstate New York*

Good morning! I couldn't help but laugh when I read this quote. Isn't it the truth? Of course, the good news is that when we are on target, and focused, and following the pathway toward our dreams, even our "ruts" become part of that journey.

The ruts also become frustrating though, because they are usually in direct opposition to our goals. We want to "break out of the rut" and "get back on track" toward what really matters most. However, one important lesson that I learned from a former colleague is that often, the harder we try to get out of a rut, the more enmeshed in the rut we get.

Sometime we need to welcome the rut. It might be telling us something. It might be telling us that we are moving too fast, or moving in the wrong direction, or it might reveal some other important lesson to us. Every rut comes with a reason. The wise goal-seeker determines what lesson the rut has to teach and then proceeds on her journey.

Your Turn:

Instead of fighting out of the rut, welcome it. Take a break and think about what lesson this rut might be trying to reveal. Honor and listen. Then you will have the strength to walk away from it.

Today's Affirmation:

I learn from the rut.

Reflection Questions

Are there any areas in your life where you feel you are "trudging through mud" where you once traveled smoothly?

What would happen if you "welcomed the rut" and instead of trying to plow forward, set still?

What reason could be behind your rut?

September 4

"It was on my fifth birthday that Papa put his hand on my shoulder and said, 'Remember, my son, if you ever need a helping hand, you'll find one at the end of your arm.'"
—*Sam Levenson*

Good morning! This quote reminded me of one of the primary traits I have discovered in people who are successful in their professional lives, personal lives, and passions. The successful person heeds this quote and understands that in order to move forward, she needs to use her own helping hand.

We cannot put the responsibility of moving forward on another, or wait for someone to help us. We have to live every day, helping ourselves, leading ourselves down the road of our dreams.

That would seem to be common sense, yet I would dare to estimate that maybe 10 percent of people actually live that way. Many people, somehow, manage to remove themselves from the process of change and forward movement (at least part of the time) by waiting for someone else's hand to lift them up, or engaging in thoughts that allow them to believe their own hands aren't strong enough to do the job.

Here are just a few examples I encountered recently:

- A person sets a career goal. She quickly realizes she doesn't have the background to accomplish what she sets out to do. She asks someone to help her, but doesn't get the help she needs. Instead of moving forward, she stops.

- A person wants to make an investment but does not know how to invest. She asks a friend for advice or guidance, but the friend doesn't have time to help her. She doesn't invest.

- A person wants their family to eat more healthily. She tries to orchestrate a meeting to get "everyone on board," but can't seem to get everyone to sit down together. She decides now isn't the time to start the new regimen.

Reread these three examples. Can you think of another way they could have been handled had the women embraced today's quote? Here are my ideas:

The woman with the career goal could make a list of the information she needs answered, and then seek out sources that have the information. If she truly wants to reach the goal, the answers are at the end of her fingertips. The person without investment knowledge could consult a local stockbroker, book, or many online resources to educate herself or create a mock portfolio. The woman seeking a healthier experience for her family might lead by example.

Your Turn:

What area of your life are you waiting for help in? Instead of spending time waiting, spend time generating a list of what you need to know, and then uncovering sources of the information.

Today's Affirmation:

I do not stall in life; instead, I seek out solutions.

September 5

"Drag your thoughts away from your troubles... by the ears, by the heels, or any other way you can manage it."
—Mark Twain

Good morning! Mark Twain certainly has some "nuggets," doesn't he? This seemingly simple sentence is a powerful prescription for living. It is important to remember that our thoughts are like water for a garden. Wherever we let them wander, they will water that area, and help it to grow.

Pause for a moment to think about the last few days. What did you spend most of your time thinking about? Worries? Troubles? Hopes? Dreams? Problems? If you spent the last few days worried about a problem, odds are that the problem grew, or your perception and stress from the problem has grown. If you spent the last few days thinking positively about the future, and about hopes and dreams, you were likely in a good mood and making positive steps forward.

Your Turn:

Remember that thoughts are like water for a garden. What area in your life needs to grow? Focus your thoughts there.

Today's Affirmation:

My thoughts are positive, constructive, and encouraging.

 *September 6*

> *"At some point during your search for the meaning of life, don't forget to do a little living."*
> —*quoted from* **A Thousand Paths to Tranquility**

Good morning! This quote made me smile, as it speaks to one of the things I have found most puzzling about people's quest for "self-discovery." As many people search for their passion, or for the meaning of life, they are wrapped up in "tomorrows." The goal is to get to that "special tomorrow" where fullness and meaning is discovered, and problems lessen. However, to think that we can find the meaning of life in any day but today doesn't really make sense.

In order to find the meaning of life, we have to live. We can't live tomorrow right now, we can only live today. If we spend our time wrapped up in thoughts of what's next, then we end up losing the gifts of today and actually moving further away from self-discovery.

Your Turn:

Remember that the path to contentment isn't a path you have to find tomorrow or next week. The path is right below your feet today. You just need to take a step on it, and then another, and another.

Today's Affirmation:

The path to the life I desire is here today—and I walk down it.

September 7

> *"Faith sees the invisible, believes the incredible and receives the impossible."*
> —*Author unknown*

Good morning! Often we turn to our faith only in time of sorrow, stress, and challenge. Then, suddenly, our faith becomes needed as a source of strength. We ask our faith to guide us through; to see clearly what lies ahead and how we should confront it. But how often do we dismiss our faith when times are calm, joyful, and untroubled... when we are resting and content?

Just as our faith can be a light post to see us through times of trouble, it can also be a pillow on which we can rest, and a light to shine and make our joyous days even brighter.

Your Turn:

What role does faith play in your life? Studies have shown that those with a faith-based outlook are more optimistic and live longer than those without. Why? I believe it is because faith teaches us how to trust and believe in a world where those values aren't seen every day. Consider your faith practices and consider if you can incorporate a daily time to exercise your faith.

Today's Affirmation:

My faith is a light, always guiding my path and my steps.

 *September 8*

> *"Cynicism is not realistic and tough. It's unrealistic and kind of cowardly because it means you don't have to try."*
> —*Peggy Noonan*

Good morning! All of my friends can attest that I have an incredibly low tolerance for those who are cynical, pessimistic, or buried beneath excuses. We all have challenges and obstacles to face, and we all have the power to overcome them.

I was having a conversation with a new friend the other day. She is a very sweet young lady who is bouncy, fun, energetic, and optimistic. I actually thought she must have had a pretty typical upbringing, because at age twenty she was vibrant and ready to tackle the world. We began sharing about our pasts: My parents were divorced shortly after my birth; her parents had never been married. Neither of us had a real relationship with our fathers, nor saw them often. We both grew up at what would be considered "poverty" level. She had lost her cousin, who was like a sister, to suicide. I had lost my brother through a fatal reaction to a bee sting. Our "nontypical" sharing continued.

I expressed my surprise at the life she had lived thus far in twenty short years (just as I remember so many expressing that same sentiment to me when I was twenty). She shared how many friends felt "sorry" for her and how she couldn't stand that. She is happy and confident with who she is and realizes that each experience, although painful, made her into the young woman she is today. I have said that exact statement many times. We can't filter life and just take the good without the bad. We are a sum of our experiences—but it is up to us whether that sum will be positive or negative.

Your Turn:

No matter where you have been, what you are facing, or what lies in your future, you can overcome. Empower yourself!

Today's Affirmation:

I empower myself to move forward and find the resources and support to do so.

September 9

"Pick battles big enough to matter, small enough to win."
—*Jonathan Kozol*

Good morning! Debbie sent in this quote, with the following note:

I've always heard to pick your battles with your kids, but I am looking at this from a new perspective now—picking my battles with my to-do list. What really matters? What is doable?

Debbie has hit on a very valid point that is essential to living in balance. We need to challenge our routines, instead of doing them on autopilot, and we need to choose to focus on what really matters. Life isn't about getting everything done—life is about completing what matters. Do not fill up your to-do list with so much "clutter" that you can't complete the tasks that give life meaning.

Your Turn:
At every turn ask yourself... does this matter?

Today's Affirmation:
I focus on what matters.

Inspirations

Need ideas on how to make today matter? Read an excerpt of my book, *The Change Your Life Challenge* online at www.brooknoelstudio.com.

September 10

> *"Life is just a mirror, and what you see out there,*
> *you must first see inside of you."*
> —*Wally "Famous" Amos*

Good morning! Want a quick way to measure how you feel about yourself and what type of attitude you have? Answer this question: How do you see the world around you today?

If you see the world as scary, worrisome, negative, or stressful, then odds are you are holding these feelings within yourself. Likewise, if you see the world as hopeful, optimistic, and joy-filled, you likely embrace those feelings within.

We can't capture the invisible. If we desire a life of peace, contentment, and happiness but cannot feel it internally, we won't be able to find it externally.

Your Turn:

How we perceive the external is a reflection of how we feel internally. If you took a picture of the external world today, what would it reveal about you? Use this technique to keep your attitude healthy and strong. Treat yourself well—remember that how you feel will be reflected into the world and to all of those around you.

Today's Affirmation:

Today I create a stronger "self" by treating myself with care, love, and respect.

 *September 11*

> *"Faith is the strength by which a shattered world shall emerge into the light."*
> —*Helen Keller*

Good morning! Sometimes our world shifts dramatically, without warning, as it did on 9/11/2001.

I wanted to take a moment today to reflect on this type of unwanted and unwelcome shift in the world. Perhaps you have experienced other dramatic and unwanted shifts, like the loss of a loved one, a job, a pet, or a move. How do we keep our thoughts, minds, and hearts in a positive place when things seem to be crumbling all around us?

This is not an easy question to answer, but I believe that the answer has two parts. The first, I believe, is to remember what we still have in our lives and to admire the courage of the human spirit. As we see pictures of the Astrodome in the wake of Hurricane Katrina; watch footage of the crumbled towers in New York, and hear the stories of sadness and loss, we also hear stories of gratitude and praise for a saved life—even if that life has lost everything within it. Why is that? Because no matter what we lose, our heart, our soul, our spirit, remains. And from that we can rebuild.

Secondly, where does that human spirit come from? It comes from our connection to something bigger than our world, than ourselves. This simple quote by Helen Keller, a woman who could have perceived life much differently than she did, is yet another admirable show of the human spirit.

Your Turn:

Today, I challenge you to take a moment of silence to reflect and pray for those who have suffered such great losses in the events we have witnessed on the news, and in the many events that we will never know about. Then, reflect on your own spirit. Are you nurturing the spirit within? In one of my books I wrote, "Faith is the soul's food. One cannot live long without it—or live well on just a little." Are you feeding your faith?

Today's Affirmation:

I find strength in my faith.

Inspirations

Take a moment to pause and reflect in remembrance of 9/11. Visit the World Trade Tribute for several memorial videos you can view online or download. www.worldtradetribute.com/yellow7/wings/index.htm

September 12

> *"One of the most tragic things about human nature is that all of us tend to put off living. We are dreaming of some magical rose garden over the horizon instead of enjoying the roses that are blooming outside our windows today."*
> —*Dale Carnegie*

Good morning! If you were to gather 100 people in a room and ask them to write down their happiest times, you would likely find that the lists had one thing in common. Our happiest times come when we connect with others and give the best of ourselves. Yet, these happy times can be hard to come by, because human nature is to acquire "this or that," or accomplish "this or that," before taking time to connect.

Taking a moment to list out what makes us truly happy can be an interesting exercise. Often we find that the items on our list aren't things that are hard to attain—they are simply things we must make time for. When we are chasing after some magical rose garden, we can forget to make time today, assuming that the time we create in this "magical someday" will be richer.

Your Turn:

Take a moment today to think about what makes you truly happy. Is it spending time with a friend or sharing a good laugh with a child? Make the time each day to find happiness instead of looking for it in a distant someday.

Today's Affirmation:

I live in a garden of happiness.

September 13

"There are no guarantees. From the viewpoint of fear, none are strong enough. From the viewpoint of love, none are necessary."
—*Emmanuel*

Good morning! So often in life we want a guarantee. You have undoubtedly realized how the business of extended warranties has become a main source of revenue for retailers. We will pay a few extra hundred dollars on a new electronic device for the comfort and safety brought by a warranty.

We often bring this same desire for a guarantee to our personal life. We want to try something new, but we are fearful. We long to know that our energy will not be wasted. We want to try a new career or implement a new idea, but we need reassurance to warrant the risk. We seek some reassurance that we will be better off for taking a chance. Without reassurance it is easy to withdraw and not take a chance.

But we have to learn to dance with life, even without a guarantee. We have to reach past our fears and embrace risk to discover the path to fulfillment. For the greatest things in life aren't backed by guarantee, but by risk and courage.

Your Turn:

What have you been withdrawing from in your own life because there is no guarantee? Is there an idea you would like to implement? A career you would like to pursue? A new hobby you want to try? A relationship you want to take to a new level? How would a 100 percent guarantee change your behavior? Consider acting that way now—even without the guarantee.

Today's Affirmation:

I embrace life as it is, not as I need it to be.

Going Further

While there are no guarantees, there are steps we can take to ensure the odds are in our favor, especially when it comes to our health. September is National Cholesterol Education month and the National Institute of Health has put together some valuable resources, recipes, and reading. Check it out at http://hp2010.nhlbihin.net/chol-month/10_Ideas.htm

September 14

> *"Adversity is the diamond dust that*
> *heaven polishes its jewels with.."*
> —*Thomas Carlyle*

Good morning! When you meet someone you find admirable, or hear an incredible story of courage or strength, you will usually find that these admirable and courageous people have faced much adversity in their lifetime. What makes them admirable is that they chose to challenge adversity and learn from it, instead of laying down or letting go.

While adversity in itself seems uncomfortable or something to run from, it truly is the diamond dust that heaven polishes its jewels with. When we face adversity, we are always presented with a chance to grow, a new life lesson to absorb, and a new lens with which to see the world, which can strengthen our soul and our spirit. Those people we find admirable are often those who grow, learn, and use adversity as a tool to strengthen their values, commitments, and priorities.

Your Turn:

Welcome adversity as a chance to learn more about yourself, your priorities, and your values.

Today's Affirmation:

I learn something new from every life experience. What I learn enriches me for every life experience to come.

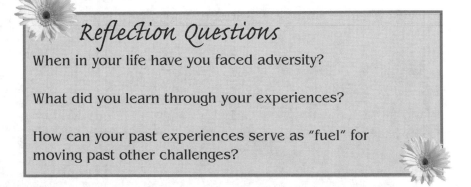

Reflection Questions

When in your life have you faced adversity?

What did you learn through your experiences?

How can your past experiences serve as "fuel" for moving past other challenges?

September 15

"A positive attitude is a magnet for positive results."
—*Author unknown*

Good morning! This quote holds a universal and simple truth that we should all remember from moment to moment.

Like will always attract like. Think about debt and what will you get? More bills. Think about negative people and what will you get? More negative people. Think about negative outcomes and guess what you will get? More negative outcomes. It is that simple. The converse is also true. Think about reaching your goals and what will you get? A step further toward your goals. Think about helping people, and what will you get? Positive and thankful people.

Your Turn:

For the rest of this week, try to practice this simple truth and notice the impact and change it creates in your life.

Today's Affirmation:

I have a positive attitude. I attract the positive in life.

Going Further

Fold a piece of writing paper in half lengthwise and write down the answers to these questions on the left-hand side.

What are three words I would use to describe my month so far overall?

What are three occurrences that have happened this month? (Either positive or negative.)

When you're finished, write the answers to the following questions on the right-hand side of the paper directly across from the first set of answers.

What are three words you would use to describe your thought patterns this month?

What activities have you been focused on this month? (Your focus could be positive, like taking a step forward or completing a task, or it might be self-defeating, such as worry or anger.)

Look at your two columns. Can you see how the actions and thoughts on the right coincide with what you recorded on the left? The month is halfway over. If you do not like what is on your paper, redirect your energy. Flip it over and answer the second set of questions first. Use these as guidelines for the days to come in the second half of the month.

September 16

> *"If you are speeding down a highway… and you are driving at the speed of light… and you turn on your lights… do they do anything?"*
> —***Steven Wright, comedian***

Good morning! I was listening to a Steven Wright monologue on the radio the other day (while I was speeding down the highway, incidentally), in which he said the above, as only he can in his drawling, drawn-out manner.

Have you ever noticed how, inside a joke, there usually lies a message—and how most jokes are most successful when they lend new insight or a nugget of truth to a contemporary condition? Inside Wright's joke lies a relevant question: *Are we going too fast for our own good?* Has our speed surpassed our ability to function at our human best and with human vision? Individually? And as a society? Do we need to slow down a little and let our headlights shine the way in front of us, so we can see where we are going, learn how we are doing, understand our orientation, and realize that we might need to adjust our journey a bit?

Sometimes in our frantic pace (thoroughly expected by today's "destination-driven" society) we lose the enjoyment of the "getting there," of our journey. "We become blindsided from experiencing all the little facets along the way that could make our lives so enjoyable, so meaningful.

Your Turn:

The next time you find yourself "driving too fast," slow down. If nothing else, slow down long enough to give yourself time to laugh!

Today's Affirmation:

I cherish the journey as much as the destination.

 September 17

> *"Everyone should carefully observe which way his heart draws him, and then choose that way with all of his strength."*
> —*Hasidic Proverb*

Good morning! It is easy to get lost in being reactive to life instead of being proactive. Our days are full and we often respond moment to moment without much time for creative thinking or self-reflection. Today's quote draws us back to self-reflection. Which way does your heart draw you? What dreams keep surfacing in your mind? Where do your thoughts wander?

I have said it before, but it is worth repeating: stress, anxiety, and depression are most commonly encountered when we stray from our core values, mission, and vision. Find some time to reflect on where life is leading you. If you are feeling stress, anxiety, worries, or out of balance, ask yourself: What am I straying from?

Your Turn:
Today, take ten minutes to journal your answer to this question: Where is my heart leading me?

Today's Affirmation:
I follow my heart.

September 18

"All I know is that you can get there from here. You can. Walk through the fear."
—*Mary Anne Radmacher*

Good morning! How often do we turn away from something out of fear? It might be something on a large scale, like a hidden dream in our heart. Or it might be on a smaller scale, like not making a phone call because a conversation makes us nervous. However, if we don't take a step forward, we will never get "there." Each time we step, we build our internal confidence and belief system.

Your Turn:

Take a step today toward "there"—wherever your "there" may be.

Today's Affirmation:

I walk through fear.

Going Further

Need direction for overcoming a fear? Check out wikihow. com, a collaborative online writing project full of valuable how-to information. Search the wiki for "overcome a fear" for a list of topics or view general suggestions at http://www.wikihow.com/Conquer-a-Fear.

September 19

> *"The mistake we make is when we seek to be loved, instead of loving."*
> —Charlotte Yonge

Good morning! I think one of the hardest lessons to learn in life is complete unconditional love and acceptance of self. Seeking love from others is easier than seeking love from ourselves, as we are the ones who are hardest on ourselves, magnifying each "flaw." But as we have all heard time and time again, we cannot love another person or be loved by another person *completely* until we first love ourselves.

What is self-love? Many times we have a hard time with this concept because we confuse self-love with selfishness. Self-love doesn't mean always putting ourselves first or living *our way*. Self-love is treating ourselves with the same compassion, forgiveness, and acceptance that we do dear friends and family. Our friends and family will undoubtedly make mistakes, and we will forgive them. They will undoubtedly stumble, and we will encourage them. But, do we do those same things for ourselves? Do we forgive and encourage ourselves?

Your Turn:

This week, practice treating yourself with the kindness, compassion, and encouragement with which you treat others.

Today's Affirmation:

I am worth complete and total love, right now, just as I am.

September 20

"Do a little more each day than you think you possibly can."
—Lowell Thomas

Good morning! This quote emulates the concept of "going the extra mile," but in fresh words. Just as we start each day with a positive thought, how about ending it with the question: "What is one last thing I can do today to make today matter?" Maybe it is a call to return, a note to write, a person to thank. Maybe it is saying "I love you" to someone in your home, or finishing one more load of laundry, or taking a long bath to refresh your soul and mind. Maybe it is taking a multivitamin or a five-minute walk, petting the dog, or writing an affirmation. It can be a little thing or a big thing and will likely change day to day based on your energy level.

Your Turn:

Tonight, ask yourself: "What is one last thing I can do today, to make today matter?"

Today's Affirmation:

I make every day matter.

 *September 21*

> *"What a wonderful life I've had! I only wish*
> *I'd realized it sooner."*
> —*Colette*

Good morning! So much is shared and conveyed in this thirteen-word quote. Odds are it doesn't need much interpreting or analysis as it probably speaks to you in the same straightforward way it spoke to me.

My heart really goes out to Colette. My heart is also inspired to realize all the wonderfulness in this world that exists right here and right now.

Your Turn:

How do you relate to Colette? What message can her words teach you?

Today's Affirmation:

Everything is just as it should be in the here and now.

Going Further

Tonight, take some time to write down all the wonderful things that have happened in your life. Consider starting a journal or keeping a scrapbook to document these blessings.

September 22

> *"The way to succeed is to never quit. That's it."*
> —*Alex Hailey*

Good morning! In 2005, I was asked to speak at the Mother of Invention awards held annually by the Whirlpool Corporation. One mother asked "What is the key to your success?" My answer echoed Alex's quote. I have found that the key to success is to be personal or professional no matter what the goal is; to never quit.

When I was building my business and ran out of money, I didn't quit. When I experienced great personal setbacks and the loss of loved ones, I didn't quit. When some of those around me told me it couldn't be done, I didn't quit. When I was diagnosed with a rare and dangerous health condition, I didn't quit. When every indicator pointed to giving up as a wise decision, I didn't quit. Even when I questioned and began to doubt myself, I didn't quit.

I believe that never quitting is an example of a very simple universal truth. The key to getting anywhere is to not stop until you get there. No excuses, no blame—it is that simple.

Your Turn:

Write down one thing in your life that is important to you and make the commitment to never quit. Post it where you will see it daily. While the path to get there might change, as long as you keep moving you will arrive.

Today's Affirmation:

I know my desired destination and I will overcome any obstacle to arrive there.

 September 23

> *"It takes less time to do a thing right than to explain why you did it wrong."*
> *—Henry Wadsworth Longfellow*

Good morning! I have always been a strong believer in doing your best at whatever it is you are doing. If you are cleaning today, clean with passion. Clean completely. If you are spending time with your child, really listen, interact and communicate. If you are working on a project, constantly ask yourself: "Is this the best I can do?" and, if not, keep going. The Earl of Chesterfield said it well in a quote I have used before: "Whatever is worth doing is worth doing well." And if you find that you aren't doing something at 100 percent, then it is time to ask yourself why you are doing it in the first place.

Your Turn:

Today, give 100 percent of yourself to each moment.

Today's Affirmation:

I always do my best.

Reflection Questions

Where in your life do you have a tendency to cut corners in hopes of gaining more time? How does this affect the end result?

How would your life change if you focused completely at the task at hand and giving it your best?

September 24

> *"Success is often the result of taking a misstep in the right direction."*
> —*Al Bernstein*

Good morning! Did you know that Levi Strauss was originally a tent maker in the 1850s? He used a heavy-duty denim fabric he had invented to make tents to make blue jeans. He failed at his tent-making endeavor. I wonder what we would all be wearing if he had succeeded?

I love hidden success stories. Most success stories are journeys that include obstacles, "failures," detours, roadblocks, and road bumps. But obstacles, "failures," detours, roadblocks, and road bumps are *key ingredients* to success. We can't get to success in a personal or professional endeavor without these ingredients. Roadblocks and the like teach us to stretch our thinking, reframe our situations, and expand our possibilities.

If I were the editor of the dictionary, I would define success as: a series of mistakes, small steps, accomplishments, detours, roadblocks, dreams, and persistence that eventually deliver us to a desired goal.

Perhaps if we expected these sidesteps, we could accept them instead of thinking they were reasons to abandon a goal. They aren't! They are just another step toward the end result.

Your Turn:

Post this new definition of success somewhere you will see it regularly: "success is a series of mistakes, small steps, accomplishments, detours, roadblocks, dreams, and persistence that eventually deliver us to a desired goal."

Today's Affirmation:

There is no such thing as a setback. A setback is a necessary ingredient in the recipe of success.

September 25

> *"Every day you must try to make yourself grow. This you can do."*
> —*Maxwell Maltz*

Good morning! Each day we are presented with many opportunities to make positive choices, take positive action, and grow. Each day challenge yourself to embrace these opportunities, and decide to choose growth.

Your Turn:

At every turn of the day, choose to embrace growth.

Today's Affirmation:

Every day I choose to grow.

Reflection Questions

Often when we shy away from a challenge or opportunity, there is an underlying need for growth. In the past when you have experienced self-growth, what was the catalyst? Are there any opportunities you are facing now that might be an inspiration for additional growth?

September 26

"It is a gift to be able to paint a particular picture or to carve a statue, and so to make a few objects beautiful; but it is far more glorious to carve and paint the very atmosphere and medium through which we look. To affect the quality of the day—that is the highest of the arts."
—*Henry David Thoreau*

Good morning! This is a quote worthy of reading several times. I fall in love with the line: "To affect the quality of the day—that is the highest of the arts." Think about that for a moment. Right now, this hour, this moment, you have the ability to affect the quality of a day. Each day then becomes part of our history—both for ourselves personally and for our world.

Why not put away the "tomorrow" attitude for good and instead grab hold of today? You have the ability to affect the world today... you are going to one way or another whether you like it or not. You are either going to do nothing, or you are going to make a positive impact or a negative impact. The choice is yours.

Your Turn:

What are you waiting for? Today is here, full of opportunities to find magic and create happiness! What can you stop and do *right now* to affect the quality of today in a positive way? Choose something. Then do it.

Today's Affirmation:

I create magic today.

September 27

"We can only be said to be alive in those moments
when our hearts are conscious of our treasures."
—*Thornton Wilder*

Good morning! When I started my Good Morning routine, my primary motive was to turn off the "autopilot" in my life. I am sure you are familiar with being on autopilot. You can see it actively in your life when one day fades into another and before you know it a week, a month, or a year has gone by and you are left wondering: "Where did that time go?" I wanted to find a way to practice living moment to moment and treasuring each moment for the true gift that it is.

I stumbled across this Thornton Wilder quote while doing a search for "Thanksgiving." It summarizes both the goals I have for my own life, and my goal to share with other women: how to turn off autopilot and make each day count. When we are conscious of all our treasures and we focus on those treasures, our lives become rich and valuable moment to moment.

Your Turn:

Today, turn off your autopilot. Be fully present in each moment. Focus on the treasures you have moment to moment instead of what is missing in your life.

Today's Affirmation:

Each moment I am present and conscious of life's many treasures.

September 28

"Be miserable. Or motivate yourself. Whatever has to be done, it's always your choice."
—*Wayne Dyer*

Good morning! We naturally want the best for those with whom we are close. Whether it is our children, our relatives, our friends, our acquaintances—as women, we are natural nurturers. It's important to realize that our views and attitudes about our world are the single biggest influence we can give to those around us—either positive or negative.

Keeping the zest alive in our own lives is one of the most influential ways to encourage passion in others. Here are some ideas to awaken the passion within.

Find a role model: Think of people you know who seem to have a natural passion for their life and their world. Spend time with these people and spend less time with people who are negative. Make positive people the models for your own days and conduct.

Discover something new: Choose an interest that you have never made time for and make time for it. Perhaps it's painting, writing, photography, or woodworking—as you rediscover the passion and joy found in creating, let that spill over into other areas of your life.

Your Turn:

Keeping the passion alive in our life is one of the best gifts of encouragement we can share with those around us. Choose and implement one of the above ideas, or create one of your own that will help awaken passion in your everyday life.

Today's Affirmation:

I encourage others through my passion for life.

Inspirations

America On the Move Foundation (AOM) is a national nonprofit helping individuals, families, and communities across our nation make positive changes to improve their health and quality of life. America On the Move provides an interactive, fun, and free way to get healthy and get motivated. AOM encourages people to move more and eat smart by making two small daily changes:

• Take 2,000 more steps (about 1 mile)

• Eat 100 fewer calories (about a tablespoon of butter)

September 29

"Every action that you perform is recorded in you, the soul. These imprints ultimately mold your character and destiny. When you understand this principle, you will pay more attention to bringing your best to everything you do."
—Dadi Janki

Good morning! Imagine that your life is one big movie that you could replay on your VCR. Then imagine you are the editor of this movie and have to create two volumes of scenes. One volume would contain clips of your "greatest hits." The other volume would be your "outtakes or bloopers."

Take a moment to think about at least five scenes that would be on each tape. After doing so, write down five lessons you learned from this exercise.

When I did this myself, I learned many things, including: my "greatest hits" often weren't huge endeavors or undertakings, but simple acts of kindness from one soul to another. My "bloopers" were when I lost sight of my vision and steered from my core values.

Your Turn:

Take some time to reflect on and complete this exercise throughout the day.

Today's Affirmation:

I am a willing student of my past, and take my lessons with me toward the future.

September 30

"'Well,' said Pooh, 'what I like best,' and then he had to stop and think. Because although Eating Honey was a very good thing to do, there was a moment just before you began to eat it which was better than when you were, but he didn't know what it was called."
—A.A. Milne

Good morning! Who knew that a cartoon bear could be so wise? I can relate to Pooh. I love having a new book released, but the time I like even better is that time when I am writing—when the words and research are driving me toward discovery.

"Life is a journey, not a destination," is a quote we often see on inspirational posters. We have to create a day-to-day life that fosters the feelings Pooh describes. Our day-to-day journey has to become the joy and richness in our life. After all, what do you do when you get to a destination? You usually don't stay there, but instead chart another course. We can't link good feelings to our destination, or we would never have as many good feelings as we deserve in our lifetime.

Your Turn:
What is one thing you can do daily to help make your day-to-day journey richer?

Today's Affirmation:
Each day of my life is rich and rewarding.

October 1

"Try a thing you haven't done three times. Once, to get over the fear of doing it. Twice, to learn how to do it. And a third time to figure out whether you like it or not."
—*Virgil Thomson*

Good morning! When we try something new, we can't base our judgment of that experience on our first attempt. Newness always brings anxiety and high emotion. We must get to an "even ground" with a "level head" to decide the value of something new in our lives.

Likewise, in business, we don't make a decision after one attempt at something. We try something again and again, gathering more information each time, to make a more informed decision.

I wonder what would have happened to the many inventions in this world, had the inventor only tried once? I certainly doubt I would be traveling 31,000 feet in the air on a regular basis!

Your Turn:

What is something that you have only tried once? Can you guess what your challenge is for October? That's right… try it two more times.

Today's Affirmation:

Anything worth trying, is worth trying more than once.

October 2

> *"It was only a sunny smile and little it cost in the giving*
> *but like morning light it scattered the night*
> *and made the day worth living."*
> —*Author unknown*

Good morning! I love it when I stumble across a quote that drives home the importance of a simple smile. Smiles make us feel better, and everyone around us, too. It doesn't take any more time to smile sincerely than it does to remain expressionless.

Your Turn:

Become a smile-scatterer. Seriously, if you have never done this, now is the time. Today, smile at least twenty times. (Try to smile at others for as many of those times as possible—but if you are not with others, just smile in the mirror.) Watch the dramatic shift in how you feel.

Today's Affirmation:

I scatter smiles throughout the day.

Inspirations

The Harvey Ball World Smile Foundation (WSF) was established in 2001 to honor the name and memory of Harvey Ball, the artist who, in 1963, created that international symbol of goodwill: the smiley face.

Harvey Ball said that a smile "… just reflects what is inside every one of us—a smile is what we want to see when we look at another human being." He said, "Sometimes we forget that. Sometimes the world seems big and filled with problems that are too hard to understand, much less solve. We start to believe that we are too small to make a difference. But that's not true. The truth is that every one of us has the ability to make a difference every day."

The first Friday in October each year is celebrated as World Smile Day. The theme for the day is "Do an act of kindness. Help one person smile." For more information on World Smile Day, visit www.worldsmileday.com.

Send a Smile: Send a smile online by visiting http://www.123greetings.com/events/smile_day/.

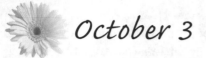

October 3

> *"It's important to give it all you have while you have the chance."*
> **—Shania Twain**

Good morning! This wonderful quote speaks to so many aspects of our lives. It's no secret that every day brings opportunity. It might be the opportunity to help a family member, assist a stranger, move toward a goal, absorb a sunset, or spend time with a favorite pet. The "it" in the above quote could be anything. "It" could refer to anything in my previous sentence about self-care: exercise, your children, any relationship, the day in general, or this very moment.

Your Turn:

Today and every day, remind yourself as often as you can to "give it all you have while you have the chance." Let down any walls that hold you back and give it all you can—the chance may not come again.

Today's Affirmation:

I recognize the opportunity I am blessed with each day, and I give each opportunity my all.

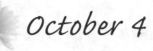

October 4

"I take nothing for granted. I now have only good days, or great days."
—*Lance Armstrong*

Good morning! I find it interesting that the power to have a good day or bad day is truly up to us. Yet very few people want to take responsibility and really own that fact. Instead, they blame the external. While the external indeed does have an influence on our lives, it doesn't have the final say—we do.

We have the ability to make choices about our life and how we feel and what we do. There are many cultures where destiny is predetermined and choice is not existent. We have the choice to make today a good day or a great day. Let's use our power of choice and choose to challenge life!

Your Turn:

Take not a single moment for granted. Let go of bad days and have only good and great days. The choice is yours.

Today's Affirmation:

I experience only good days or great days.

Going Further

Staying safe in the moment: With 91 percent of employees commuting to and from work and 18 percent of all motor vehicle trips being work-related, the Drive Safely Work Week (recognized the first week in October) offers important reminders for commuters. The Network of Employers for Traffic Control promote ten positive steps for responsible driving:

1. Plan YOUR Route

2. Maintain YOUR Vehicle

3. Focus YOUR Attention

4. Minimize YOUR Distractions

5. Know YOUR Surroundings

6. Share YOUR Space

7. Watch YOUR Speed

8. Keep YOUR Distance

9. Signal YOUR Intentions

10. Always Wear YOUR Seat Belt

Visit www.trafficsafety.org for interesting articles on all aspects of work and commuting

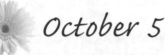

October 5

"Heart is what separates the good from the great."
—*Michael Jordan*

Good morning! Today's quote is a beautiful reminder about the key component to excellence, whether that excellence is found in our personal lives, social lives, spiritual lives, or professional lives. How many times have you felt that something was missing or that an activity once enjoyed doesn't bring the same joy now that we are at another point in life? Often we make the mistake of thinking that something is wrong with us, or that we are in a funk or depression. Of course, this type of thinking only saps joy and energy from our days.

Or, if our lack of joy is work-related, we might think that if we could just do something better, or learn more, or make more money, that the empty void would be filled.

Being our best is the only way to fill that void. It is difficult to be our best, though, when we feel that void. This quote from Michael Jordan provides a key—though often overlooked—component for filling the void within.

When we feel that emptiness, it isn't just a matter of doing more or doing less, and it isn't a matter of trying harder. That void is always a sign that reflection is needed, because our heart is not fully present in the endeavor we are pursuing. Only when our hearts are as present as our minds will we feel "great" instead of "good."

Your Turn:

You can test this theory by looking back at some of your happiest moments, or at times when you felt everything was "clicking." Think about where your mind was and where your heart was—odds are they were operating in tandem. When you feel an emptiness in any area of your life, take a moment to take stock of what your heart is telling you. It might be requesting a little adjustment in your routine, more self-care, or a desire to lead you down a different path altogether.

Today's Affirmation:
I listen to my heart.

 October 6

> *"Two men look out the same prison bars;*
> *one sees mud and the other stars."*
> —*Frederick Langbridge*

Good morning! Positive thinking does not spiral and grow as fast as negative thinking. I believe this is because most people are trained to prepare for the worst instead of expecting the best. Because we live like that (or live around people who do), negative thinking has the power to build quite quickly—like the first little snowball that is soon rolled into the belly of a big snowman.

We are trained like this from a young age. "Don't talk to strangers." Why? Because something bad might happen. We don't view strangers as friends we have not yet met; we view them as potentially dangerous villains. As children, we are right to be taught caution: If we did not have these protection mechanisms when we were young, many of us would have been endangered or hurt. But we aren't children now. We don't need the same defense mechanisms we once had. Now we are adults—now it is up to us, every moment, to make our own choices.

Your Turn:

Where have protection or defense mechanisms limited your choices? Today, make a conscious choice to put down a self-protection tool you have outgrown.

Today's Affirmation:

I know the choices I make become my future.

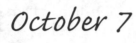

October 7

> *"Who I am makes a difference"—a Good Morning reader*
> *found this message on a ribbon that came home from*
> *school with her seven-year-old son.*

Good morning! What positive reinforcement that school is practicing! Perhaps we should each make a ribbon or card displaying those six important words to remind ourselves that each and every day, *who we are makes a difference*!

One of my favorite quotes has always been, "Those who are crazy enough to think they can change the world usually do" (author unknown). We get to the place where we can make positive change by believing and embracing the concept that who we are makes a difference.

In today's world, it is so easy to forget our own power and fall into the rut of blame or negativity. That's why it is so important to focus each morning through the power of a Good Morning, and to remember all that is good and right about ourselves and our world.

Your Turn:

Write today's quote on a piece of paper and place it where you will see it each morning.

Today's Affirmation:

Who I am makes a difference.

Going Further

Celebrated on the last Saturday of each October, Make a Difference Day is a national day of helping others—a celebration of neighbors helping neighbors. Created by *USA Weekend* magazine, the day has inspired millions of people to participate in both small and large-scale projects. Visit www.usaweekend.com/diffday/ to find a project, submit a project, or come up with an idea using the online project generator. You can also download guides and resources to assist in coordinating a Make a Difference Day project.

October 8

"You gain strength, courage, and confidence by every experience in which you really stop to look fear in the face. You must do the thing which you think you cannot do."
—*Eleanor Roosevelt*

Good morning! This past week I saw a dear friend confront a deep-rooted fear with excuses. He was faced with making a very big life decision. He had already made his decision, committed to it, and committed to many other people as well—all that was left was "to dot his I's and cross his T's." The change he was challenging himself to make wasn't one done on a whim. He had spent many months preparing and talking with others to make sure it was for the best. Yet the final steps to make this change would require him to come face-to-face with a deep-rooted fear he had held since childhood. He would have to look that fear in the eye and take the last step to move past it. In the final moment, he looked his fear in the eye and, instead of stepping past it, he stepped backward and let the fear live. He then created a list of reasons as to why his decision made sense. Yet he knew, and all of us who were aware of it, knew, in our hearts, that these were just excuses—what had happened in reality was that his fear had won.

I am not passing judgment on him—no one can pass judgment on anyone, for each of us has to fight our own battles, and we can only truly understand the battles when we are in the shoes of the battler.

However, what became abundantly clear to me after watching this struggle play out in his life, was how often I have seen people within a similar struggle: seeking truth, finding it, and then letting fear take it away. Is that right or wrong? I believe that it is neither. All I know is this—*if we do not change, we will not get different results than we already have.* If your life is full and rich and helping others and mattering—then perhaps continuing to walk down the same road is the best course. But if your life is less than its potential, if you have backed down when you might have risen up, if you have chosen safety over risk, if a voice inside you cannot be quieted—perhaps it is time to look fear in the eye... and move past it.

I believe that we can only overcome fear when we embrace it. We acknowledge we are scared and terrified, but we look at the situation from all angles, make the best decision we can, and then we take a deep breath and go forward.

Your Turn:

When in your life have you faced fear and overcome it? What was the result? When have you faced fear and stepped backward? What was the result? Is there any area in your life now where you need to—as Susan Jeffers says in her book title— "Feel the fear and do it anyway?"

Today's Affirmation:

I accept fear as a calling to grow.

Going Further

One of the scariest times for two hundred thousand women in the United States each year is the day they learn they have breast cancer. Just as relevant today as it was more than twenty years ago when the organization was founded, National Breast Cancer Awareness Month (NBCAM) wants women of all ages to know that breast health is a year-round concern.

Visit the Susan G. Komen for the Cure website for downloadable breast self-examination cards at www.komen.org or call (800) 462–9273. For in-depth information on breast cancer, visit the newly redesigned National Breast Cancer Awareness Month website at www.NBCAM.org.

October 9

"Perhaps the greatest enigma of time is that nobody has enough of it, yet we almost always succeed in wasting it. Time is different from every other resource we utilize. When we don't have money, we don't buy excess clothing. Yet when we don't have time, we still fritter it away on whatever may pop up. Perhaps the explanation behind such odd resource waste is that we don't think of time as a resource. Everybody knows that time is precious and should be utilized carefully, but few people treat time with the respect that it deserves."
—**Pete Mockaitis, author of The Student Leader's Field Guide**

Good morning! An acquaintance of Pete's who is also a Good Morning reader sent in this quote. Debbie shared that:

Pete went to high school with my daughter. He read leadership books as a hobby, served as president of a ton of organizations, was a National Merit semifinalist and went on to my alma mater, the University of Illinois. While there, he continued to assume leadership roles and was frustrated by the lack of leadership books aimed toward students. He ended up writing a book himself and having it published before his college graduation.

Like Debbie, I am struck by the sentence: "Perhaps the greatest enigma of time is that nobody has enough of it, yet we almost always succeed in wasting it."

Almost daily, I hear complaints of people running out of time or not having enough time to get things done. Yet Pete is right: We still manage to fritter time away instead of managing it as the asset it is. This isn't to say that we should be working around the clock or goal, chasing every hour of every day, but we should make sure we are spending our time in alignment with our personal priorities. When we spend out time more wisely, we release ourselves from the "never enough time" trap.

Your Turn:

Where have you been letting time escape that doesn't align with your priorities? What can you do to change that this week?

Today's Affirmation:

I value and spend my time wisely.

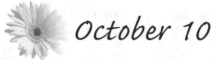

October 10

> *"If you don't change your thoughts your life will be
> like this forever. Is that good news?"*
> —*Dan Miller,* **Releasing Principles
> for Work/Life Excellence!**

Good morning! This morning's quote is quite a reality check and eye-opener, isn't it? Odds are when you read it, you had an immediate reaction... either positive or "Oh, no!" The quote is so true though: Our thoughts become our actions and our actions become our history and our history becomes our legacy. Given that this begins with thought, what type of legacy are you creating?

What have your recent daily thought patterns been like? Are you feeling mostly positive and influencing those around you in positive ways? Have you been somewhat self-absorbed, missing chances to help others? Are you wrapped in negativity or stress without a plan to break free?

Your Turn:

What was your reaction to today's quote? Use the self-check technique of auditing your thinking each hour on the hour if you want to answer today's questions differently.

Today's Affirmation:

I control my thoughts; they are positive and supportive to myself and others.

October 11

"Character is the ability to carry out a decision, after the emotion of making that decision has passed."
—Author unknown

Good morning! I smiled when I read this quote—and I think many of you will nod in recognition of the truth contained in this simple sentence. How often do we make decisions based on a moment of clarity and inspiration, only to find that the energy we put into its implementation doesn't match that original moment of inspiration?

It is in these moments that character is built. When we make a decision and then follow through, despite life's hurdles, we strengthen our minds and souls. We develop perseverance and commitment. We move past the "imaginary" and into the "reality" of seeing our inspiration come to fruition.

For this reason, we should be careful in our commitments. Let us only commit and decide to do those things that align with our priorities and that we hold dearly. Then, once the decision is made, let us build our character by transforming our inspiration into reality.

Your Turn:

In what area of your life have good intentions led to little results? What commitments do you hold most dear? What steps do you need to take to see them through?

Today's Affirmation:

I thoughtfully follow through on each decision I make.

 ## October 12

> *"Limitations live only in our minds. But if we use our imaginations, our possibilities become limitless."*
> —*Jamie Paolinetti*

Good morning! Did you know that the story of your life creates a movie in your mind? The movie you have created thus far goes with you everywhere. Each time you meet a new experience or moment, it is broadcast onto this "movie screen of the mind" and interpreted through the lens of your life. Not only do you have your own personal movie, but so does everyone else you meet. Because no two life experiences are the same, no two movies are the same. Each of us sees and interprets the moment based on our unique experiences.

Understanding this concept can help us learn a lot about ourselves and about our interactions with others. Differences of opinion and disagreements are easy to explain, given we are all operating from our unique experience.

Just as a television screen has controls for "brightness" and "contrast," our screen has controls. Our beliefs, emotional state, physical energy, needs, history, and genetic disposition act as controls. Each control can fluctuate, creating many different ways our moments can be viewed. Our focus and priorities are the channels of our lives. An even-more-important similarity between your mind and a television: If your television is not working, displaying only static, or has bad coloring, guess who is in charge of fixing it?

Your Turn:

What channels are playing in your mind? Where is your focus? If you do not like what you are seeing in your life, change the contract or change the channel.

Today's Affirmation:

I make healthy and enriching choices.

October 13

> *"Death is not the biggest fear we have; our biggest fear is taking the risk to be alive—the risk to be alive and express what we really are."*
> —*Don Miguel*

Good morning! When I was in my late teens I read Susan Jeffers' book, *Feel the Fear and Do It Anyway*. The book changed my life and the title became one of my personal guidelines for living. I knew that to get from point A to point B, I would have to learn to *love* fear. Fear would have to be my friend and something that would propel me forward and encourage me to challenge myself, instead of something that would make me cower in a corner.

Fair enough: Fear can be scary. Fear can cause people to get very creative in how they deal with it. Instead of confronting fear, many people come up with excuse after excuse to avoid the discomfort that fear brings. These people view fear as a negative emotion instead of a positive one. Many people make decisions in an attempt to avoid fear. They don't walk the tight-rope; they don't cross the line; they don't take a chance, or a risk, because something scares them. Sometimes it is external. More often, it is the monsters they make themselves.

Your Turn:

Where in your life has fear been influencing your choices? Today, take a moment to separate your fear from reality. Are you making any monsters in your life?

Today's Affirmation:

I live fully and without fear.

Inspirations

Read articles on facing fear and learn more about Susan's great book at www.susanjeffers.com.

October 14

"Act as if failure is impossible, and your success will be assured. Wipe out every thought of your not achieving your objectives, be brave and set no limits on the workings of your imagination. Never be a prisoner of your past. Become the architect of your future ... and you will see that nothing can stop you."
—*Author unknown*

Good morning! How would your life change if you realized that 90 percent of the obstacles you face in reaching your dreams are created by your mind? I don't know what the actual percentage is, but I truly believe that the obstacles thrown in our way from life are incredibly outnumbered by the obstacles thrown in our way by ourselves.

If I compare goals I have pursued where I entered them with self-doubt, to goals that I pursued with complete conviction—the results are always the same. I succeeded when the conviction was there, and I faltered when it wasn't. How can we expect the world to line up and be on our team, if we aren't even on our own team?

Before we chase a dream, we need to encourage, believe, and trust in ourselves. We need to come face-to-face with our doubts and fears, and then overcome them, step-by-step—that is what challenging life is all about.

Your Turn:

Where in your life have you been sabotaging yourself? What steps do you need to take to get out of your own way? Who can support you?

Today's Affirmation:

I confidently pursue my dreams.

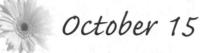 *October 15*

> *"Your vision will become clear only when you look into your heart. Who looks outside, dreams. Who looks inside, awakens."*
> —*Carl Jung*

Good morning! If, this morning, you were asked to make a list of anything holding you back from your dreams, what would it look like? Do you need more time? Do you need more knowledge? Is someone preventing you from getting where you want to be or not assisting you as you desire? Is your location holding you back? Is a friend or family member unsupportive? How many of the items on your list are external issues?

If you find that your list holds many external issues—you are likely suffering from "excuse syndrome." There is always, always, always, a reason not to do something or proceed down a certain path. Many people walk around this world seeking out these excuses, because then they don't have to challenge life. Comfort is comfortable, but it isn't where we find our full potential.

When I entered book publishing and the author world, I had absolutely no knowledge of what I was doing. I didn't have a degree in publishing (actually, I didn't have a degree, period). I didn't have any business, marketing, website, or sales courses. I didn't have any money, so I had to work full-time as a waitress while learning the ins and outs of the field I wanted to enter.

Yet I had one thing that would ensure that nothing would stand in my way—faith that if I wanted to accomplish something, I could and I would. I read book after book after book on every area I needed to develop. I read through complete and boring technical manuals to learn web programming. I called people who had done what I wanted to do and I asked for their advice. I ran away from excuses and ran toward the reality that I wanted to create.

As I come into contact with many people who are struggling to move forward, I can often see where the struggle stems from, from a mile away. Many of these people are waiting for some "external alignment" and won't move forward until that occurs. Of course, when you run into these people a year later, guess where they are standing? In the same place. Comfort is comfortable, but it isn't where our full potential is found.

Your Turn:

Where have you used excuses or waiting for "something else" to happen in order to avoid the time, energy, and risk involved in chasing a goal? How is that working for you? What if, today, you decided to stop waiting for something else to happen and instead made it happen yourself? How would that change where you would be in one year?

Today's Affirmation:

I rid my life of excuses and put that energy toward action steps.

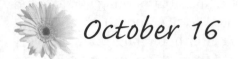 *October 16*

"You're all obliged to do what you love because that's where your gifts lie and those gifts belong to all of us."
—*Barbara Sher*

Good morning! This quote puts a new perspective on cherishing and nurturing our unique gifts and talents.

As women, many of us put our own interests aside in our natural instinct to care for others. Some women have a deep-rooted love or goal, but shy away from it due to fear of failure. Barbara's quote points out that our unique gifts, when nurtured, are gifts for the world to enjoy. When we choose to put our unique gifts on the back burner, or to shy away from them, we rob not only ourselves of that gift experience, but everyone else as well.

Undoubtedly, we each have unique gifts and qualities to bring to this world. If doubt and neglect were replaced with belief and respect, I can only imagine how much better the world would be.

Your Turn:

What gifts do you have yet to give? What step can you take today to nurture those gifts?

Today's Affirmation:

I nurture and share my unique gifts with the world.

Going Further

The Meyers-Briggs Type Indicator (MBTI) is one of the most well-known tools to help you uncover your unique abilities. The results can help you in relationships, learning, choosing a vocation, self-growth, and more. To read the history of this Jung-based model visit www.myersbriggs.org/

You can take a paid assessment online at www.mbticomplete.com/ which is approved by the Meyers-Briggs Foundation. (Sample reports are available at www.cpp.com/samplereports/reports.asp#mbti.) Alternatively, there is a free test based on the MBTI at www.humanmetrics.com/cgi-win/JTypes2.asp

October 17

> *"Failure seldom stops you. What stops*
> *you is the fear of failure."*
> —*Jack Lemmon*

Good morning! I would encourage everyone to read today's quote several times. Then, recall some times where you perceived the results of your actions as a "failure." Did you actually fail, or did you simply never try? Most often, it is the fear of failure that stops us from committing wholeheartedly and trying. We don't actually fail, we just fail to try.

One of the most beautiful freedoms we can attain is the ability to accept what result will come our way—and try wholeheartedly anyway. Releasing ourselves from the result and focusing instead on our effort creates focus, clarity, and a rich future.

Your Turn:

Where are you so busy looking at the result and whether it is attained or not that you are avoiding giving your all to the moment? Put on your blinders and block out the future so you can focus on the now.

Today's Affirmation:

Nothing stands between me and giving my best effort daily.

October 18

"The man is richest whose pleasures are cheapest.
—Henry David Thoreau

Good morning! I was enjoying lunch with two friends and my daughter when our conversation turned to winning the lottery. The jackpot had reached a record high and one of our friends had purchased several tickets. She was posing the infamous question: What would you do if you won the lottery?

One of my friends seemed a bit surprised when Sara and I said that we wouldn't change much about our lives. As the discussion went on, I realized that Sara and I are in the right spot, doing the right things, and truly living a rich life. I knew this because with all the money in the world, there were very few alterations we would seek. We had found true wealth without mountains of money.

What is wealth anyway? True wealth, heart-wealth, cannot be connected to money (thank goodness), otherwise it could disappear in an instant. A rich life comes from within. I believe a rich life is composed of self-value and self-esteem, making a difference, laughter, rewarding connections with others, and commitment to purpose. If I had the opportunity to trade in those qualities for the winning ticket, I would not even be tempted. That isn't to say we can't have monetary wealth and heart-wealth. Many people have both. But it is important to remember that the two are not dependent on one another.

If I could break down true wealth, I believe it is:

W - Working with passion and commitment on something you love

E - Esteem in your worth, purpose, and value

A - An attitude that keeps a smile on your face and the faces of others

L - Love for those around you and for yourself

T - Time to engage in your life priorities

H - A heart big enough to give and receive freely

Your Turn:

Our happiest moments often revolve around finding joy in simple day-to-day activities such as laughing with a child or dinner with a girlfriend. Take some time today to think about what wealth means to you. What are three things you can do this week to create more heart-wealth in your life?

Today's Affirmation:

The best wealth in the world is a wealth money cannot buy.

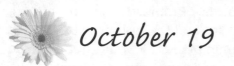 # October 19

> *"Anyone can carry his burden, however hard, until nightfall. Anyone can do his work, however hard, for one day. Anyone can live sweetly, patiently, lovingly, purely, till the sun goes down. And this is all life really means."*
> *—Robert Louis Stevenson*

Good morning! I love this quote. How often do we put our energy into tomorrow's issues instead of focusing on what is on our plate for today? When we spread our energy between to-day and tomorrow, it is hard to carry the challenges of the day or enjoy the fruits at hand. However, when we walk with focus, step-by-step, we find that in one day—sunset to sundown—we can carry whatever we must, love and enjoy to the fullest, work and share at our full potential. This focus is the single most important ingredient for living a wonderful day.

Your Turn:

Draw your attention to today and the joys and challenges at hand. Whenever tomorrow or yesterday drift into view, refocus on the matters at hand. Live richly in the moment.

Today's Affirmation:

I accomplish everything I need to accomplish today.

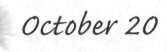

October 20

*"Strong, positive beliefs are the foundation upon which
all great lives are built. Such beliefs are magical.
They can turn the ordinary into the extraordinary,
the simple into the profound, and a single
step into a giant leap."*
—*Beth Mende Conny,* **Dare to Believe**

Good morning! I have met many positive people in my life and they all seem to have extraordinary tales to tell. I also have met many pessimistic people in my life, and their stories rarely capture my attention beyond the telling; for, somewhere along the way, they have fallen sour to their circumstances and are not willing to budge from their lower ground, no matter what you say.

Make a point to surround yourself with positive people—their strength is magnetic, infectious, invigorating, and often magical. Surrounding yourself with pessimistic people can be draining, even exhausting, and will only, if not sooner then later, pull you down and decrease your "mind-set."

Your Turn:

Take a moment today to make a date with an optimistic person who inspires you.

Today's Affirmation:

I surround myself with people who inspire and encourage me.

Inspirations

It began as a week-long party. It became a nationally celebrated event. Now it's a movement for change. In 2007 over 5 million kids in fifty-one countries celebrated Character Counts week (the third week of October). To learn more, view the online PDF brochure at charactercounts.org/pdf/charactercountsbrochure.pdf or register online at www.charactercounts.org to access many free resources.

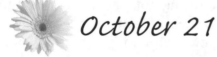

October 21

> *"Never forget that the first step in getting help is asking for it."*
> *—Brook Noel*

Good morning! We are not Superwoman: She had a cape. Most superheroes even have sidekicks: Batman has Robin, Superman can count on Lois Lane, Luke Skywalker has Yoda and Obi-Wan. I don't know why so many women feel the need to be Superwoman, or do it all on their own. While it might seem that that makes us more independent or stronger, it doesn't make a lot of sense if you step back a minute and think about it.

How many people in this world operate completely independently, capable of doing it all themselves? I can't think of a successful CEO who isn't backed by talented executives. I am unaware of a politician that isn't helped by aides or campaign managers. Schools and churches have boards for guidance. So why do we think that we can, or should, "do it all?"

Instead of striving to "do it all" or "beating yourself up" when you can't do it all, switch to a "team-spirit" mentality. Find supportive players to be a part of your team and ask for help when you need it. Doing everything ourselves doesn't make us stronger—it makes us more lonely and needlessly stressed.

Your Turn:

How have you tried to "do it all" in your life? What were the results? Who can be a part of your support team? Who can you ask for help?

Today's Affirmation:

Today I let go of trying to "do it all" and focus on building a network of support and encouragement.

Going Further

Take a look at your to-do list. Choose at least five items to ask for help with this week.

October 22

"If you want happiness for an hour—take a nap.

If you want happiness for a day—go fishing.

If you want happiness for a month—get married.

If you want happiness for a year—inherit a fortune.

If you want happiness for a lifetime—help others."
—***Chinese Proverb***

Good morning! I enjoyed this proverb: It contains so many of the things we try in our pursuit of happiness. Yet, its bottom line reveals what we quickly realize to be true if we review our happiest moments—we create happiness when we help others. When we continually give of ourselves, we will be hurt from time to time, but we will also realize very rich rewards—a type of happiness that can't be taken away because we know we made a difference.

Your Turn:

As you go about your day, be observant of opportunities to help others. Watch how those acts of kindness bring an unparalleled joy to the soul.

Today's Affirmation:

I am never too busy to lend a helping hand.

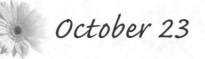

October 23

> *"Do not ask God to guide your footsteps*
> *if you are not willing to move your feet."*
> **—Unknown**

Good morning! When I first read today's quote, I immediately wished I could print it in neon across the sky. Some people pray to God for change or guidance. Others just *want* change or guidance. Either way, there is always one very important question that needs to be asked: "What are you prepared to do?"

While we might desire, yearn, or wish for change, if we aren't prepared to be an active participant, then we should not expect much. Being open to change is an important first step; meeting change halfway with action is the next.

Your Turn:

How active have you been in pursuing change? Make sure your actions are equal to, or exceed, your desire.

Today's Affirmation:

I do not wait for change, I create it.

October 24

"Christmas, children, is not a date. It is a state of mind."
—Mary Ellen Chase

Good morning! Christmas Eve is officially sixty days away, and this morning I want to encourage you to plan ahead for the festivities! For many years, I longed to host holiday festivities, but somehow it was always December 16th when I arrived at my planning. Choose and lock-in a date now! Send your invites... the earlier the better! Here are seven ideas for holiday entertaining.

Christmas Cocktails: Invite families over to enjoy cocktails and appetizers. If there are many young children in the group, consider hiring a babysitter or two to help out. Providing a babysitter will encourage those with young children to attend, as it is one less detail to organize during a busy season. If some of the children attending are older, set up a Christmas craft area for them to work on projects while the adults are visiting.

Caroling Party: You don't need to have a spectacular vocal range to enjoy caroling! We caroled every year when I lived in Portland, even though none of us could carry a tune. That actually made it all the more fun as each house tried to listen and lavish us with praise... only to finally encourage us to keep quiet by feeding us Christmas treats. All you need is a group of six or more "singers" who aren't scared to belt out a tune. This is by far one of my favorite Christmas activities and it always ends with cherished memories and laughter.

Have people meet at your house and dress for a night outside. Serve appetizers and cider while waiting for guests. Once assembled, enjoy the caroling and regroup at your house for Christmas cookies and cocoa, cider, or an after-dinner drink.

Gingerbread House Party: I don't know about you, but even when I buy the ready-to-assemble kits, my gingerbread houses never quite look like the ones on the package! Every year my scrapbook has a picture of "my" gingerbread house, and then a picture of the one featured on the ready-to-assemble box. I must get a box missing some walls or something every year... One year, I actually took to super gluing my building together! Fortunately, through a Gingerbread House Party, I have discovered there are others whose houses suffer the same fate.

To host a Gingerbread House Party: supply Gingerbread House ready-to-assemble kits or have each person bring their own. Take an afternoon to build your houses. People can build in teams or families. Vote for the favorite house.

Ornament Party: Have a make-your-own ornament party. Visit a craft store and choose a project sheet. Have each person make two ornaments: one to take home, and one to put in an exchange, so that each person leaves with a "gift ornament."

Decorating Party: Have a garland party and ask each person to bring a bag of items that could be used in a garland. Mix-and-match items to create garlands for all.

Holiday Potluck: Potlucks create a fun party any time of year! To add a holiday note, have attendees bring a recipe that has a story behind it from their family. Share recipes and stories. You can also ask guests to bring copies of their recipes on 8.5 x 11 paper. Compile recipes into sets so each guest can take home a full set of recipes. Set out folders to place recipes in.

Your Turn:

What holiday festivities would enrich your season? Plan now to make them a reality.

Today's Affirmation:

I celebrate the season through early preparation.

Going Further

http://www.evite.com/app/cms/ideas/christmas

The crew at Evite has put together some wonderful planning tools. They have planning guides and tools to help you create a budget, decide how much of specific beverages to have on hand, menu plans, party checklists, and more. Combine these online tools with your invitations for an easily organized festivity.

October 25

"Dare to believe—because believing makes it so."
—Beth Mende Conny

Good morning! Take time this week to focus on what you truly believe. Dare to dream, to cast away all doubts, to just believe—in yourself, your family, your talents, your strengths, and all the positive forces at work around you. This power to think positively will catapult you toward success, renewed vigor, less stress and anxiety, and the ability to be self-fulfilled. Think of your positive thinking as a powerful energy—a prophecy of sorts: that if you will it to be positive, it will be! If you will it to be less than satisfactory, it probably will be that instead!

Your Turn:

We are but the authors and the tellers of our own stories... the architects and the builders of our own dreams. Think only the best for yourself and then go out there and put those thoughts to good use! You'll be amazed at how you can tackle even the toughest situations.

Today's Affirmation:

I dare to believe.

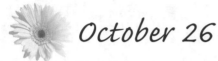

October 26

> *"How beautiful a day is when kindness touches it."*
> —*Author unknown*

Good morning! When I was ten, I was a math whiz. My mother was always helping kids in our neighborhood and we often took in a child who might have been having problems in his home. One year, we took in a young man who had just turned eighteen and wanted to begin a military career. Unfortunately, his education had been lacking and he had been unable to pass the math test.

I went to my school principal and asked if he could loan me elementary math books. I started tutoring "my" soldier-to-be for two hours each night, beginning with first-grade math and gradually working toward military requirements. A year later, when he took his test, he passed and began a successful military career.

We lost touch after he entered the military. Then, a decade later he left a message on my mother's answering machine. The message was short and sweet, thanking us for taking him in and specifically for the tutoring. He shared that he had since married, had children, and continued to enjoy his service for our country. The call was a blessing my mother and I will remember forever.

Sharing our thankfulness with others dramatically enriches our lives and the lives of those we thank. This can be done in person, through a phone call, or through a card.

Your Turn:

Take a few minutes to generate a list of people you would like to thank. They can be current people in your life or people from long ago. Throughout the holiday season, aim to thank one person from this list each week.

Today's Affirmation:

I am never too busy to thoughtfully express my thankfulness.

Inspirations

Need ideas on how to express your thanks? Visit these websites for ideas:

http://www.cardsshoppe.com/wording.asp

http://www.brownielocks.com/notes.html

Tip: I keep a set of thank-you cards and a pen in a plastic bag in my purse and use unexpected time openings (traffic, waiting for a doctor's appointment) to send sentiments of thanks.

October 27

*"There are costs and risks to a program of action,
but they are far less than the long-range risks
and costs of comfortable inaction."*
—John F. Kennedy

Good Morning! Often, when our attitude is suffering, it is because we have not connected purpose with our actions. Many people make the mistake of believing that only great feats have purpose—world peace, feeding the hungry, organizing a protest or petition, holding a fund-raiser, donating to a blood drive. While these are great achievements, we can also bring purpose to everything in our lives—including tasks like doing the laundry or grocery shopping—with Mini Mission Statements.

For many people, the only real introduction to the idea of mission statements has been through the movie *Jerry McGuire*. Mission statements are not stuffy or dry corporate documents, but rather well-articulated visions that are meant to energize people and help us hone in on our core purpose. Most companies use a mission statement to help remain focused on their core values or purpose.

Let's use grocery shopping for our example. Since grocery shopping is not my favorite task, I could easily sigh, drag my feet, and pout when I have to go to the grocery store. Or I could use a Mini-Mission Statement like: "Today is the day I always do my grocery shopping. Grocery shopping is a way for me to promote my family's health by selecting nutritious foods."

Whether it is in work or home life, most people are used to mission statements that are made once, and then occasionally glanced at. I strongly encourage you to make a million mission statements. You can create a mission statement for every errand, every task, or for a goal, for a day, for a week, for a month, or for a life. The more purposeful statements you make, the more focused and energized you will become. The reason is simple: Mission statements clear away all the "mind clutter." When your mind is presented with a mission, it will act like a computer and work to complete it. Successful businesspeople are masters at using mission statements to stay on course while avoiding diversions and distractions. We can use this business template to achieve success in our personal lives. Adapting regular mission statement use in our daily lives will help us stay on course while avoiding diversions, distractions, and destructive thinking.

Your Turn:

Today, create a positive mission statement for the majority of the activities you do. A mission statement should be something easy enough to commit to memory and strong enough to give you a purpose. Writing down the statement will increase its effectiveness.

Today's Affirmation:

I bring the power of purpose to my daily activities.

 October 28

> *"To poke a wood fire is more solid enjoyment than almost anything else in the world."*
> —*Charles Dudley Warner*

Good morning! How many times have you found yourself getting angry at a disobedient computer? What about getting tired of a ringing phone? Have you ever heard a child get frustrated with a video game? Do you have a spouse or child whose cell phone seems to ring incessantly? Just as we choose to have these technologies that make our lives easier (said tongue in cheek), we can also choose to turn them all off once in a while.

In Wisconsin, we have many thunderstorms, and with them many power outages. We are all amazed at how quiet the house is when the power goes out. There isn't any "hum" of electronics, beeping instant messengers, radios or televisions left on—there is just silence. We navigate the house by candle-light and flashlight without the option of electronics. Depending on what we were doing at the time of the power outage, it is sometimes frustrating. Yet after ten to twenty minutes without electricity, we all slow down, and then start laughing and talking. (The only part that is truly frustrating is resetting all the digital clocks in the house!)

After a particularly stormy spring, one summer I began to miss the storms and our "quiet time." As a result, I began scheduling "power outages" once a week for our family. Once a week we turn it all off. Once a week we slow down and enjoy. Try implementing an electricity and phone-free night in your home once per week or month. If your family won't join you (although young kids quickly embrace the idea) do it a couple of hours one day when you are home alone. Create a time and space for life to be simple.

Your Turn:
Choose a time this week to "turn it all off" and enjoy quality time without interruptions, either by yourself or with your family.

Today's Affirmation:
Each week I take time to rejuvenate and connect by turning off technology and turning on heartfelt communication.

Inspirations:

Here are a dozen technology-free ideas for you to consider:

Do a puzzle

Read a book

Take a nature walk

Write in a journal

Look through photographs

Tell stories

Create or build something

Skip rocks at a lake

Plant a tree

Play cards

Build a campfire and enjoy s'mores

Star-gaze

Carve a pumpkin

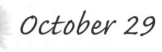

October 29

> *"God, grant me the serenity to accept the things I cannot change; the courage to change the things I can; and the wisdom to know the difference."*
> —*The Serenity Prayer*

Good morning! One of the many gifts that we are able to share with others is a positive mental attitude. People who can hold their head high and believe in the world live more fulfilled, healthy, and happy lives.

Every morning when we wake up, we have the choice of being positive or negative, happy or grumpy. Every moment of every day, we have that choice. Each time we encounter someone, we have the ability to choose how we react to them. Happiness and fulfilled living lie within these choices.

Likewise, we will run into people throughout our lives who we do not understand, would like to change or help, but are resistant. Our own peace of mind can be found in the knowledge that we have the choice of how to interact with these people. It is not our job to try to change or control their behavior: It's only our job to choose our response to them.

Your Turn:

The Serenity Prayer has brought hope, encouragement, and peace to people for decades. If you do not know it by heart, memorize it now. Recall it when you are faced with the question of how to respond in a trying situation.

Today's Affirmation:

God, grant me the serenity to accept the things I cannot change; the courage to change the things I can; and the wisdom to know the difference.

 ## October 30

"There is no better way to thank God for your sight than by giving a helping hand to someone in the dark."
—*Helen Keller*

Good morning! I have always been moved by the courage, strengths, and compassion Helen Keller shared, both in word and deed. She lived a life that many couldn't imagine (and many couldn't handle) and she lived her life with more passion and bravery than many of us who have more blessed lives do. Her words offer an insight into her guiding principles.

I find this quote to be profound and one I will remember daily. How rich we could make this world if we not only "give thanks" for our blessings, but also "live thanks" for our blessings. While we can be thankful for our sight (or any blessing), let us also live thankfully by sharing our blessings. Need ideas on how to reach out and share with others? Visit www.volunteermatch. org to get started.

Your Turn:

What are you grateful for? How can you "live thanks" as well as "give thanks"?

Today's Affirmation:

Today, I live and give thankfully.

October 31

"Be who you are and say what you feel, because those who mind don't matter and those who matter don't mind."
—*Dr. Seuss*

Good morning! I stumbled across this quote on the Internet while reading a graduation speech from a college I have never heard of. I thought it was interesting advice. How often do we catch ourselves censoring what we might say, or trying to suppress or change how we feel because we are worried about how someone might respond? When we do this long enough, we begin to lose our connection with our self.

To live an authentic life and be true to our journey, we have to be able to express and share how we feel. We have to be able to be the real "us." Dr. Seuss has been right about many-a-thing, and I think he is right-on in this quote, as well.

Your Turn:

Do you find yourself trying to change your actions or words to please others? Remember that each of us is unique and one of the greatest gifts we can give in life is being true to who we are.

Today's Affirmation:

I appreciate my uniqueness and express it openly and thoughtfully.

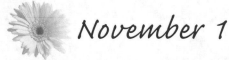

November 1

> *"We make a living by what we get but we make a life by what we give."*
> —**Winston Churchill**

Good morning! The first-ever Christmas card was posted in England in the 1840s, and the practice soon became an established part of the buildup to the Christmas holiday. Over a billion Christmas cards are now sent every year in the United Kingdom, many of them sold in aid of charities. By starting early in the season, sending holiday greetings is a chance to journal, reflect, and connect.

Here is my system that helps me achieve my card-goal with ease:

I purchase a spiral notebook, about five inches wide by eight inches high, with colored paper, or paper with some sort of nice feel or design. It needs to be spiral and preferably also have a perforation mark to remove the pages easily.

On the inside cover, I list all of the people to whom I want to send special letters. (I have two card lists—one for a nonpersonalized card with the standard Merry Christmas wish, and another list for people who I want to send a special message to.) I then keep this with me—all the time. If needed, I switch to a larger purse to keep this with me.

During unexpected breaks in my day, such as waiting for my daughter to emerge from an after-school event, waiting for a doctor appointment, train rides, etc. I pull out my notebook. I look through the names on the inside cover and, almost always, I immediately think of something I would like to share with one of the people on my list. I then turn to a blank page and begin writing. I don't worry about finishing my entire letter in one sitting; I simply share the compelling "thought" of the moment. I continue doing this, switching "people" as inspiration strikes.

Typically, my letters end up being two-to-four pages in length. (I am a writer—would you expect anything less?) When I check my progress weekly, if a letter is done, I remove it, place it in an envelope with THE ADDRESS AND THE STAMP, and tuck it in the front pocket of my holiday notebook. I then cross the name off the inside cover.

Your Turn:

This week, begin creating your own holiday card-sending notebook and generating a list of people you would like to send a special greeting to. Challenge yourself to send two to three letters per week.

Today's Affirmation:

I slow down to connect with those I love this season.

November 2

> *"Treat people as if they were what they ought to be and you help them become what they are capable of being."*
> —*Goethe*

Good morning! A lot of women have asked me: "How do I stay positive and focused when everything seems to be falling apart or becoming challenging?" Some of these women are battling unsupportive husbands or family members. Other women are struggling with gossip and negativity. Some women are fighting illness; others, depression. Other women are plagued by so many "minor" issues that they have developed a "major" weight on their shoulders.

I have been at that place, where choosing old patterns and turning away from progress seemed easier than turning toward challenging life to be the best it can be. Here are some of the tips and tools I have used to stay positive, regardless of what is going on in my life at the moment.

Let go of "fair": Sometimes when we get down, it is because we don't feel things are going as they should, or that we are getting the help we deserve. We can easily focus on the injustice of the situation or what is wrong with people or the situation around us. Focusing on the external won't help you internally. Instead, focus on what you can control and how you can positively influence others.

Remember that a lot can happen in a day: Just because this moment isn't ideal, doesn't mean the next moment can't be. Instead of focusing on what isn't working, be open to the idea that something great can happen today.

Count your blessings: When our surroundings or situation gets us down, it is easy to count the many things that are wrong with our life. Switch perspectives by counting your blessings. Like attracts like. Count how many things are wrong with your life and surely the list will multiply. Count the many things that are positive in your life and they will multiply instead.

Take a break: When we are tired (either emotionally or physically), staying positive can be an uphill battle that leaves us feeling frustrated. Instead of forcing it, take a break to recharge. Whether it is ten minutes or a day, find some space to relax and nurture yourself. Enjoy lunch or coffee with a positive friend. If you don't have a positive friend, have lunch or coffee with a positive book or inspirational audio.

Get a cheerleader: A community of like-minded, positive women can do wonders! Consider joining our e-group for a wonderful community of positive women to turn to for ideas and support.

I will survive: I love that song! Create a CD of music that is uplifting to you and listen to it when the weight of the world is on your shoulders. Recall other situations you have overcome and realize that you have the power to overcome whatever you are currently facing.

Your Turn:

Action is one of the greatest remedies for frustration, fear, worry, or sadness. Choose one area in your life that needs improvement right now and make improvement a priority in your life. Make a list of seven action steps you can take this week so that by next week the situation will be different.

Today's Affirmation:

I choose how I feel each day—and I choose to be positive.

 *November 3*

> *"Christmas, children, is not a date. It is a state of mind."*
> *—Mary Ellen Chase*

Good morning! One of my favorite holiday traditions is hosting a cookie exchange. A cookie exchange is a small holiday gathering where each guest prepares a designated number of their favorite cookies prior to the gathering. The day of the gathering, each guest receives a dozen of each attendee's cookies, and gives each attendee a dozen of their own. Recipes are also attached, so that your family can add new holiday favorites to your repertoire. Typically, at the gathering, guests sample cookies, share stories, and fun is had by all.

The cookie exchange is a great way to have some holiday time with the girls, stock up on many different kinds of cookies without preparing each one on your own, and enjoy the stories and recipes of others.

Scaled down version: You can do a scaled-down version of this. Consider hosting a "Cookie Tasting," where each person brings a dozen of their favorite cookies and copies of the recipe. This is more of a "tea party" event, where all of the goodies are shared at the actual event. This "scaled-down version" also works great for an office party.

How many people should I invite?

Use this handy table to determine how many people you would like to invite and how many cookies to ask them to bring. (Note: these calculations include enough cookies for each guest to have one of each cookie for tasting at the party.)

	Have each person prepare:	
Invite six people	three-and-a-half dozen cookies	six-and-a-half dozen cookies
Each guest will leave with	three dozen cookies	six dozen cookies
Invite eight people	four-and-a-half dozen cookies	eight-and-a-half dozen cookies
Each guest will leave with	four dozen cookies	eight dozen cookies
Invite ten people	five-and-a-half dozen cookies	ten-and-a-half dozen cookies
Each guest will leave with	five dozen cookies	ten dozen cookies
Invite twelve people	six-and-a-half dozen cookies	twelve-and-a-half dozen cookies
Each guest will leave with	six dozen cookies	twelve dozen cookies

Your Turn:

Simplify your holiday baking while enjoying a get-together with friends by hosting your own cookie exchange.

Today's Affirmation:

I celebrate the season.

Inspirations

You can find step-by-step checklists for hosting a cookie exchange at

allrecipes.com/HowTo/How-to-Host-a-Cookie-Exchange-Party/Detail.aspx

http://content.scholastic.com/browse/article.jsp?id=1322.

November 4

> *"A smooth sea never made a skillful mariner."*
> **—Unknown**

Good morning! I have a magnet that my mother gave me on my fridge, which says, "Whatever you are—be a good one." Becoming "good" or an "expert" on whatever mission we choose for ourselves is never an easy path. To truly be an expert, we have to be able to handle both the good and the bad. Life will never serve us just one or the other: It is always a mixed batch. Our ability to deal with what we are served will be the predominating factor in our level of happiness.

When you meet someone you find admirable, or hear an incredible story of courage or strength, you will usually find that these admirable and courageous people have faced much adversity in their lifetimes. What makes them admirable is that they chose to challenge adversity and learn from it—instead of laying down or letting go.

Your Turn:

Welcome the challenging times as a chance to sharpen your skills. You will need a varied tool set to deal with the ups and downs of life.

Today's Affirmation:

I challenge adversity.

November 5

> *"A peaceful home is as sacred a place as any chapel or cathedral."*
> —*Bil Keane*

Good morning! This Sunday, take a moment to think about your home and the comfort of your home. As we head toward the season of holidays, it is a perfect time to think about how you can make your home more peaceful and enjoyable for the family.

Is there a clutter-filled room you can simplify? (If you are a pack rat and the thought of throwing something away makes you cringe, just box up some items for now. You'll likely love the simplicity, but if not, you can easily put them back!)

Would adding a new painting or a plant (or, if you aren't a green thumb, a nice silk plant) give a fresh look to a tired room? How about new pillows to add color? Or rearranging the furniture? Perhaps some candles to light at night instead of bright lights?

Your Turn:

Think of one way to make your home more comfortable and welcoming this week, and then take action to achieve your goal.

Today's Affirmation:

My home is peaceful and welcoming and a place to rejuvenate.

 *November 6*

"If your everyday life seems poor, don't blame it; blame your-self; admit to yourself that you are not enough of a poet to call forth its riches; because for the creator there is no poverty and no poor indifferent place."
—*Rainer Marie Rilke*

Good morning! When I was twenty-one, I remember being profoundly moved by the words in Rainer Marie Rilke's book, *Letters to a Young Poet*. This one small volume contained some of the best advice I have ever read for living a rich life. I have made a habit of rereading it each year. It only takes an afternoon, and I think my entire copy is now highlighted, as different phrases have "spoken" to me at different times.

Rilke's words challenge us to take responsibility for our lives. He confronts us with many of our "mind games," and challenges us to move past them. If you have not read *Letters to a Young Poet,* I wholeheartedly recommend doing so. The book offers a series of letters between Rilke and a young poet in which he shares advice on living a full life. Although written many years ago, the book's advice is timeless. I have given the book as a gift many times, and have yet to find a bookstore that does not have several different copies on hand.

Often, we blame outward circumstances for our inner feelings. Rilke challenges us with: "Don't blame it, blame yourself." He knows that each life is beautiful, but we have to call forth the riches. Our life will only be poor and indifferent, if we choose to let it be so.

Your Turn:

You needn't be a poet or artist to "call forth the riches in life." Take a fresh picture. Change your perception. Count your blessings instead of your obstacles.

Today's Affirmation:

Each day, I uncover the many riches in my life.

Inspirations

Letters to a Young Poet can be read online here: http://www.carrothers.com/rilke_main.htm.

The letters were originally written to Franz Kappus, a nineteen-year-old student at the Military Academy of Vienna, of which Rilke was an alumnus. Discouraged by the prospect of military life, Kappus began to send his poetry to the twenty-seven-year-old Rilke, seeking both literary criticism and career advice. Their correspondence lasted from 1902 to 1908. In 1929, three years after Rilke's death, Kappus assembled and published the ten letters.

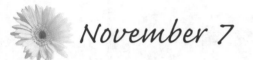

November 7

"Where so many hours have been spent in convincing myself that I am right, is there not some reason to fear I may be wrong?"
—*Jane Austen*

Good morning! Being right all the time takes incredible amounts of energy. It also entails a lack of listening skills, closed-mindedness, and generally makes a person unpleasant to be around. After all, no one can be right all the time—certainly none of us have all the answers. While offering advice and guidance is important, remember to be open to new ideas and know that there is great power in making mistakes and admitting to them.

Likewise, in personal situations we will often defend our actions. We may have had an argument with another person, and we go over and over the details, analyzing why our actions were "justified" or "correct," while the other person's weren't. It's important to realize that "being right" doesn't do you any good if you lose a friend or destroy a relationship.

Your Turn:

The next time you are focused on being the expert or being right, pause for a moment. Look at the situation through the other person's perspective and see if there is opportunity for growth and understanding.

Today's Affirmation:

Being caring and fair is more important than being right.

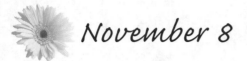 # November 8

> *"Who does not thank for little will not thank for much."*
> —*Estonian Proverb*

Good morning! On a recent trip, after a long day of meetings and a red-eye flight (and four-hour drive) the day prior, I hopped in my elevator. I played "elevator-woman," asking each person what floor they would like while juggling a binder, a briefcase, and a very, very, very big purse. Soon we were talking and sharing—as much as you can share in an elevator only operating between seven floors—but it was a simple act of courtesy and caring and I believe it brightened some other weary travelers today.

As I tucked myself into my hotel room that night, I wondered if true contentment is found in consistent courtesies. There is great warmth to be found in reaching out to strangers and family alike with a simple word, nod, or touch.

Your Turn:

Today, be consistently courteous. Reach out to each person you encounter with a simple kindness.

Today's Affirmation:

I am courteous and caring to all whom I encounter.

November 9

> *"Never underestimate the power of simple courtesy.*
> *Your courtesy may not be returned or*
> *remembered, but discourtesy will."*
> —*Princess Jackson Smith*

Good morning! With Thanksgiving just around the corner, I have been thinking a lot about ways to make more time in our busy lives to "give thanks."

When I think of giving thanks it is always elaborate... I want to celebrate someone or the gift they have brought to my life. But as we get busy, and busier still, often our elaborate plans of thanks, or homemade gifts, or handwritten notes, sadly get lost in the hustle and bustle. This quote is a wonderful reminder of how powerful a simple sentence, spoken or written from the heart, can be.

Your Turn:

Let's make "thanks" simple today. Tell as many people as you can "thank you" for whatever they have done, large or small. Buy some cards, send some emails, pick up the phone, sincerely thank the person at the drive-thru window—keep it simple. Look as many people in the eye as you can, and give them two heartfelt words that make all the difference: "Thank You."

Today's Affirmation:

I am thankful for my life and for all the people in it.

November 10

*"Sometimes you have to take the leap,
and build your wings on the way down."*
—*Kobi Yamada*

Good morning! Have you ever had a "hunch" about something? You know, that gut feeling that has words on the tip of your tongue, or an action you think you should do, but you squelch it? Then days, weeks, or months go by—and you realize the intuition you ignored was right? Maybe you had a reason to ignore it. Maybe everyone else disagreed with you and you couldn't find one fan of your idea or action. Maybe self-doubt got in the way, or fear, or anxiety. Whatever the reason, you ignored the hunch, only to learn later, that it was there for good reason.

Maybe the only thing more frustrating than not knowing an answer is realizing we knew the answer but didn't act on it. For whatever reason, we didn't listen to intuition's whisper.

Kobi's quote reminds me that intuition always has a purpose, though sometimes we can't see it right away. But these "heart messages" should be heeded and considered. Even without support, sometimes we have to "Take the leap and build our wings on the way down."

Your Turn:

Is there anything in your life right now where you have that "gut instinct" about what to do next? Take a moment today and honor that intuition. Listen to it; don't squelch it. These moments of intuition are blessings about the directions we need to take in our lives.

Today's Affirmation:

I honor, heed, and consider each of my intuitions.

 *November 11*

> *"A bad habit never disappears miraculously;*
> *it's an undo-it-yourself project."*
> *—Abigail "Dear Abby" Van Buren,*

Good morning! Raise your hand if you have ever discovered a bad habit and wanted it gone *now*! Examples:

- Eating too much
- Eating unhealthy foods
- Stress
- Negativity
- Negative self-talk
- Add your own

In today's world, we often look for instant gratitude. When we want change, we want it *now*! We seek a magic wand to make it "all better." The self-help and self-improvement industry is booming as we seek solution after solution to ease the areas where there is discomfort in our lives.

When we try to hunt down an instant solution to a problem that has grown over time, we might find ourselves frustrated or doubting our ability. We don't build these bad habits in a day, and nor do we remove them in a day. Instead, as Abigail Van Buren writes, "It's an undo-it-yourself project." We choose a course of action and take daily steps until we walk out of the bad habit and into the new habit.

Your Turn:

Choose a habit that needs some work. Spend twenty minutes today brainstorming small steps you can take to move yourself away from the bad habit and toward the good habit you desire to put in its place.

Today's Affirmation:

I can accomplish anything I set my mind to accomplish.

November 12

> *"Don't forget to salt the rice."*
> *—Artris Kelone*

Good morning! Jadenda shared the following when she sent me this quote:

This is something my father has been telling me since I was old enough to help in the kitchen. Since then, he and I have repeated it to my children, also. It was not until last week while putting a pot of rice on to cook and pondering the actions of my twenty-year-old that I heard my father's voice in a different light.

To most people, this advice might not mean anything except a reminder to put salt in the rice while it is cooking, because afterward it matters not how much you add: It will not turn out the same. But to a mother of a twenty-year-old, I now look at it as a word of warning about raising children. I also see how it could apply to all relationships. At twenty, it is too late or at least really hard, to instill good values. So if you do not do it while you're cooking the rice—or raising the child—sometimes it is too late. This applies to showing love, respect, and discipline.

And yes, it is hard sometimes to wait to see if I added just the right amount of salt to the rice.

Your Turn:

What relationships in your life need tending? Don't put off until tomorrow what you need to share today.

Today's Affirmation:

I pay close attention to the needs of those around me.

 ## November 13

> *"The smallest act of kindness is worth more than the grandest intention."*
> —Oscar Wilde

Good morning! While still within this seasons of thanks, let's keep that thankful spirit going. Yesterday, we focused on sharing our thanks through words. Today, let's share them through a deed.

Your Turn:

What is one deed you can do today to express your thanks to a deserving someone?

Today's Affirmation:

I make and take the time to thank those who are vital in my life.

November 14

> *"This is the moment you own."*
> *—submitted by Good Morning reader Julie*

Good morning! What a powerful six words. I think I am going to print this out, frame it, and put it on my desk! It is so easy to get sidetracked by what is coming around the corner, or the path we have traveled in the past. As our thoughts spiral and move away from the present, we lose the value of this very moment, because our focus is somewhere else.

Your Turn:

The most powerful place we can be is right here, right now. Let us "use this moment we own."

Today's Affirmation:

This is the moment I own. I spend it wisely.

November 15

> *"Never worry about the size of your Christmas tree.*
> *In the eyes of children, they are all thirty feet tall."*
> —*Larry Wilde,* **The Merry Book of Christmas**

Good morning! While Charles Dickens images might flash through your mind, most families also experience *War of the Roses* moments during the holiday season. A few conscious steps pre-holiday can maximize your memorable moments and minimize your headaches.

Dream a little: Take an hour to clearly think about what type of holiday you want to create and what memories you want to last. What's most important to you? We can't have the holiday we desire, if we don't know what it is we want.

Let go: Don't let external expectations extinguish your holiday spirit. Focus on the list you made each day to keep your priorities in focus.

Create versus compete: Instead of trying to outdo last year (or any other year), have a contest to add a new tradition. Choose a simple prize and have all the family members reveal their idea at dinner.

Your Turn:

In mid-November, have each family member share his or her favorite holiday moments (excluding gifts received!) from years passed. Talk about how you can all pitch in to create many more memories this season.

Today's Affirmation:

I take time to reflect on what the holidays mean to me.

November 16

"Courage is only an accumulation of small steps."
—*George Konrád*

Good morning! People often crave a feeling of confidence to support difficult steps. Many of us would like to feel that, when faced with adversity, we act in courageous ways. Many of us search for a strong "center" to guide our actions. Konrád's quote offers the simple formula for developing courage, and it is within reach for all of us.

We build courage not by taking risks, but by taking steps. As we take small steps forward in our lives, we build confidence. We master the art of taking the small step, and then we can take a little bigger step, and then another. Courage is the art of moving forward instead of standing still.

Your Turn:

What area of your life has been challenging you to develop courage? Where have you been caught in indecision or blame instead of action? We cannot accomplish anything, or move forward, when we are rooted in indecision. What steps will you take this month to foster a courageous life?

Today's Affirmation:

I am courageous. Each day I challenge myself to be my personal best.

November 17

"Happiness will never come to those who fail to appreciate what they already have."
—*Author unknown*

Good morning! For as many times as we have said, "patience is a virtue," you would think that the message would be drilled into our brains, and our society. But look around. Take any day, of any year, and see how little patience exists in the world we live in.

If you really want to see how lacking in patience the world is, get about twenty items and try going through the express lane at the grocery store. A loud chorus of sighs will start behind you.

How about road rage? Everyone is so intent on getting there, fast, faster, fastest. Or watch someone with a modem on the Internet. If it takes a computer screen more than twenty seconds to load, they'll start adjusting cords, wondering what is wrong and why the Internet is so slow. Never mind that not even a decade ago, most people had to journey to the library for the afternoon to gather information that is now delivered to the savvy web-surfer in seconds.

My mother is famous for pointing out how the lack of patience is so foolish when driving. Up in northern Wisconsin where I grew up, the roads were only occasionally speckled with traffic. Despite the beauty of the scenery around them, cars would zoom and race by. Once we got to the city and found ourselves at a traffic light, the car that passed us at ninety miles per hour was just a matter of a few feet in front of us. My mom would always laugh at how the drivers were so focused on the road and passing others that they missed the fall colors or spring blossoms.

Your Turn:

When you are charging around in daily life—ask yourself where exactly you are going. Is crossing the "finish" line a bit quicker worth missing the view?

Today's Affirmation:

While engaged on any journey, I remember to enjoy the view.

 ## November 18

> *"The happiest and most-efficient people in this world are those who accept trouble as a normal detail of human life and resolve to capitalize on it when it comes along."*
> —*H. Bertram Lewis*

Good morning! How do you react when trouble or difficulty come your way? Do you rise up or shrink back? Many people do not realize their true strength and power, and as a result they shrink back when trouble or conflict arises.

I can guarantee we will likely live more days that have some essence of conflict or trouble within them than days that are trouble-free. We have to own our strength and power, and develop skills to rise up. As trouble surfaces, accept it as a natural part of life. Then, capitalize on it by asking yourself: What can I learn or try that will make me stronger for the next thing that comes my way? Use troubles to experiment with creative problem solving and creative thinking. You will likely be surprised how many problems you can solve and you will be liberated by your positive action.

Your Turn:

Today, as trouble surfaces, accept it as a natural part of life. And then capitalize on it by asking yourself: What can I learn or try that will make me stronger for the next thing that comes my way?

Today's Affirmation:

Challenges are gifts to build my problem-solving ability and personal strength.

 *November 19*

> *"It is the personal thoughtfulness, the warm human aware-*
> *ness, the reaching out of the self to one's fellow man that*
> *makes giving worthy of the Christmas spirit."*
> —*Isabel Currier*

Good morning! Last night I was sharing with my friends stories, memories, and traditions of childhood holiday seasons. All of my favorite memories were not of gifts I had received, but of gifts I had given.

I especially remember one Christmas when a very good friend's father was stricken too ill to go out and get a tree. He was a very proud man (and up north, you went out into the woods and cut down your tree!) but he was now immobilized by multiple sclerosis, and his family's house was filled with concern and sadness.

My mom (who didn't go out and cut down her tree, but had hers delivered right to our door, by an old lumberjack in need of extra money) ordered two trees that year. As soon as they were delivered, we piled the largest one into my brother's truck and dashed over to our friend's house, caroling all the way.

That was many years ago now, but I can still feel the hugs, and the tears, and see the joy on the dad's face. He said it was the most beautiful tree he'd ever seen. We stayed for some hot chocolate, helped position and admire the tree—then we dashed home (caroling all the way) to decorate our own.

Your Turn:

What is one way you could reach out to someone in need this holiday season? Take action and watch how the gift of yourself is the greatest gift of all.

Today's Affirmation:

I enrich my holiday season through thoughtfulness.

November 20

> *"Some think it's holding on that makes one strong;*
> *sometimes it's the letting go!"*
> —*Sylvia Robinson*

Good morning! Oh, what a lesson today's quote holds! I can't tell you how many times I thought holding on would make me stronger, when in reality it was the letting go that helped me grow. I have learned that life is fluid—each moment is a gift.

Your Turn:

What have you been holding onto that is hurtful or that weakens you? Most likely these are things that keep us from moving forward. Perhaps we are holding onto an unrequited love; or an unrewarding friendship prevents us from making new friends or finding more fulfilling love. Identify something that you need to let go of—and then repeat today's quote while visualizing the letting go.

Today's Affirmation:

I let go of anything that hurts me. I welcome all things that encourage me.

 *November 21*

"What is Christmas? It is tenderness for the past, courage for the present, hope for the future. It is a fervent wish that every cup may overflow with blessings rich and eternal, and that every path may lead to peace."
—*Agnes M. Pharo*

Good morning! My mom began creating a Family Christmas book to collect our holiday recipes and stories. This family story, titled "The Woman and the Postman" is one I wanted to share with you this Thanksgiving season.

Once again the tiny, rural post office in our Northwood's Wisconsin town had been properly notified. The Postmaster, simply known as John, had received his yearly letter (addressed to "John"—first name only—"Post Office"—no street and number, no zip code, only the word "Town") asking him to select five little girls "from Santa's List" who would love to receive a Christmas Doll. Now, John knew everything and everybody—if you wanted to find out something, or get the local scuttlebutt, you went to John—so he set about checking his postal routes, making his recommendations, and had the season's list secretly delivered to the woman.

From about November 1st on, the woman's dining room table became covered with snippets of lace and ribbons, buttons and bows, velvets and satins—along with the five Madame Alexander dolls that had been ordered that year through the mail.

Her needles and thread in hand, and an old Singer sewing machine by her side, the woman began to weave her yearly Christmas magic. Party clothes, sportswear, ball gowns, warm winter coats—she fashioned them all—until each doll had a wardrobe beyond any girl's dreams.

A week before Christmas, she would have the dolls delivered to the stoop of the Post Office, beautifully wrapped and tagged for each child with a note from Santa. John would notify the families that a special package had arrived and needed to be picked up, before he closed on Christmas Eve.

The week after Christmas, John would usually receive a thank-you note, or two, or three, that needed to be delivered in return. Sworn to secrecy, he would pass on the child-scribbled notes to "whom it may concern."

Then, one fall a funeral came to pass. November came and went, and the list hadn't been asked for. The Christmas dolls didn't arrive, and the magic faded. Not long after that, John put in for retirement. The post office became renovated, with zip codes + 4, an automated sorter, updated routing and regulations, and rules too numerous to count or accept; a new postman was brought up from the city—all in the name of "progress." Still bound by his oath of secrecy, John's knowledge about the woman and the dolls retired with him.

Every year, when we'd go to my aunt's for Thanksgiving dinner, I'd always notice that her table had just been cleared of a sewing project. She would set a fine table and our family would eat and feast until we could barely eat any more. And then, over her delicious pumpkin pie, my talk would turn to speculation about the mystery dolls that would surely arrive (just as mine had) at the post office—just in time for Christmas. My Aunt Joan would just give me a wink and her yearly reply, "Surely, my dear, you'll have another piece of pie."

Your Turn:

While in the hustle and bustle of daily life, we often think that life is about gain, or accomplishment, or maintaining the *status quo.* It isn't. Life is about relationships, about love, about kindness, about caring. Those are the moments we all long for more of. As we move through the Thanksgiving season, remember what life is truly about. Find a way to "invisibly bless" someone.

Today's Affirmation:

I build blessings into every day.

November 22

> *"Feeling gratitude and not expressing it is like wrapping a present and not giving it."*
> —*William Arthur Ward*

Good morning! The *Journal of Personality and Social Psychology* conducted a three-week study, in which researchers found that participants who wrote a list of up to five things they were grateful for each day were not only happier and more satisfied with life, but also got more sleep and felt more refreshed when they awoke each morning than people who didn't.

Your Turn:

Have you been keeping up with a gratitude journal? If not, renew your commitment to do so today. If so, take some time today and scan the pages, realizing all the blessings life has given you.

Today's Affirmation:

I express my thankfulness daily, through word and action.

Inspirations

The top five Thanksgiving activities, according to Hallmark Research, include:

1. Spending time with family/spouse's family.

2. Enjoying a big meal.

3. Cooking/entertaining people in my home.

4. Going to someone else's home.

5. Involving friends and/or neighbors.

November 23

"A man too busy to take care of his health is like a mechanic too busy to take care of his tools."
—*Spanish Proverb*

Good morning! Today is Family Health History Day. As you gather with relatives over the holidays, set a special date to get together to build an accurate family health history. Having this information on hand can be a great screening tool for present and future generations.

In 2006, both my mother and I faced health challenges that could have been minimized by having an accurate family health history. My mother spent four days in ICU with high blood pressure later determined to be tied to pernicious anemia. Because my grandmother had passed away when my mother was four, she had not had this information. My challenge fell on the opposite end of anemia: iron overload. Having records of my grandparents or father would have helped the doctors detect clues to the cause and potentially reduced the number of tests I underwent.

To avoid my daughter having to face a similar challenge as an adult, I requested all of my health records and put them together in a family folder. I also did the same for my husband and mother. Health histories can be requested from the medical-records department of any health care provider. Usually, you will need to sign a release, and if you are collecting the records for personal safekeeping, they typically charge a nominal copying/processing fee.

Your Turn:

Make a list of your blood relatives. Do you know the basic health history of each family member? If the history is hazy, consider visiting the online tool mentioned in "Going Further" to build a more comprehensive health history.

Today's Affirmation:

I proactively take healthy steps.

Going Further

A computerized tool has been developed by the U.S. Surgeon General, the United States Department of Health and Human Services, and other agencies. This tool will make it easy for you to organize your family history information to share with family members or your doctor.

Visit http://www.hhs.gov/familyhistory/ for more information.

November 24

> *"Unselfish and noble actions are the most radiant pages in the biography of souls."*
> —David Thomas

Good morning! I have always enjoyed the Thanksgiving season, as it hasn't yet been diluted with gifts and commercialism. It speaks to one of the soul's greatest riches—*gratitude*.

So I will keep today's message short, but the "Your Turn" will be a little longer.

Your Turn:

Today say *thank you*! Contact ten people by phone or email, and express a heartfelt thank you. Life is wonderful and we have so many things to be grateful for. What are you waiting for? We have a lot of thanking to do!

Today's Affirmation:

Thank you, world, for all my blessings.

Going Further

Creating a tree of thanks: Purchase a large sheet of poster board or other large paper and some leaf stickers or leaf cutouts. Draw a simple tree base with many branches, so that most of the room is available for leaves. Have kids or guests write something they are thankful for on a leaf, along with their name, and then glue it to a branch on the poster board. Or, you can use decorative paper cut into circles and put a hole punch at the top. Place these, ornament-style, on a real or artificial tree to enjoy through-out the season. You can fill the tree up at Thanksgiving dinner, or have each family member add a couple of "leaves" per week. These paper ornaments can later be combined into a scrapbook along the theme of thankful-ness. (Note: you can keep this thankfulness theme going all-year long by using different ornaments: hearts for Valentine's Day, pumpkins at Halloween, Easter Eggs, etc.) This is a great way to remain aware of all the things to be thankful for as a family, while also creating a neat keepsake of life's blessings.

November 25

> *"Some men have thousands of reasons why they cannot do what they want to do, when all they need is one reason why they can."*
> **—Willie R. Whitney**

Good morning! You likely know the people to whom Willie is referring. No matter what it is that they desire, they can create a list of reasons that is longer than Santa's wish list as to why their goal is out of reach. You might even have some of those tendencies yourself. Most people do.

At some point, we all embrace the "I can" attitude. As babies learning to walk, we don't sit down after that first fall, plop our thumb in our mouth, and count the reasons we will never be able to walk like the "big people" all around us. But somewhere between those young years and adulthood, many of us do just that. We plop doubt in our minds and count the reasons why we will never be able to have the dreams that we truly desire.

How is it that we have become addicted to thinking: "I cannot" instead of "I can"? Of course, when we are babies we have a team of cheerleaders. Parents or relatives help us stand again, they hold our wobbly legs, and they shriek for joy as we make those first steps. Video cameras roll and lights flash in our eyes, as if our parents or support team has become paparazzi!

In our lives as adults, we often don't have that support network saying, "Get up and try again;" "Of course you can;" "You can do it!" And, in the absence of those positive voices, doubt creeps in.

I wonder what the world would look like if tomorrow we could all create a list of reasons "we can" versus reasons "we cannot."

Your Turn:

Your challenge for the day is twofold. Find someone you believe in and tell them today: "You can do it!" whether by email, phone, in-person, or a thoughtful card. Then, choose something you want in your life and create an ongoing list of the reasons that you can reach that goal.

Today's Affirmation:

Each day, I tell myself: "I can!"

November 26

> *"Happiness is in the heart, not in the circumstances."*
> —*Author unknown*

Good morning! The vision of the happy family eating home-made meals every night, having family time once a week, and anticipating the annual family vacation is a great one. But for the most part, it's just that: a vision. We are much more likely to go through "spurts" where we feel we are pulling together as a family, and go through times where it seems no matter what we try, we're falling apart.

Occasionally, our vacations will be wonderful. Other times they'll be filled with sick kids, sunburn, or lost luggage. Sometimes we will all sit down to eat together. Other times there is bound to be a last-minute meeting, an after-school sport, or, if we do all sit down—a burnt dinner because the chef is in shock at everyone's arrival.

But what makes the difference between the good trips and the bad? Take, for example, two families who have excitedly planned a picnic. The day for the picnic arrives—and storms arrive with it. There is no hope of the outdoor jaunt that the family craved. Why does one family complain about the weather, mope and pout, while another family throws the picnic blanket down on the living room floor, grabs the snacks and a board game and enjoys a day in?

It all ties back to priorities and attitude. If your priority is truly your family, sure it will be a disappointment that it's raining, but you can focus on the fact you still have your family together, and there are plenty of other ways to spend your time. If your focus is elsewhere, you are likely to mope, since the picnic probably became a vehicle for "using up the time," because you felt it necessary.

Your Turn:

When plans change and good intentions go awry, don't give up. Step back and look for ideas to make the most of what you have in the here and now.

Today's Affirmation:

I promote happiness and togetherness.

November 27

"We are not powerless specks of dust drifting around in the wind, blown by random destiny. We are each of us, like beautiful snowflakes—unique, and born for a specific reason and purpose."
—Elizabeth Kubler-Ross

Good morning! How tempting it can be to forget that we are each "unique, and born for a specific reason and purpose." Often, we compare ourselves to those around us, measuring our differences, instead of embracing our own uniqueness.

Truly internalizing that we "are born for a specific reason and purpose" means that we must embrace life, instead of hiding from it. We must get up: sometimes, when we would rather lay down. We must bounce back at times when we aren't feeling resilient. We must risk, when we would rather hide. That isn't an easy job to accept.

Many people choose to play the victim. "Surely, my purpose has been stripped from me after all of life's turmoil." Still others do not want a purpose. Leave the purpose-driven stuff to someone else, they think. You will recognize these people from their negativity or their numbness. They often lack passion for life and all the gifts that can be found within it. They are too scared to challenge life, so they convince themselves that those "purposes" and "rewards" are for "everyone else."

Hiding from our own purpose is a double-edged sword. While we minimize the risks we take and the bruises we get, we are left with a gnawing ache for "something more" in our lives.

The word "purpose" can be misleading. Obviously we aren't all going to be Martin Luther Kings, Mother Theresas, or Einsteins. That doesn't make our purpose any less important. Each of us has something distinct to contribute while we are here. It is something only we can give. And each gift, whether small, medium, or large, by whatever measure you use—impacts the world for eternity.

If you choose to hide from your purpose or not discover it, that also impacts the world for eternity. Erica Jong said it well, "And the trouble is, if you don't risk anything, you risk even more."

Your Turn:

Take some time to think about what "purpose" means in your own life. Can you clearly articulate your purpose in a sentence or two?

Today's Affirmation:

My purpose guides my priorities.

November 28

"Don't spend your precious time asking 'Why isn't the world a better place?' It will only be time wasted. The question to ask is 'How can I make it better?' To that there is an answer."
—*Leo F. Buscaglia*

Good morning! How often do we run into people who are complaining about the world around them, or notice that we have negative words about the situation we are in (or those situations surrounding us)? I have long believed that the quickest way out of emotional turmoil and negativity is to take a positive step forward—even if you aren't sure what direction to step in! I rarely ask, "Why is my role so difficult?" and instead ask: "What is my role for improvement?"

Your Turn:

One of the keys to successful living is to ask good questions. Try asking, "What can I do?" instead of "Why is this happening to me?"

Today's Affirmation:

I believe everything happens for a reason, and I move forward.

November 29

> *"The difference between great people and everyone else is that great people create their lives actively, while everyone else is created by their lives, passively waiting to see where life takes them next. The difference between the two is the difference between living fully and just existing."*
> —*Michael E. Gerber*

Good morning! When we create our lives, we are filled with energy. When we passively react to our lives or wait for "our ship to come in," we become tired and bored.

Just like everyone else on this planet, I have a long list of sorrowful experiences that could leave me feeling pessimistic, with a chip on my shoulder. I, like everyone else, have excuses that could allow me to reasonably choose to wait for life to bring me something instead of going out and risking heart and soul day after day.

You know what, though? When we disengage and become passive, we also become negative and complain a lot. I tried it once and got tired of listening to myself within two days. I didn't want to be around myself, so why would anyone else—or life's gifts—want to come to me? Furthermore, doubting life and doubting ourselves is a dark place. No one can bring the light to get out of that darkness to you. You have to choose to ignite the light—and you have to choose that day, after day, after day. It is the only way to live fully.

Your Turn:

No matter what obstacles you face or have faced, realize you can't live fully if you choose to stay in the darkness. And if you choose to stay in the darkness, darkness is all you will see. There is always a light. Realize that you have the power to light up your life.

Today's Affirmation:

When I encounter darkness or difficulty, I do not dwell—instead I turn on the light.

November 30

> *"Discipline is the bridge between goals and accomplishments."*
> —*Jim Rohn*

Good morning! This quote speaks to a problem that many of us face—while we desire a specific result, a foreboding gap may stand between our goal and our accomplishment.

Over the years, I have met many women who will chalk this up to "lack of willpower" or "lack of self-discipline." I prefer to take a more positive approach—it is called "growth."

Imagine for a moment a child in kindergarten. That child decides he wants to be president of the United States. That probably happens hundreds of times around the country each day—a child proclaiming their intent to run the country. Yet this child is different: He wants to accomplish that goal *next month*.

Well... a month comes, and a month goes. You might have already guessed how this story ends: He doesn't become president in those thirty days. Why do you think that is? Would it be chalked up to lack of self-discipline or willpower? Of course not. However, it could be attributed to growth and process. Every goal and desire is a growth and a process—a journey.

We live in an instant-gratification society. We have figured out how to have food *now* versus cooking it (drive-thru), we can have information *now* (via the Internet) instead of researching or going to a library. We can book trips around the world *now* rather than going to a travel agency. We can communicate in written form *now* (through email, versus handwritten letters). Somehow, many of us feel we should thus be able to accomplish our goals and change *right now*.

Until we find a way to order our favorite goal, predone and delivered at the local drive-thru, let us remember that it is a process of many steps. It is not a matter of self-discipline or willpower, but a matter of focus, daily action, and time.

Your Turn:

Where have you been belittling yourself for not "getting more done," or not having "self discipline" or the "required willpower" to achieve your goals? Consider that goals and desires are a journey, and the place you are now is one required step on that path.

Today's Affirmation:

I cherish the journey.

December 1

> *"A Christmas candle is a lovely thing; it makes no noise at all, but softly gives itself away; while quite unselfish, it grows small."*
> —Eva K. Logue

Good morning! When my daughter was eight years old, she created a wonderful tradition. Seemingly out of the blue, Samantha asked if I would take her to the store so she could get some "supplies." When we left the store, we had twenty-five glass votive holders and twenty-five candles.

When we arrived home, I still wasn't sure of Samantha's plans. (She insisted it be a surprise.) She cleared an area of the side table in our dining room and set each votive, with a candle, in a line. Then she sat down at the table and stared at them, while studiously writing some notes. The next day she invited us all in and lit the first candle declaring, "This candle is for peace." The next day, she lit both the first and second candle. Each day she lit another candle in addition to the previous candles, as she added to the "traits" she wanted to remember during the holiday season. As Christmas Eve neared, this grew into a twenty-minute daily routine, which helped us all to truly slow down and remember what the season was all about. On Christmas Day, we lit a large candle and let all the candles burn for the day of celebration.

Here is the original list of Samantha's candle representations at age eight years old:

Peace	Joy	Love
Gratitude	Giving	Listening
Hope	Harmony	Growth
Understanding	Health	Trust
Those we have lost	Compassion	To cherish
Sharing	Serenity	Freedom
Life	Friends	Spirit
Faith	Family	Celebration
Jesus		

Your Turn:

Create your own list of holiday traits. Make a special page in your journal and add one trait per day throughout the season.

Today's Affirmation:

I take time to remember and reflect on the reason for the season.

Going Further

Visit www.brooknoel.com to see a picture of "Samantha's Candles" and download a project worksheet on how to incorporate this idea into your home.

December 2

> *"If you don't have time to do it right,*
> *when will you have time to do it over?"*
> —*Author unknown*

Good morning! Ever find one of those quotes that really hits home? This one makes me pause and reflect whenever I see it. With all the different directions I often go, and the many things I have going on, it can be tempting to make my goal "completing the task" in order to move it to a to-do list, instead of completing the task in my own best and unique way.

Your Turn:

Instead of trying to transfer items to a to-do list, focus on giving every task your own personal best and unique ability. It is better to let the task sit there a few days longer, and for it to receive that special attention, than to simply push it off the list, have it resurface later, and need to do it again.

Today's Affirmation:

I take each to-do seriously and to heart, giving my best.

December 3

> *"There is no such thing in anyone's life*
> *as an unimportant day."*
> —*Alexander Woolcott*

Good morning! I love this quote by Woolcott, because it is a reminder to me that every day is very important—no matter what the day holds. Often, we believe that only the days holding significant events are important. We forget that even the simplest and unstructured days are important, too. Each day etches a slice into our history. And besides, we never know what can happen in a day! Even a quiet, unscheduled day, can bring a revelation.

Your Turn:

Let each day unravel and reveal itself to you, without your deciding whether it is important or not. You will likely be pleasantly surprised by all the magic contained within a twenty-four-hour period.

Today's Affirmation:

I seize the day!

December 4

*"Whatever in your life gives you joy and happiness
just for you, do it. Everyone around you will notice
if you are happy, healthy, joyful, and positive."*
—Cristen, a reader

Good morning! I received a wonderful email on self-care from Cristen that I wanted to share with you.

Don't forget to make sure you are "feeding" yourself, first. Someone reminded me recently that we have to make sure our needs are being met before we can effectively give to others. In my industry, we are taught not to rush in to help someone in crisis until we make sure we are safe ourselves.

Here is the scenario for the analogy: One person is overcome by oxygen-deficiency. A coworker, seeing the person collapse, will rush to help them and become overcome themselves, thus requiring rescue efforts for two people versus the original one person. The training we receive tells us to stop and secure our own safety, i.e. put on a respirator, before attempting to go help and becoming another hazard to the rescue personnel, thereby putting them into greater danger also.

Please, everyone, take a moment to think about what you are doing to protect, feed, and nourish yourself while you are in the midst of helping everyone around you. If we collapse from mental/physical/emotional exhaustion, who will take care of them? Whatever in your life gives you joy and happiness just for you, do it. Everyone around you will notice if you are happy, healthy, joyful, and positive. Conversely, if you are depressed, anxious, nervous, or upset, that will also overflow onto everyone you come into contact with during your journey.

I had to learn to be a little selfish in order to be happy. I was trained to sacrifice myself for the good of my family, but I got to the point that I wasn't happy and, as the old saying goes, "If Mama ain't happy, ain't nobody happy." That is truth!

Now, scheduled into my day are three things: (1) my Good Mornings and Nightly Reflection; (2) (most) every night I read for about twenty to thirty minutes. Something just for me; (3) workout time, and, once a week, I go to a class just for me. No kids are invited to go with me! Out of a twenty-four-hour day, I spend maybe one-and-a-half hours total on ensuring my well-being (the biggest chunk goes to working out). It was really hard to make it a priority at first, but I am seeing the benefits.

Because I schedule it, I am more likely to stick to it. Out of our abundance, we are able to give joyfully, not grudgingly.

Your Turn:

What do you need to do to increase your self-care? Divide a piece of paper into two columns. On the left, list out all the ways you have not been caring for yourself in the past thirty days. Where are you coming up short? How are you helping others, without helping yourself? On the right column, list a positive action step you can take in each area. Then, schedule some time in your catch-all notebook to do just that.

Today's Affirmation:

I know that caring for others begins by caring for myself.

December 5

> *"It's pretty hard to tell what does bring happiness.*
> *Poverty and wealth have both failed."*
> —*Frank McKinney "Kin" Hubbard*

Good morning! What is on the list you mentally keep of "things that will make you happy?" I used to have a long list. I needed some more "me" time, I needed more one-on-one time with my daughter or spouse or friends. I needed more money, or less debt. Interestingly, one of the things that I have found that is most helpful in creating happiness right here and now is to throw out your list of "what I need to be happy."

Happiness isn't gained when we achieve something. When we achieve something, we gain only that which we were trying to achieve. Happiness is created, moment-to-moment, by choice. It isn't waiting anywhere for us: It is already here.

Your Turn:

Let go of the concept that happiness comes with achievement. Realize that happiness is right here, right now. Commit to discovering it.

Today's Affirmation:

Instead of expecting happiness, I create happiness.

Going Further

As we head into the holiday season, take a moment to think through what is most important to you for a happy seasonal celebration. Write a one- to three-sentence mission statement for the season and keep it in your daily calendar.

December 6

> *"Happy, happy Christmas, that can win us back to the delusions of our childhood days, recall to the old man the pleasures of his youth, and transport the traveler back to his own fireside and quiet home!"*
> —**Charles Dickens**

Good morning! Often we think "visually" when decorating, but sound and scent both appeal to the senses, too, and can help set the stage for the holidays.

Fa, la, la, la, la: Dig out your Christmas music or find a local station that carries twenty-four-hour Christmas music. Whenever you are at home, make sure to turn on some Christmas carols in the background.

Jingle all the way: Adding jingle bells to your main doors is another way to use sound in your decorating.

Simmer Scents: Kitchen potpourri is easy to make and a delight to have filtering throughout the house. Place a pot on the simmer burner of your range. Add oranges studded with cloves and cinnamon sticks to some water. Let the pot simmer on a cold winter day, to infuse your house with spicy aromas and a little extra humidity.

Candles: Burn candles or use air fresheners scented with cinnamon, cranberry, orange, pine, coffee, cocoa, cider, or other scents loved by your family.

For the birds: Use bread dough to make circular wreaths. Press wild-bird seed into the wreaths, then bake as directed. Tie a ribbon and Christmas bow for hanging. Decorate an outdoor tree for a feather-friendly holiday.

Your Turn:

Schedule some time to implement one of these simple tips to enhance your home for the season.

Today's Affirmation:

I enjoy all the senses of the season.

Going Further

Choose a new holiday tradition to add to your season. Check out this neat idea for creating a cookie advent calendar at www.wikihow.com/Make-an-Advent-Calendar or the Good Deed Advent Jar project at familycrafts.about. com/cs/adventcalendars/a/bladventjar1.htm

December 7

> *"It is Christmas in the heart that puts*
> *Christmas in the air."*
> —*W. T. Ellis*

Good morning! Undoubtedly the holiday wishes will begin rolling in through the mailbox soon, if they haven't done so already. Maximize the joy of cards by incorporating them into your home decorating. My favorite two ways to enjoy holiday cards:

Hang an evergreen garland to display cards: Paint clothespins in red and green and attach cards to the garland as they arrive.

Create your own Christmas book: I have created a Christmas book featuring the holiday cards we receive. After enjoying the cards, I mount each "front" card onto a page of cardstock or thick paper. Sometimes I collage several cards together. Below the cards, I write down who sent it and include a Christmas quote. You could also use Christmas cards as backgrounds in scrapbooking your holiday memories. For quote ideas, try these websites:

www.quotegarden.com/christmas.html

www.quotelady.com/subjects/christmas.html

Your Turn:

Choose an out-of-the-box way to enjoy your cards throughout the season.

Today's Affirmation:

I cherish and appreciate every gesture of kindness I receive.

 *December 8*

> *"Every action in our lives touches on some chord that will vibrate in eternity."*
> *—Edwin Hubbel Chapin,*
> *American clergyman (1814–1880)*

Good morning! Chapin's words can be somewhat scary if we truly embrace them. For his words affirm we are important and that what we do—no matter how small—matters. Each step, each word, each thought will "vibrate into eternity" in one way or another.

Your Turn:

As you go about your day, listen to your own "echo into eternity." What type of music are you leaving? Happy and joyous? Creative? Stress-filled? Angry? You hold the tuner in your hands. If you do not like what you are hearing, change the channel.

Today's Affirmation:

I create beautiful music.

Inspirations

Here are a few sounds of the season you may want to tune into:

For those of you who love Christmas music, here is a link so you can listen while working on your computer.

http://www.ylw.mmtr.or.jp/—johnkoji/hymn/xmas/

A reading of *How the Grinch Stole Christmas*, along with the written story.

http://www.santas.com/grinch/grinch.html

December 9

"A house is made of walls and beams;
a home is built with love and dreams."
—**Author unknown**

Good morning! Today we are going to do something simple and practical to warm our home. When we think of the senses, we often think of taste and touch, but we forget scent. Scent is a wonderful way to enhance the home, especially with the holiday season upon us.

"Aromatherapy for the Kitchen"

One-half small can whole allspice

One-half small can whole cloves

One-half can stick cinnamon

Two or three star anise

Rind of a small orange

One or two cups water

Simmer in an open pan on the stovetop during the holidays.

This makes a wonderful, festive-yet-soothing aroma to filter through the house. Do not leave simmering potpourri untended anymore than you would a burning candle.

Your Turn:
Try the potpourri recipe to freshly scent your home.

Today's Affirmation:
My home is a peaceful and sacred place.

December 10

"Never give up a dream just because of the length of time it will take to accomplish it. The time will pass anyway."
—*H. Jackson Brown*

Good morning! So often our goals and time schedules may not match that of what the world or life has planned for us. Unexpected interruptions happen. Delays are common. We all face life's bumps in the road.

But that does not mean we should abandon our dreams or goals. Instead of giving up, we need to uncover the lessons of perseverance and persistence. For any goal worth getting to should have a worthy destination, either in one day or one decade.

Your Turn:

When you miss a benchmark for your goal, do you give up, turn away, lose enthusiasm or become hard on yourself? Encourage yourself to take a moment to learn patience, persistence, and perseverance. See what lessons can be found in the unexpected. Ultimately, they will make you stronger when you reach your goal.

Today's Affirmation:

I pursue my dreams with patience, perseverance, and persistence.

December 11

"It's easy to have faith in yourself and have discipline
when you're a winner, when you're number one.
What you've got to have is faith and discipline
when you're not yet a winner."
—*Vince Lombardi*

Good morning! Today, I want to encourage you to begin the process of self-coaching. It isn't complicated; you don't need a coaching degree. The only "tool" required is a mindfulness of your thoughts and a commitment to "take stock" of your thoughts. Let's take a look at the typical roles of a team coach.

Is a coach expected to show up for each practice, or does he just show up when it is convenient or he is in the mood? A coach has to be consistent and dedicated to the purpose of his team. Like a coach, we need to "show up" and be ready to manage our thoughts consistently and with dedication.

When a player doesn't perform well, even though they practiced hard, does the coach ignore the performance or belittle the player? A good coach does assess the performance, but he does so while building up the player, rather than belittling him. When we make a mistake or fall short of a goal, we need to evaluate our performance, and analyze how to positively move forward, without belittling ourselves.

Does a coach (such as an Olympic coach) go to a competition expecting to lose? Of course not: Why go or try if losing is the goal? The quickest way to lose is to do nothing. Vince Lombardi said, "Perfection is not attainable. But if we chase perfection, we can catch excellence."

Does a coach change teams if his players lose the first game that he has coached? Certainly not if he wants to make a career out of coaching! A good coach knows that practice and perseverance are vital. We have to practice our newly acquired tools regularly. Again, I defer to Vince's coaching wisdom: "Once you learn to quit, it becomes a habit."

If a football team is losing at half-time, does the coach stay for the second half? A good coach not only stays, but brainstorms and analyzes new ideas for the second half. We have to recognize that every day is not going to be perfect. Instead of walking away, we do our best.

Your Turn:

What techniques can you use from this list to begin coaching yourself toward success?

Today's Affirmation:

I support myself through self-coaching.

 ## December 12

> *"Yesterday is history, tomorrow is*
> *mystery… today is a gift!"*
> *—Eleanor Roosevelt*

Good morning! This quote fits perfectly with the holiday season at hand. So often in our daily lives, we get bogged down with waiting for the weekend, or a vacation, or some event in the future. As we look forward, we forget to be present. Ask anyone who has lost a loved one, or anyone who is very ill, and they will often wish they had been more present each day.

This quote would be a wonderful reminder each morning to treat each day as the true gift it is. Often we don't realize the value of a day until we don't have any left; it is then that we see the importance contained within a twenty-four-hour period.

Your Turn:

As we navigate this hectic time of year, treat each day as a gift. Unwrap all it has to offer with a grateful heart.

Today's Affirmation:

Each day is a gift and I unwrap it gratefully.

Inspirations

Speaking of gifts, if you are planning on creating any homemade presents, make sure to get started soon! Need some ideas? You'll find over one hundred great ideas at jas.familyfun.go.com/guestsubmit?action=display&topic_id=11

December 13

> *"Like the person you see first, in the mirror, each morning!!"*
> *—A Good Morning Reader*

Good morning! Let's start this morning with a question. If you have children, are they perfect? If you have a spouse or significant other—is he perfect? If you have pets, are they perfect? What about friends... are all of your friends perfect? Or do they have little things that get on your nerves sometimes, maybe a couple of areas where you would like to see change, or a few flaws here and there? Yet despite those flaws and little things, you still accept them, right?

Why, then, do we have such a hard time accepting ourselves? Just as those around us have quirks or flaws, we are never going to be perfect, either. Yet we are often relentless and demanding in our self-expectations, whereas we are accepting of those around us.

Your Turn:

Today, practice loving yourself first. Accept your imperfections as part of what makes you lovable, rather than unlovable. Our soul and spirit is a compilation of our good traits as well as our not-so-good traits. We can only find inner peace when we accept all that we are.

Today's Affirmation:

I love myself.

 *December 14*

> *Gifts of time and love are surely the basic ingredients of a truly merry Christmas."*
> —*Peg Bracken*

Good morning! Today is my birthday, so I thought I would share a personal story to offer some comic-relief when faced with holiday stress.

In my world, Christmas preparations can never come too early. As soon as the turkey is cleared from the table on Thanksgiving,

I am hauling out box upon box of Christmas ornaments. At 6:00 a.m. the following day, while other women are racing for the best sale, I am hunting down the perfect Christmas tree. But what is more interesting is how my tree-loving spirit has continued—in spite of myself.

It was my first year with my husband in our new home. We were playing house, as newlyweds do, and I was determined to decorate floor-to-ceiling in the festive way my family always had while I was growing up. My husband wasn't into the preparations the same way I was, but I was convinced that my enthusiasm would be so contagious that surely the festive spirit would waft his way.

Together, the day after Thanksgiving, we went to pick out our first tree and tree stand. I quizzed the tree salesman about the ins and outs of tree care and we left, confident, with our beautiful evergreen on top of our car. When we arrived home, my husband was ready to take the tree directly into the house, but I reminded him he had to cut the bottom to create the Yule log.

I waited patiently inside, as I had already piled box upon box of ornaments waiting for their new home in our living room. My husband informed me he really "wasn't into tree decorating," and he proceeded to meet some friends that evening while I hung each ornament with care.

For several hours I danced in the holiday spirit. I turned from the tree to open the last box of ornaments, when suddenly, I found myself facedown, flat on the floor, my gigantic Christmas tree on my back. I paused for a moment in shock, wondering what I should do next. I was scared to move. I had heard a few ornaments breaking, and I didn't want to move and cause any more to break. My husband would not be home for several hours. Thoughts swirled in my head of how merry I had imagined my first Christmas to be. Somehow, the image of me being flattened by an evergreen, with sap gluing me to the needles, hadn't really been in that picture.

Although pinned to the floor, I stretched and was just able to reach our cordless phone. I called my husband's brother and asked him to drive over and rescue me. I ignored his laughter when I explained the problem...

After twenty minutes of bonding with the tree, Bobby arrived and carefully lifted the tree back up. We then set about repairing the tree, adjusting the lights, and affixing the ornaments to their branches once again. After another hour of the Christmas spirit we were satisfied with our work and I took Bobby into the kitchen to show him a project I was working on. As I excitedly rambled on about my project, we heard a loud thump, like an exclamation at the end of my sentence. We both turned in horror: The tree once again lay belly up on the floor.

Bobby and I once again resurrected the tree. This time we weren't so eager to repair it for redecorating. Instead, we leaned it against the wall and stared at it, puzzled. Then I saw it. The trunk of the tree was cut at an angle that would make an isosceles triangle jealous. While the tree salesman had told us to cut the base at an angle to maximize the tree's water intake, I don't think he meant for my husband to make it look like a ski slope.

My husband arrived home a long hour later. "How was your night? How's the tree?" he asked enthusiastically. I greeted him with a Medusa-like stare that a newlywed should not know. I took him by the hand and showed him the trunk of the tree. "Well, no one told me 'exactly' how to cut it," he said defensively. That night we removed all the ornaments, and all the lights, and hauled the tree back outside. Andy recut the base and our well-traveled tree once again went back inside.

It was nearly 4:00 a.m. when I finished "trimming" the tree—for the third time that Christmas. I had long since turned off the holiday music and switched to an angst-ridden music channel that better matched my mood. Too exhausted to admire my tree, I went to bed, cautiously hopeful that it would still be standing tomorrow.

Our tree was beautiful that year and it was to receive many a compliment, but very few people would ever know the turmoil that came with that beauty. Not everything is as easy as it looks.

Moral of the Story: "Sometimes the third time is indeed the charm, but it isn't always as much fun."

Your Turn:

My mom started a tradition of a family Christmas book, and every year, each family member contributes a story or memory. This entry is from that cherished collection. Consider adding a Christmas storybook to your holiday traditions.

Today's Affirmation:

I celebrate wonderful memories.

December 15

"He who has not Christmas in his heart
will never find it under a tree."
—Roy L. Smith, (from Joy to the World, *2003;*
Hallmark Books)

Good morning! While we check our light strings for working lights, and gather cookie-making recipes, and confirm event dates, and dress children for concerts and plays, let's not forget to look for the Christmas spirit in its most important place—our hearts. With everything going on this time of year, it can be easy to be checking externally for signs of the holiday, but we should be mostly concerned with the signs within.

What is the Christmas spirit, anyway? I posed this question to my daughter when she was ten years old. I asked her, "If you could capture the Christmas spirit on little pieces of paper, and tuck them into a bottle to last all year... how would you define the Christmas spirit?"

She said, "What are you talking about Mom?"

I tried again. "If someone were to ask you, 'what does the Christmas spirit mean,' how would you answer?"

First she said, "Bah, humbug." Then she started laughing, saying she was just kidding. She went on to answer: "It is about giving to other people more than to yourself."

"The Christmas spirit is being jolly and remembering all the things to be jolly for."

"The Christmas spirit is about getting excited, and having belief, and magic, and faith."

"The Christmas spirit is about having everybody available in your family together... except if it is a really big outdoor dog."

"The Christmas spirit means, even when you don't get what you want, you're still grateful for what you did get." She paused thoughtfully. "I don't think I've ever had that happen, but if you don't get what you want, don't start yelling at the person, as they tried their best."

So, what is the Christmas spirit? It is all of those things Samantha came up with and more. The themes underlying all of her statements are gratitude, caring for another, taking time to be present with one another, giving of ourselves, expecting, and believing, and receiving magic.

Your Turn:

Today, take a moment to bring the Christmas spirit alive in your household. Ask each family member, over dinner, to define the Christmas spirit. Then post their answers on your refrigerator as your personal family reminder of what this season is all about. Please send along any lists you make with the subject line "Christmas spirit" to brooknoel8@aol.com. I would love to include a few lists in the Good Mornings as we head toward the holidays.

Today's Affirmation:

I cherish and nurture the spirit of Christmas within my heart.

 December 16

> *"Never let yesterday use up too much of today."*
> —*John L. Mason*

Good morning! Learning to break the cycle of anxiousness and worry isn't simple. It takes time, practice, and persistence. Worries about finances follow many of us throughout the day. We feel guilt over "not getting everything done." Household commitments sometimes seem endless. We worry about our children; we worry about our loved ones. And that worry and preoccupation ends up robbing the joy from the magic of today.

There is nothing more freeing than finally "letting go." You'll recognize the feeling, because the little things you have been missing will begin to shine and glisten like never before. So, how do we learn to do that? How do we practice letting go?

To practice letting go, make a list of three things you need to let go of. Focus on events that you cannot control—those which your endless fretting will not advance. Each time your mind drifts to one of these three items, remind yourself to "let go." I like to say in my mind, "Let go and let God." It helps me to feel I am not giving up, but instead giving my items over to something with much more power than I will ever have.

Continue to practice this daily, until the "letting go" becomes automatic. No doubt, at times you will stumble and struggle. In those times, come back to this written practice.

Your Turn:
Write down three things you could benefit by from letting go of.

Today's Affirmation:
I let go of the past and stay in the present so I may experience happiness now.

 December 17

> *"It is what a man thinks of himself that really determines his fate."*
> —*Henry David Thoreau*

Good morning! What a true quote this is. When we send ourselves positive energy and think positive thoughts, we re-alize positive things within our life. When we have negative thoughts, we realize negativity in our life. Take a look at your life today. What are you manifesting from your thoughts? How are you treating yourself, your world, and those around you?

Your Turn:
Today and every day, remind yourself that what you think about, you bring about. Treat yourself with esteem, love, and respect.

Today's Affirmation:
I treat myself with love, esteem, and respect.

 December 18

> *"Never sacrifice the permanent on the altar of the immediate."*
> —*Dr. Bob Jones, Sr.*

Good morning! I thought this quote was especially relevant as we talk about dreams and goals.

When we first conceptualize a new dream or goal and take the first few steps toward achieving it, we are full of excitement, expectation, and hope. The change seems welcoming and fresh. But change is never easy. As we go further down the path, it can be hard to maintain change: Giving up seems easy, and we often choose the path of least resistance.

And so it is with our dreams. As obstacles and challenges surface, we can find ourselves doubting our ability to rise to the challenge. That is why it is so important to create a concrete vision of where you want to go at the beginning, when hopes are high. At that point, we need to capture why we want to make a change in our life, or reach a dream. Then we need to turn back to that vision and embrace it during difficult times. From that vision, we have to derive the energy to take the next step, and the next. We cannot sacrifice that dream for immediate relief—for, in the long term, that will not take us to where we want to be.

Your Turn:

Take a moment to clearly visualize your dream. Begin writing down all the reasons this dream is important to you. Keep adding to this list. When the road gets tough, come back to this list for inspiration to take the next step.

Today's Affirmation:

Nothing will stop me from reaching my dreams.

December 19

> *"Life is not easy for any of us. But what of that? We must have perseverance and, above all, confidence in ourselves. We must believe that we are gifted for something, and that this thing… must be attained."*
> —*Marie Curie*

Good morning! So often, we become sidetracked by looking at what is unfair or not "just" in our lives. We can count our bruises and wonder "why isn't this easier?" But this quote holds the realization that, "Life is not easy for any of us. But what of that?"

It is important to accept that fact and quit looking for the "easy way" in life—because there isn't one. Instead, we need to develop the traits that Curie suggests: "perseverance, confidence, and our special gifts." Life itself will never be easy, but we can develop the strengths and skills to make our life easier.

When we approach life with a centered and confident purpose, obstacles become stepping stones and fears become smaller. Life itself hasn't changed, but we have. We have learned to look past our immediate ego to the bigger purpose of contributing and living fully.

Your Turn:

On a scale of one to ten, how well do you know your purpose? Likewise, on a scale of one to ten, how strong is your confidence? What is one step you can take today to build in either of these areas?

Today's Affirmation:

I approach life from a centered and confident self.

 ## December 20

"We don't remember days; we remember moments."
—*Cesare Pavese*

Good morning! This is the time of year when we see moments more clearly, as we cherish the holiday season and our time with friends and family. Perhaps one of the things that makes this time of year so magical is that, instead of counting days, we accumulate memorable moments that will last for years to come. Several years from now, when we look back at this season, we aren't likely to say: "Remember that December twentieth when we..." Instead, we might say something like, "Remember when we made those cookies and the frosting turned out khaki-colored?"

Your Turn:

During the holiday season, it is easy to focus on moments

rather than days. Use this time of year to practice your "moment recognition." Try to carry this ability into next year, capturing the wonderful, magic moments offered by each day of our lives.

Today's Affirmation:

I pay attention to magical moments.

December 21

> *"Hem your blessings with thankfulness*
> *so they don't unravel."*
> *—Author unknown*

Good morning! My daughter often calls me a "Thank-you vigilante." Whether we are in a restaurant, or at school, or anywhere else, as soon as a kindness is extended, my ears perk up, listening for the "thank you" to follow.

I believe that when we are thankful, we attract more goodness into our lives. When we forget to be thankful, the "blessings begin to unravel." We need to thank those we interact with. We need to thank God for our blessings, large and small. We need to be thankful for the lives that we have. And our thanks must be heartfelt. We don't practice thankfulness just to attract or cement good into our lives; we practice thankfulness because it makes us whole.

Your Turn:

Remember to thank everyone you encounter today for their kindness.

Today's Affirmation:

I practice thankfulness daily.

December 22

> *"In the depths of winter I finally learned*
> *there was in me an invincible summer"*
> *—Albert Camus*

Good morning! While tonight is technically the darkest night of the year, it is a great time to light things up around the house. Celebrate this solstice by creating your own *luminarias* (decorative lanterns).

Here is our household solstice routine:

- Pre-dinner: Enjoy hot apple cider and appetizers while we make *luminarias* (instructions below)

- Enjoy dinner together

- After dinner: Light the *luminarias,* bundle up and go star-gazing (or cloud-gazing) depending on the weather. Take turns making a wish for the holidays as we look up at the stars.

- Later that night: Warm up by a fire and hot chocolate with marshmallows to boot. Talk about wishes and dreams and the spirit of Christmas.

How to make a luminaria:

Materials:

- Brown lunch bags

- Sand

- Votive candles or small pillar candles (any candle with a sturdy base)
- Scissors and stencils or decorative hole punches (like those used for scrap booking)

If using hole punches, randomly punch holes in the bag or do so in a pattern—create enough holes to let some light shine through. If using stencils, you can create a design and then cut out the design. Or you can gently fold the bag either vertically or horizontally and cut random snippets from the bag (similar to how you make paper snowflakes). When done, place the bags outside and pour an inch or two of sand into each of them. Secure a candle in the middle of sand. Light and enjoy. Typically *luminarias* are set out to mark a path up to the house, placing one on each side of the walkway up to the house every four to six feet. (Of course, keep an eye on the candles throughout dinner and make sure to snuff them out when done.)

Your Turn:

Whether you make your own *luminaria* or simply step outside to stargaze, take a moment to celebrate the solstice.

Today's Affirmation:

Each day holds special joy and something to celebrate.

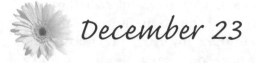

December 23

"Ordinary riches can be stolen, real riches cannot.
In your soul are infinitely precious things
that cannot be taken from you."
—*Oscar Wilde*

Good morning! As many of us make our last-minute Christmas preparations, tying ribbons and bows, I thought that this Oscar Wilde quote was a nice reminder about "real riches."

While we give gifts and save gift receipts, let us remember that the best gift we can give doesn't fit in a box... and it certainly doesn't need a gift receipt. It isn't the opening of the presents, or the surprises inside that bring true and lasting joy. It's the moments around the edges, the laughter, the winks, and the touch of one person to another.

Both sadly and ironically, it is often easier to see what really matters, when it isn't there to see. Ask a family that has lost someone this past year, and they know for certain what is missing, and they know for certain what matters, and they know for certain that it isn't under the tree, or tucked carefully in a package wrapped with gold ribbon.

We have to learn to see love, and touch love, and make it just as visible as any other icon of the season. Perhaps if it were tangible, if we could see how fragile moments really are, we would be more careful not to drop them.

In 2005 I faced an especially trying holiday season. I lost my father that year, after losing my brother eight years before. As the holidays approached that one loss greatly compounded the other. Yet, I always feel that when we lose something, we also stand to gain something. Life is balance. In my search to gain, I did something new this year. Instead of opening doors on an advent calendar each day and anticipating a piece of chocolate inside, I opened my eyes to a magical moment each day. It was much more rewarding, and each day brought more than one moment. Of course, I had to open my eyes and choose to see them. Otherwise, I would have only seen another pound on the scale from eating some chocolates.

Your Turn:

What can you do today, and every day, to make love visible in your life? Imagine your love is carefully contained within a fragile, heirloom glass ornament; imagine love from others in the same way. Handle love carefully, give it freely and treat it for what it is— the greatest gift we will ever have the power to give or receive.

Today's Affirmation:

Today, I make my love for others visible, realizing it is the only gift that truly matters.

December 24

Good morning! Today's inspiration is also the quote of the day. A bit longer than usual, but carrying a special message and reminder.

"A Soldier's Christmas Poem"

The embers glowed softly, and in their dim light,

I gazed round the room and I cherished the sight.

My wife was asleep, her head on my chest,

My daughter beside me, angelic in rest.

Outside the snow fell, a blanket of white,

Transforming the yard to a winter delight.

The sparkling lights in the tree, I believe,
Completed the magic that was Christmas Eve.
My eyelids were heavy, my breathing was deep,
Secure and surrounded by love I would sleep,
in perfect contentment, or so it would seem.
So I slumbered, perhaps I started to dream.
The sound wasn't loud, and it wasn't too near,
But I opened my eye when it tickled my ear.
Perhaps just a cough, I didn't quite know,
Then the sure sound of footsteps outside in the snow.
My soul gave a tremble, I struggled to hear,
and I crept to the door just to see who was near.
Standing out in the cold and the dark of the night,
A lone figure stood, his face weary and tight.
A soldier, I puzzled, some twenty years old
Perhaps a Marine, huddled here in the cold.
Alone in the dark, he looked up and smiled,
Standing watch over me, and my wife and my child.
"What are you doing?" I asked without fear
"Come in this moment, it's freezing out here!
Put down your pack, brush the snow from your sleeve,
You should be at home on a cold Christmas Eve!"
For barely a moment I saw his eyes shift,
Away from the cold and the snow blown in drifts,
To the window that danced with a warm fire's light
Then he sighed and he said "It's really all right.
I'm out here by choice. I'm here every night."
"It's my duty to stand at the front of the line,

That separates you from the darkest of times.

No one had to ask or beg or implore me,

I'm proud to stand here like my fathers before me.

My Gramps died at 'Pearl on a day in December,"

Then he sighed, "That's a Christmas 'Gram always
remembers.

My dad stood his watch in the jungles of 'Nam

And now it is my turn and so, here I am.

I've not seen my own son in more than a while,

But my wife sends me pictures, he's sure got her smile."

Then he bent and he carefully pulled from his bag,

The red, white, and blue... an American flag.

"I can live through the cold and the being alone,

Away from my family, my house and my home,

I can stand at my post through the rain and the sleet,

I can sleep in a foxhole with little to eat,

I can carry the weight of killing another

Or lay down my life with my sisters and brothers

Who stand at the front against any and all,

To insure for all time that this flag will not fall.

"So go back inside," he said, "harbor no fright.

Your family is waiting and I'll be all right."

"But isn't there something I can do, at the least,

Give you money," I asked, "or prepare you a feast?

It seems all too little for all that you've done,

For being away from your wife and your son."

Then his eye welled a tear that held no regret,

"Just tell us you love us, and never forget

To fight for our rights back at home while we're gone.

To stand your own watch, no matter how long.

For when we come home, either standing or dead,

To know you remember we fought and we bled

Is payment enough, and with that we will trust.

That we mattered to you as you mattered to us."

—Michael Marks, Christmas 2000

To all of our troops and their families, I send a special thanks that, because of your strength, my family and friends are enjoying a peace-filled Christmas.

Your Turn:

Take a moment today and send a note of support and encouragement to members of our armed forces. You send a note online at www.americasupportsyou.com.

Today's Affirmation:

I am thankful for my freedom.

December 25

"There is only one Christmas. The rest have been anniversaries."
—W.J. Cameron

Good morning! This morning, I thought I would keep things simple and just share a handful of Christmas thoughts and quotes to inspire your day. Merry Christmas!

"It is the one season of the year when we can lay aside all gnawing worry, indulge in sentiment without censure, assume the carefree faith of childhood, and just plain 'have fun.' Whether they call it Yuletide, Noel, Weinachten, or Christmas, people around the earth thirst for its refreshment as the desert traveler for the oasis."—D.D. Monroe

"I am not alone at all, I thought. I was never alone at all. And that, of course, is the message of Christmas. We are never alone. Not when the night is darkest, the wind coldest, the world seemingly most indifferent. For this is still the time God chooses."—Taylor Caldwell

"Christmas—that magic blanket that wraps itself about us, that something so intangible that it is like a fragrance. It may weave a spell of nostalgia. Christmas may be a day of feasting, or of prayer, but always it will be a day of remembrance—a day in which we think of everything we have ever loved."—Augusta E. Rundel

"I sometimes think we expect too much of Christmas Day. We try to crowd into it the long arrears of kindliness and humanity of the whole year. As for me, I like to take my Christmas a little at a time, all through the year. And thus I drift along into the holidays—let them overtake me unexpectedly—waking up some fine morning and suddenly saying to myself: 'Why, this is Christmas Day!'"—David Grayson

"We hear the beating of wings over Bethlehem and a light that is not of the sun or of the stars shines in the midnight sky. Let the beauty of the story take away all narrowness, all thought of formal creeds. Let it be remembered as a story that has happened again and again, to men of many different races, that has been expressed through many religions, that has been called by many different names. Time and space and language lay no limitations upon human brotherhood."—*New York Times*, 25 December 1937, quoted in *Quotations for Special Occasions* by Maud van Buren, 1938, published by The H.W. Wilson Company, New York.

"Christmas is most truly Christmas when we celebrate it by giving the light of love to those who need it most."—Ruth Carter Stapleton.

"The star of Bethlehem was a star of hope that led the wise men to the fulfillment of their expectations, the success of their expedition. Nothing in this world is more fundamental for success in life than hope, and this star pointed to our only source for true hope: Jesus Christ."—D. James Kennedy ("Following the Star" in *Christmas Stories for the Heart*)

"Late on a sleepy, star-spangled night, those angels peeled back the sky just like you would tear open a sparkling Christmas present. Then, with light and joy pouring out of Heaven like water through a broken dam, they began to shout and sing the message that baby Jesus had been born. The world had a Savior! The angels called it 'Good News,' and it was."—Larry Libby ("The Angels Called it Good News" in *Christmas Stories for the Heart*)

Your Turn:
It is your turn to enjoy this special day.

Today's Affirmation:
I enjoy all the magic of today.

December 26

$\mathbf{G}$ood morning!

MAYBE YOU HAVE OTHER PLANS:

I work up early today excited over all I get to do before the clock strikes midnight.

I have responsibilities to fulfill today.

My job is to choose what kind of day I am going to have.

Today I can complain because the weather is rainy,

OR—I can be thankful that the grass is getting watered.

Today I can feel sad that I don't have more money,

OR—I can be glad my finances encourage me to plan my purchases wisely and guide me away from waste.

Today I can grumble about my health,

OR—I can rejoice that I am alive.

Today I can lament over all my parents didn't give me when I was growing up,

OR—I can be grateful they allowed me to be born.

Today I can mourn my lack of friends,

OR—I can embark upon a quest to discover new relationships.

Today I can whine because I have to go to work,

OR—I can shout for joy because I have a job to go to.

Today I can complain because I have to go to school,

OR—I can eagerly open my mind and fill it with new knowledge.

Today I can murmur dejectedly because I have housework to do,

OR—I can feel honored because the Lord has provided a shelter for me to live in.

Today stretches ahead of me waiting to be shaped. And, here I am, the sculptor who gets to do the shaping. What today will be like is up to me. I get to choose what kind of day I will have.

Have a great day, my friend,

OR—maybe you have other plans.

Your Turn:

What type of day will you have today? Make a decision now to have a great one.

Today's Affirmation:

My attitude and my responses determine the day I will have.

 December 27

> *"Letting go is an act of strength and courage. It helps healing begin, frees you of the weight of the past, and opens doors to a new future."*
> —**Stephanie Tourlea**, **Lift Me Up**

Good morning! Forgiveness is not a topic we talk about regularly, like gratitude and thankfulness, but it is very important, nonetheless. We cannot be our best when we are holding on to grudges. An unforgiving mind or heart is like a heavy anchor and, whether we feel it or not, it will pull us down.

I run a support network for the bereaved at www.griefsteps. com. In my extensive work with grieving individuals, I came across a man who changed my view of forgiveness for all time. He had lost two children to an intoxicated driver. These were his only two daughters and they were on the way to the rehearsal dinner of one of the girls. Despite all of this, he had forgiven the driver. I asked him how he had forgiven him—and I also asked him why. He looked me straight in the eye and said, "I had no choice. To hold on to my anger would have tied me to him forever. To hold on to my anger would have killed me, too."

This man knew at the depth of his soul, that his anger could never help him, but it could destroy or distract him for the rest of his days.

As we head toward the New Year, what do you need to let go of? What anger do you have within you that is a weight in your life, whether you realize it or not? Let's clear out the clutter in our souls to make room for a wonderful year to come.

Your Turn:

With the year coming to a close, what is an experience you need to forgive? Write about it, and then rip the paper into tiny shreds as a way to release and symbolically let go.

Today's Affirmation:

I am free of harmful emotions.

December 28

"Don't be fooled by the calendar. There are only as many days in the year as you make use of. One man gets only a week's value out of a year while another man gets a full year's value out of a week."
—**Charles Richards**

Good morning! Here we are on the cusp of a new year, and I can imagine these comments being said in homes around the world:

Wow! The holidays really snuck up on me this year! Can you believe how quickly the year went by?

It seems like just yesterday we were celebrating the New Year!

How right Charles Richards is, though, in his analysis of time and the calendar. It truly isn't the number of days we have that matters, but what we bring and take away from each of those days.

Your Turn:

How efficiently did you use your days in the last year? If you had to give yourself a report card for effort, enthusiasm, giving, patience, and hope, what would your grades be? What can you learn from the current year that can make next year a more fulfilled year for you and yours?

Today's Affirmation:

Every day matters, because I choose to make it matter.

December 29

"When you come to the end of all the light you know, and it's time to step into the darkness of the unknown, faith is knowing that one of two things shall happen: either you will be given something solid to stand on, or you will be taught to fly."
—Edward Teller

Good morning! In the next couple of days, our Good Mornings will challenge you to begin thinking about the new year, what dreams you have in your heart, and what dreams you are ready to commit to making a reality.

Of course, envisioning a dream or goal is the first part. Action is the third part. But there is a very important second step that we often miss—that step is belief. Between our dream and our actions, we need to decide, we need to believe, we need to learn the art of faith, we need to see that our dream can rightfully become reality. Without this important second step, our fate is uncertain. Our actions will likely lead us to whatever we imagine, and if we don't decide and believe—who knows where we will end up!

Your Turn:

As we begin to think about goal setting and moving forward into a new phase of our lives, remember the crucial step of decision and belief.

Today's Affirmation:

I believe that I deserve my dreams to come true.

 ## December 30

> *"As long as you're going to think anyway, think big."*
> —*Donald Trump*

Good morning! I truly believe that this seemingly simple quote could very well be a key to Trump's financial success. I don't know a lot about his personal life, so I certainly can't speak to his overall life success—but I have sat at the Starbucks in New York City at Trump Tower, and I do know he must have been thinking big with that building!

It is such a simple guideline, but such a true one. We are going to think all the time—that's what makes us humans, and not barnacles. Science has shown that what we think directly correlates to our quality of life. Optimists live longer than pessimists. Optimists have a lower incidence of heart disease. The scientific data is starting to pile up that our thoughts directly correlate to the life we live, and its quality.

We spend the majority of our time thinking—sometimes these thoughts are random and wandering, other times they are reflections of those we spend time with. Sometimes it is talk from an internal critic that seems to know how we can do better at every turn. Every thought is like a building block. Are you building a foundation for today and tomorrow, or are you building a brick fortress around yourself that keeps out the light?

Your Turn:

If your thoughts are wandering into places that don't inspire and encourage you on a regular basis, then you need to make a decision to change and follow through—that is the single most important decision and commitment you can make for yourself and everyone around you. It won't necessarily be easy, but it will be worth it.

Today's Affirmation:

I control my thoughts and direct them toward the positive.

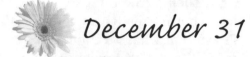

December 31

*"What would you attempt to do if you
knew you could not fail?"*
—Judy Vilmain

Good morning! Good morning! With the New Year on the horizon, take a few minutes today to dream big and think about what you want to accomplish. Spend ten or twenty minutes reflecting on the question contained in today's quote. Let your inhibitions go and answer truly from the childlike place in your heart that remembers how to dream. Dream big. The world awaits you.

Your Turn:

Take some time to thoughtfully reflect on today's question. From your reflections, choose your top goals for the year ahead and place your list where you will see it often. Let's make this the year our goals and dreams become realities.

Today's Affirmation:

Anything is possible!

Reflection Question

In the book *Calm Me Down*, authors Stephanie Tourles and Barbara Heller encourage readers to "Write your own horoscope." Today, start a new journal and begin by writing your own horoscope for the year ahead.

Acknowledgments

More than any other book I have written, this book has truly been a team effort. I cannot find the words to express how blessed I feel and how grateful I am to my tens of thousands of Good Morning readers who share their stories and quotes. You are all my constant well of inspiration.

I would like to express a special thanks to all of the women featured in this book by name or anonymously.

Additionally, I would like to thank Paige Garrison Kullman who has been following my work since the beginning. Thank you for your email saying "Hey... I could use a Good Morning inspiration each day!" Well, look how far we've come! Although we have never met I will always think of you as a friend.

I would like to thank reader Debbie Schwer, who I nicknamed the Quote Queen. (Many of the quotes throughout this book were those she emailed to me.) Thank you for your constant support and sharing.

In addition to my readers, I would like to thank the great behind-the-scenes team at Sourcebooks. To Shana Drehs and Dojna Shearer: Thank you for the time and care you have invested into these words. I would also like to thank Liz Kelsch for her help in "getting the word out." May the years ahead hold many Good Mornings and good times for you all.

About the Author

Brook Noel is the author of nineteen books, specializing in life management and balance for today's busy woman. Noel is known for going "beyond the book" by creating a whole experience to interact and support her readers. She delivers free motivational podcasts, online Q&A chats, message board interaction, in-person free "coffees" when she travels, and free newsletters delivered regularly to tens of thousands of readers.

Her greatest passion is the Make Today Matter Life System Online, which is the basis for *The Change Your Life Challenge*. "I feel like everything I have done or experienced in life has culminated in this program and book. The program isn't just about family time, or menu planning, or procrastination, or organizing—it is about every major area of a woman's life."

Noel was recognized in 2003 as one of the Top 40 Business People Under the Age of 40 by the *Business Journal*. She is a spokesperson for the Home Business Association and was featured in their top entrepreneur issue. She is an expert for Club Mom and a spokesperson for the Whirlpool Corporation specializing in the time crunch of busy moms.

Noel has conducted workshops for and/or appeared on/in: *CNN Headline News, ABC World News, FOX Friends, Woman's World, Our Children* (National PTA Magazine), *Los Angeles Times,* Cedars-Sinai Medical Systems, *Parent's Journal, Booklist, Foreword, Independent Publisher,* University of Washington, UW-Milwaukee, University of Michigan, Single Parents Association, AM Northwest, *Town & Country, New York Post,* "Ask Heloise," Bloomberg Radio—and hundreds of other publications, shows, and stations.

Brook lives in Wisconsin with her husband, their twelve-year-old daughter, a golden retriever, a black lab who thinks her name is "Kitty," a Puggle named Roxie, and one very large cat named Tom. She invites readers' feedback at www.brooknoel.com.

Also Available from Brook Noel

THE CHANGE YOUR LIFE CHALLENGE

- Are you struggling to keep up with life?
- Do you have a list of to-dos that you'll get to "someday?"
- Are you tired of mood, attitude, and energy swings?
- Have you tried other "life management" programs with little success?
- Are you overwhelmed by the needs of others, leaving little time for yourself?

Over 100,000 women, many of whom felt the same way, have CHANGED THEIR LIVES for the better using the strategies in this book.

Created by life management expert Brook Noel, *The Change Your Life Challenge* offers easy but effective step-by-step solutions for implementing lasting change in every major life area:

Housework · Health · Energy · Joy and purpose · Friends · Family · Money · Sanity and Centeredness · Chaos and Clutter Clearing · Time Management · Organization

The three-part journey begins with a written "before" snapshot to identify what areas are holding you back and to create an action plan tailored to your personal needs. Next, you'll find fifteen steps that can revolutionize virtually any area of your life. Then you'll work through a series of Mini-Makeovers, with each makeover offering five practical strategies for how to apply the idea to your life today.

More from Brook Noel

To receive Good Morning messages by email, stop by www.brook noelstudio.com/goodmorning.

To download additional inspirations and printables, visit Brook's free resource area at www.maketodaymatter.net.